Contemporary Christian Travel

ASPECTS OF TOURISM
Series Editors: **Chris Cooper** *(Leeds Beckett University, UK)*, **C. Michael Hall** *(University of Canterbury, New Zealand)* and **Dallen J. Timothy** *(Arizona State University, USA)*

Aspects of Tourism is an innovative, multifaceted series, which comprises authoritative reference handbooks on global tourism regions, research volumes, texts and monographs. It is designed to provide readers with the latest thinking on tourism worldwide and in so doing will push back the frontiers of tourism knowledge. The series also introduces a new generation of international tourism authors writing on leading-edge topics.

The volumes are authoritative, readable and user-friendly, providing accessible sources for further research. Books in the series are commissioned to probe the relationship between tourism and cognate subject areas such as strategy, development, retailing, sport and environmental studies. The publisher and series editors welcome proposals from writers with projects on the above topics.

All books in this series are externally peer-reviewed.

Full details of all the books in this series and of all our other publications can be found on http://www.channelviewpublications.com, or by writing to Channel View Publications, St Nicholas House, 31-34 High Street, Bristol BS1 2AW, UK.

ASPECTS OF TOURISM: 85

Contemporary Christian Travel

Pilgrimage, Practice and Place

Amos S. Ron and Dallen J. Timothy

CHANNEL VIEW PUBLICATIONS
Bristol • Blue Ridge Summit

DOI https://doi.org/10.21832/RON6645
Library of Congress Cataloging in Publication Data
A catalog record for this book is available from the Library of Congress.

Library of Congress Cataloging in Publication Control Number: 2018026114

British Library Cataloguing in Publication Data
A catalogue entry for this book is available from the British Library.

ISBN-13: 978-1-84541-664-5 (hbk)
ISBN-13: 978-1-84541-663-8 (pbk)

Channel View Publications
UK: St Nicholas House, 31-34 High Street, Bristol, BS1 2AW, UK.
USA: NBN, Blue Ridge Summit, PA, USA.

Website: www.channelviewpublications.com
Twitter: Channel_View
Facebook: https://www.facebook.com/channelviewpublications
Blog: www.channelviewpublications.wordpress.com

Copyright © 2019 Amos S. Ron and Dallen J. Timothy.

All rights reserved. No part of this work may be reproduced in any form or by any means without permission in writing from the publisher.

The policy of Multilingual Matters/Channel View Publications is to use papers that are natural, renewable and recyclable products, made from wood grown in sustainable forests. In the manufacturing process of our books, and to further support our policy, preference is given to printers that have FSC and PEFC Chain of Custody certification. The FSC and/or PEFC logos will appear on those books where full certification has been granted to the printer concerned.

Typeset by Deanta Global Publishing Services Limited.

Contents

Figures and Tables	vii
Acknowledgments	ix
1 The Context of Christian Travel	1
2 Evolving Patterns of Christian Travel: Denominational and Geographical Perspectives	18
3 Commoditizing Holy Places and Commercializing Sacred Experiences	43
4 Promoting Christian Tourism	64
5 Christian Volunteer Tourism: Solidarity, Spreading the Gospel and Humanitarian Service	82
6 Christian Themed Environments	103
7 Heritage Trails and Cultural Routes	121
8 Christian Events and Gatherings	145
9 Conclusion	157
References	163
Index	203

Figures and Tables

Figures

Figure 1.1	The spectrum of sacred to profane in the religious tourism experience	6
Figure 1.2	The parish church of St Michael, Poland – a UNESCO WHS folk shrine	10
Figure 1.3	A typology of contemporary Christian travel	12
Figure 2.1	Mexican pilgrims arriving at Our Lady of Guadalupe shrine in Mexico City – now an extremely mainstream Catholic destination	21
Figure 2.2	Church of Saint Lazarus in Larnaca, Cyprus	23
Figure 2.3	The still functioning New Valamo Finnish Orthodox Monastery is a well-known tourist retreat	25
Figure 2.4	Mamertine Prison in Rome where St Peter and St Paul were imprisoned	28
Figure 2.5	The Family History Library in Salt Lake City, Utah	38
Figure 3.1	The extreme commercialization of Lourdes, France, is part of its tourist appeal	46
Figure 3.2	Christian travelers being baptized in the Jordan River at the Qaser el-Yahud site	53
Figure 3.3	Olivewood carvings in Bethlehem, Palestine, are among the most favored Holy Land souvenirs	55
Figure 3.4	Shops in Medjugorje sell an eclectic range of religious and non-religious souvenirs	58
Figure 3.5	The gate demarcates the border between the sacred and the profane at Lourdes	60
Figure 4.1	Tourists can buy Christian-themed bus tours of Rome on coaches such as the one shown	66
Figure 4.2	Medjugorje and its Marian history is a major tourism brand for Bosnia and Herzegovina	80
Figure 5.1	A continuum of justice tourism	93
Figure 5.2	An advertised Holy Land tour with obvious solidarity undertones	94

Figure 5.3	A volunteer guide at the Garden Tomb	98
Figure 5.4	A volunteer worker at Nazareth Village	99
Figure 5.5	Pilgrims with physical disabilities and volunteers at Lourdes, France	100
Figure 6.1	A typology of themed tourism spaces	105
Figure 6.2	The Bible Garden in the Vatican Gardens, Vatican City	109
Figure 6.3	The Life of Christ Museum in Fatima, Portugal, is an example of a themed Christian space	110
Figure 6.4	Common features of a Protestant theme site in Israel	116
Figure 7.1	Evolution of original tracks to developed routes and trails	123
Figure 7.2	The Way of Saint James crosses the French–Spanish border at the location shown	130
Figure 7.3	The Way of Saint James and its various routes	131
Figure 7.4	Christian pilgrims symbolically 're-enacting' the burden of the cross in Jerusalem	134
Figure 7.5	The terminus of the Mormon Trail near Salt Lake City	137
Figure 7.6	A Station of the Cross along St Patrick's Trail in Northern Ireland	139
Figure 7.7	Jesus Trail guides and souvenirs in Israel	141
Figure 7.8	The head of the Gospel Trail on the outskirts of Nazareth	141
Figure 8.1	Tourists clamber to photograph jumbotron images of Pope Francis in the Vatican City	148

Tables

Table 3.1	A sample of Catholic tours sold by Opera Romana Pellegrinaggi, 2015	49
Table 5.1	Types of Christian volunteer travel	87
Table 5.2	A sample of Bible-related archaeology sites in the Holy Land and Mediterranean seeking volunteers, 2015–2018	96
Table 6.1	A sample of Christian-themed environments and theme parks in the United States	111
Table 6.2	A sample of Christian-themed environments and theme parks outside Israel and the United States	117
Table 7.1	Top origin countries of Santiago de Compostela pilgrims in 2017	130
Table 8.1	Apostolic voyages of the last three popes (1979–2017)	149
Table 8.2	Chronology and geography of WYD celebrations	152

Acknowledgments

This research would not have been possible without the help and support of family, friends and colleagues from the tourism academy and the tourism industry. The list is long, but we would like to extend special acknowledgements to Professor Jackie Feldman, the late Dr Wayne E. Brickey, Dr Daniel H. Olsen, Pastor Connie Pack, Ms Yisca Harani, Michael Hodgson of Maranatha Tours (UK), Hani Abbu Dayyeh of Near East Travel (Jerusalem), and Jimmy Abu Sbeih of Jimmy's Bazaar (Jerusalem), as well as our numerous other work colleagues, academic collaborators, Christian leader associates and travel industry friends all over the world. We also gratefully acknowledge financial and time assistance for the research upon which much of this book is based from Kinneret College on the Sea of Galilee, Ashkelon Academic College, and Arizona State University.

We wish to express our deep gratitude to the exceptional personnel at Channel View Publications, especially Elinor and Sarah, for their endless patience during our extended delays. We are also grateful to the series editors, Professors Michael Hall and Chris Cooper, for their support throughout.

Our most heartfelt thanks goes to our families, especially Myriam and Carol, who were patient with us during this writing project and put up with our many complaints, extended deadlines, days and weeks away from home, and inattention while we were writing at home. Even when working at home, we were not always 'there'. Thank you for being our strength.

1 The Context of Christian Travel

Introduction

Since the beginnings of human history, people have sought knowledge and enlightenment in the divine with belief in a god or gods, the divine nature of oneself, the spiritual existence of inanimate objects or nature gods that controlled the elements. A large number of archaeological sites were originally places of god and nature worship and locations of spiritual transformations. Some of the world's most visited heritage sites today (e.g. Stonehenge and Machu Picchu) are believed to have been sites of ancient spiritual worship.

For thousands of years, people have traveled to locations they deem sacred. Evidence suggests that ancient peoples traveled to hallowed natural areas or human-built places to worship, pray, appease the gods or beseech deity for needed blessings. Pilgrimage has long been one of the most salient manifestations of religious devotion and one of the most influential forces in generating human mobility. Göbekli Tepe, Turkey, built more than 10,000 years ago, is believed to be the oldest built place of worship on earth and was evidently constructed by hunters and gatherers who probably returned to the site from time to time throughout the year to worship (Schmidt, 2000). Approximately 5000 years ago, river-based religious rituals and celebrations began as precursors to Hindu pilgrimage during the Vedic Age of South Asia (Bhardwaj, 1973). There is ample evidence to suggest that ancient peoples traveled to venerate natural and human-made sites for a variety of spiritual reasons.

In the modern world, worshippers from almost every religion on earth travel to search for God or their own spiritual selves in places officially or unofficially deemed sacred. They visit places that are revered for their connections to gods or holy men and women, their capacity to heal or their blessed existence as a place where miracles happened. Religious tourists, or pilgrims, travel to build faith, to pray more fervently, to witness miracles, to obtain forgiveness for moral transgressions, to be healed, to fulfill religious obligations or vows, or just to visit places of historical importance to their own religions. While some religions require travel in the form of pilgrimage for salvation or eternal life, others encourage it as a means of growing faith. Alternatively, some faiths discourage religious travel as a waste of money, time and effort, which could be used more effectively in seeking godliness and inner peace at home (Cohen Ioannides & Ioannides, 2006; Jutla, 2006; Olsen & Timothy, 2006; Rinschede, 1992; Smith, 1992; Timothy & Iverson, 2006).

Christianity is the largest religion in the world with approximately one third of the world's religious adherents claiming to be Christians. There are thousands of individual Christian churches, sects and varied denominations with a multitude of similar, yet varying, doctrinal and historical foundations. Aside from basic doctrine, one thing nearly all Christians have in common is their preponderance to travel. In some churches, pilgrimage, or religious travel, is strongly encouraged as a way of building faith and seeking divine blessings. Sacred sites are officially sanctioned and formally declared places of pilgrimage. Other denominations encourage or facilitate faith-based travel but have no formal doctrines or rituals associated with pilgrimage, *per se*. In these cases, while certain places might be considered sacrosanct, they are not designated officially as pilgrimage destinations (Olsen & Timothy, 2006).

Scholars and observers have noted a drop in church attendance in the past few decades in the more traditional Christian countries of Europe and North America (Pew Research Center, 2011; Dowson, 2017; Nolan & Nolan, 1992). This is due, in large part, to increased levels of affluence filling certain human needs in place of organized religion and resulting in declining birth rates, increasing numbers of people turning to non-Christian spiritual philosophies (e.g. the New Age movement, paganism and the spiritual philosophies of East Asia), growing numbers of non-Christian immigrants and general complacency (Olsen & Timothy, 2006; Poulston & Pernecky, 2017; Ross, 2009; Timothy & Conover, 2006). Even though many traditional churches have seen a decline in North America and Europe, some Protestant, Millenialist and Restorationist churches on an individual basis have seen considerable growth in the developed parts of the world, and in the less-developed parts of the world and Eastern Europe, Christianization and church attendance are on the rise.

Despite the overall drop in official church adherence in the Western world in recent years, there has been a simultaneous growth in Christian pilgrimage tourism and mega-events (Bywater, 1994; Dowson, 2017; Eade, 2016; Jackowski, 1987, 1990; Kosti, 1998; Olsen & Timothy, 1999; Post *et al.*, 1998; Reader, 2007; San Filippo, 2001; Saayman *et al.*, 2014). This is a result of multitudinous socio-economic and political reasons. For example, more than half of all Christians live in the developed world where standards of living are relatively high and where many people have higher levels of disposable income. While there are large numbers of Christians in the Pacific Islands, sub-Saharan Africa, Latin America and a few locations in Southeast Asia (e.g. the

Philippines, parts of Indonesia and Timor Leste), most economically prosperous Christians are concentrated in Europe, North America, Australia and New Zealand (Hsu *et al.*, 2008). This geographic situation alone indicates levels of affluence that facilitate international travel, including pilgrimage or other forms of faith-based travel. Another reason for the growth is that religious tourism is no longer seen strictly as traditional pilgrimages, wherein suffering, penitence and travail are important elements of the cleansing experience. Instead, faith-based tourism takes on a variety of forms as will be discussed later in this chapter and throughout the book.

This introductory chapter examines some initial patterns of Christian travel, introduces important concepts and ideas related to Christian pilgrimage and other forms of faith-based tourism and provides an outline and rationale for the entire book.

Pilgrimage and Religious Tourism

Pilgrimage has long been viewed as journeying away from home for spiritual or religious reasons: fulfilling a religious obligation or visiting sacred places to petition deity for forgiveness, to seek divine help with life's problems, to be blessed or healed, or any combination of these. As noted in the introduction, pilgrim travel has a long history of human movement to sacred places for a multitude of pious reasons, although most scholars concur that pilgrimage is more about an inner transformation than a journey to sacred places. The physical travel is only a manifestation of the inward journey. Traditional pilgrimage has had an undertone of being arduous, burdensome and laborious – conditions that help humble, cleanse and purify the pilgrim as he or she prepares to commune with God. In religions that have required or officially sanctioned pilgrimage practices,

> For every pilgrim making a physical journey, the sore feet, enforced detours and flea-ridden hostelries, as well as the companionship and acts of generous hospitality represent in microcosm the woes and weals of life. The pilgrim's final arrival at the shrine, the source of holiness, signifies the soul's entering a state of blessedness, a rehearsal on earth for what heaven has in store. (Harpur, 2002: 11)

Since medieval times, Christian pilgrimage has existed along set routes or trails that were sanctioned and sanctified by the Church as spaces, which, if traversed in the proper spirit, could consecrate the soul and body in preparation for encounters with the divine (Gonzáles & Medina, 2003; Graham & Murray, 1997; Kelly, 2012; Pruess, 1976; Santos, 2002; Stone, 1986; Swatos & Tomasi, 2002; Timothy, 2012). Sparse supplies of food; walking, crawling or horseback riding; and stays in rustic cabins or in tents along the way were part of the experience. Typically, the pilgrim way itself was either more important, or at least as important, as arriving at the final destination because of the inward changes it effected (Turner, 1973). Similar conditions have been an important part of Hindu, Buddhist and Muslim pilgrimages for centuries. Many Christian pilgrimage routes have become modern tourist trails followed not only by the faithful in search of deity, but also by leisure tourists in search of landscapes, heritage and solitude.

Today, the notion of pilgrimage has changed to a considerable degree. While many faith traditions still encourage adherents to labor along a set pilgrim trail for the humbling experience it provides, modern adaptations now allow people to forego these burdensome aspects and travel by car, air or train to the final destination. Some religions today have approved luxury pilgrimages, wherein people arrive at the spiritual goal by airplane, air-conditioned coach or car and stay in lavish accommodation. They can even purchase pilgrimage tour packages, which also include golf, theater, shopping and visits to other tourist attractions. Virtual pilgrimages via the internet (webcams and Skype) are even sometimes considered adequate surrogates for first-hand experience, when financial or physical challenges constrain people from traveling (MacWilliams, 2002; Timothy, 2011; Timothy & Iverson, 2006).

All major religions of the world have had or continue to have varying forms of pilgrimage. The Kumba Mela (Kumbh Mela) in India is the world's largest religious pilgrimage with upwards of 70 million participants gathered in key cities in India every 3, 6 or 12 years. The hajj in Mecca, Saudi Arabia, takes place each year during the month of Dhu al-Hijjah and typically involves approximately 2.5 million pilgrims. Muslims are required to undertake the hajj, although exceptions can be made for people with special needs. Buddhist pilgrims are known travelers in India, Nepal, Sri Lanka, Thailand, Tibet and several other countries in Asia. Christian pilgrimages are commonplace at Roman Catholic sites in Europe, the Holy Land and church history sites in North America, Latin America, Europe and the Mediterranean.

There has been a long academic discourse related to religious pilgrimage. One source of contestation from both academic and religious perspectives has been the often confused relationship between pilgrimage and tourism (Badone & Roseman, 2004a). Several observers, including faith organizations and churches, have suggested, even argued, that pilgrims are not tourists because they are pious and are driven by spiritual motives that emanate from a deep-seated desire to improve their spiritual lives, whereas tourists travel for pleasure, behave hedonically and are not motivated by spiritual development or required rituals (Cohen, 1992; Collins-Kreiner, 2002, 2010a; Fish & Fish, 1993; Morinis, 1992; Pfaffenberger, 1983; Shinde, 2007; Smith, 1992).

Unfortunately, this view illustrates a clear misunderstanding of who tourists and pilgrims are. According to the tourism industries, most destinations and many international tourism-related agencies, tourists are essentially people who travel to destinations away from their home regions. The World Tourism Organization (UNWTO, 1995) refined this definition to be anyone who travels away from his or her home environment for more than a day but less than a year. A tourist can be motivated by pleasure, leisure, business or *any* other purpose, as long as he or she is not financially remunerated from within the destination visited. Thus, tourists are not defined by motives or activities, although subtypes of tourists are (e.g. sport tourists, ecotourists and cultural tourists). Tourists are not intrinsically hedonic and pleasure-seeking in their behavior but include individuals traveling for business, participating in sports, attending a funeral, visiting relatives, visiting sacred sites or participating in an official pilgrimage (Ahmed, 1992; Olsen & Timothy, 2006; Stausberg, 2011; Timothy, 2002, 2011; Vukonić, 1996; Zamani-Farahani & Henderson, 2010). Thus, overnight travel for any purpose, including pilgrimage, is part of the tourism system.

Given this broad-based and standard definition, pilgrimage is simply one form of tourism; pilgrims utilize commercial transportation, stay in commercial lodgings, shop for souvenirs, visit museums and historic sites, and dine in restaurants and cafes (Gupta, 1999; Sizer, 1999). In this sense, pilgrims are not only tourists from a statistical perspective, but they are also tourists from a demand and supply perspective as they demonstrate touristic tendencies in transit and while at the destination, and they fully utilize the tourism infrastructure. Pilgrimage should not be viewed as being different from tourism. Instead, it is one type of tourism, more commonly referred to as religious tourism, pilgrimage tourism or faith-based travel. For the purposes of this book, Christian travelers are referred to interchangeably as travelers, tourists and pilgrims.

Despite the conceptual debate, which continues to dichotomize tourists and pilgrims superficially, visitors to sacred sites may be placed on a scale of piety (Figure 1.1) (Smith, 1992). On the left end of the spectrum are the most devout visitors. These represent the purest type of pilgrims, who are required to travel or who are divinely motivated to visit hallowed ground to demonstrate godly devotion or to seek personal edification. They often bring their own food and stay in pilgrim rest houses or sleep under the open sky. The journey is heartfelt, spiritual and, for many, anguish-laden. Some of these religious tourists shun the commercial aspects of tourism, although they might purchase icons or other religious symbols from the plethora of souvenir shops and vendors that typically surround sacred places. At the other extreme are non-religious tourists, who visit holy places out of curiosity or as part of a larger cultural itinerary. They visit locations deemed sacred to others to experience the places' architectural aesthetics, heritage value or some element of living culture. The majority of these 'secular tourists' are fascinated by

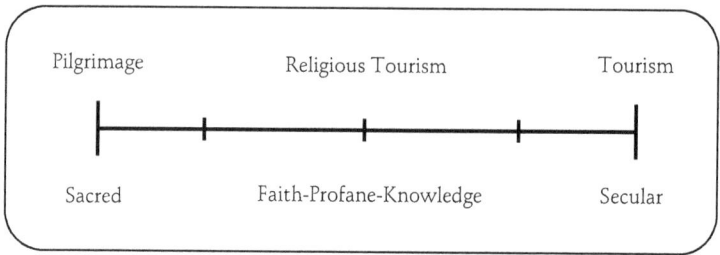

Figure 1.1 The spectrum of sacred to profane in the religious tourism experience (Source: Modified from Smith, 1992)

what they see, but few have personal connections to the site and may not be spiritually nourished by visiting it.

Between the ends of the continuum are millions of tourists who are motivated by a mix of spiritual and secular forces, many of whom might be pilgrims but who also participate in secular endeavors during their journeys, such as sightseeing, spending time at a beach, seeing a play, shopping, bungee jumping or watching a bullfight. Although devout pilgrims and secular tourists are tourists by definition, this spectrum makes clear that there are many levels of motivation for visiting sacred sites, from pure devotion to simple curiosity.

Christianity in the Modern World

The central belief of Christianity is the divinity of Jesus Christ and his important role as savior of the world. Christians believe that Jesus Christ is the son of God and that through his atoning sacrifice (crucifixion) and by his grace, all of humankind can rise above their sinful state and gain salvation and eternal life. Christians follow the teachings of Jesus as documented in the Bible and adhere to a common set of foundational doctrines, although various churches practice somewhat different rituals and adaptations of the basic Christian creed. The intention of this chapter, and indeed this book, is not to define which denomination or faith tradition should or should not be considered Christian. Instead, it deals in general terms with the religions and churches that designate themselves as Christians through their belief in the divine nature of Christ.

Christianity is the world's largest organized religion, with approximately 2.2 billion adherents, or one third of the earth's population claiming to be Christian (Central Intelligence Agency, 2018). Within Christianity there are thousands of sects or individual churches with different practices, doctrinal variations and rituals. Many of these are a part of larger denominations, while the trend toward independent churches (especially among evangelical Christians) is growing. There are many classifications of Christian churches (Miller *et al.*, 2009), but none of them adequately addresses the multiplicity of faiths and sects within this broader religious classification. The current denominational map of Christianity is complex and varied, and it is not our intention to delineate or describe every faith tradition that falls within the scope of Christianity. Nonetheless, Christianity is comprised of numerous individual faiths, churches and religious organizations that preach the divinity of Jesus Christ and his saving grace.

Keeping in mind that any classification will necessarily be exclusionary to some degree, the most customary groupings of traditional Christian churches are Catholicism, Protestantism and Orthodoxy. The Catholic tradition includes Roman Catholicism, the largest Christian denomination with some 1.2 billion adherents, and various Eastern Catholic churches, such as the Armenian and Russian Catholic churches. Most traditional Protestant denominations separated from the Catholic churches in the medieval period beginning with the Reformation movement and today include many organized denominations that have developed out of the Catholic churches and from Protestant denominations (e.g. Baptists, Pentecostals, Lutherans, Anabaptists, Quakers, Methodists, Presbyterians, United churches and Congregationalists). Part of Protestantism is the growing evangelical movement, which spans a number of faith groups and emphasizes activism, biblicism, conversionism and crucicentrism (Bebbington, 2008). The Orthodox churches (Eastern and Oriental) are united by a common creed, with very little variation in theology. Rather than being individual denominations, the Orthodox churches are designated most commonly based on national title or language most widely used by clergy and in scripture. Thus, the Greek, Georgian, Macedonian, Ukrainian, Romanian, Bulgarian, Finnish and Russian Orthodox churches, for example, have similar theologies but are designated by their national orientations (Binns, 2002).

In addition to the three traditional sets of Christian faiths is a growing population of adherents who belong to various other Christian churches that do not fit within this customary tripartite classification. These include a sometimes overlapping mix of Protestant, Nontrinitarian, Latter Day Saint, Restorationist, Sabbath-Keeping, Millennialist, Bible Student, Unitarian and Jewish Christian faiths, which do not consider themselves to be fully Protestant, Catholic or Orthodox, but which do consider themselves to be Christian. While there are many churches within these categories, some prominent examples include the Church of Jesus Christ of Latter-day Saints, Jehovah's Witnesses, Seventh-day Adventist Church and Church of Christ, Scientist. Denominations within this 'other' category number in the thousands and consist of small groups ranging from less than 100 adherents to large groups with memberships in the millions.

Because of the size of Christianity, its diversity, the multiplicity of individual denominations and varied differences in doctrine between sects, it is not our intention to examine every church and its travel practices and patterns. This is not a result of lack of interest or a statement of importance of one group over another, but instead it reflects the need to treat Christian travel in more general terms. It also reflects the availability of past and present research to help lay the foundations of a book such as this one; some denominations' travel patterns have been well researched by scholars, while others have been virtually ignored. Where empirical examples are provided, they are based on extant knowledge as available in the academic and popular literature.

Christian Travel in Perspective

Historical evidence hints at Christian pilgrimages to the Holy Land beginning within one or two centuries after the death of Jesus, although according to Harpur (2002), perhaps the earliest Christian pilgrimage was manifest in the magi, who traveled from the East to visit the baby Jesus at his birth in Bethlehem. During the first few centuries CE, the Christian faithful assembled to pay homage at tombs of martyrs and saints, as well as at locations where the icons and relics of the saints and the Holy Cross were kept by Jewish leaders and Christian clergy in Europe and the Caucuses (Metreveli & Timothy, 2010; Stone, 1986). Once the Roman emperor Constantine had converted to Christianity in the 4th century, the European portions of the Roman Empire began the Christianization process (Curran, 2002; MacMullen, 1986), so that by the High Middle Ages most of Europe had become Christianized (Fletcher, 1997).

With the conversion of Constantine and the early Christianization of Roman Europe, visits to the Holy Land and sacrosanct sites throughout Europe by people from around the empire grew considerably (Harpur, 2002; Timothy & Ron, in press). By 600 CE, Christian pilgrimage was, together with trade, one of the most widespread manifestations of long-distance travel in the Mediterranean region (Timothy, 2010). Christian pilgrimage reached its zenith during the Middle Ages but waned following the Reformation of the 15th and 16th centuries, largely because the practice was challenged by religious reformists who believed pilgrimage, like much of the church, had lost its meaning and value. In their view, pilgrimage had become simply a sightseeing journey (Bremborg, 2013; Harpur, 2002).

Martin Luther eventually condemned pilgrimages, suggesting that they should cease. In his words, 'there is no good in them: no commandment enjoins them, no obedience attaches to them. Rather do these pilgrimages give countless occasions to commit sin and to despise God's commandments' (quoted in Dyas, 2014: np). It was not long before most English shrines had been destroyed and their relics desecrated. The monasteries, which had supported place-based pilgrimages by maintaining shrines and providing hospitality for pilgrims, were subdued. 'Implementing change at the level of popular devotion and parish worship took time… place pilgrimage v. inner journeying/life pilgrimage remained a powerful and fruitful image' (Dyas, 2014: np).

Owing to these criticisms, pilgrimage in the Protestant countries of Europe greatly diminished. According to Harpur (2002), this commoditization of traditional pilgrimage resulted largely in such 'quasi-pilgrimage' replacement activities as the 18th-century Grand Tour.

However, as religious fervor grew among Protestant and Catholic groups, and with a more mobile population owing to transportation innovations (e.g. steamships and trains), pilgrimage in Europe and the Holy Land saw a major resurgence during the 1800s and 1900s. Modern-day miracles and Marian visitations brought about the establishment of several important Marian shrines and officially designated holy places in the 20th century, including Lourdes, Knock, Medjugorje and Fatima at which Roman Catholics began to congregate and worship (Fedele, 2009, 2014; Nolan & Nolan, 1989; Shackley, 2006b; Turner & Turner, 1978; Vukonić, 2006). As well, there was a general revival in a significant number of medieval holy places, such as Walsingham, England and St Andrews, Scotland (Harpur, 2002). In the 1860s, Thomas Cook, the 'father of modern tourism', began to offer ship and train tours of the Mediterranean regions of Europe and the Holy Land (Palestine and Egypt) (Brendon, 1991; Timothy, 2011). According to Hamilton (2005), after 1869, Cook brought more British people to the Holy Land than anyone since the Crusaders.

Christian tourists still pour into the Holy Land by the millions to visit the sites and relics associated with the life and ministry of Jesus Christ and his apostles (Wright, 1999). Catholics, Orthodox and Protestants continue to visit thousands of official pilgrimage centers and saints' relics in Europe, the Caucuses, North America and Latin America (Konstantinovna & Nikolayevich, 2014; Metreveli & Timothy, 2010; Ostrometskaia & Griffin, 2018; Ron, 2009), as well as many ecclesiastically unrecognized sites of religious devotion that are known locally as 'folk shrines' to which visits are encouraged on a small scale and informally by local clergy with visitation at such locales being referred to sometimes as 'folk religiosity' (Afferni *et al.*, 2011; Banica, 2016; Černá, 2014; Maddrell *et al.*, 2015; Ostrometskaia & Griffin, 2018; Rodosthenous & Varvounis, 2014) (Figure 1.2). According to Nolan and Nolan's (1989) account, there are more than 6000 Christian pilgrimage shrines in Europe, including folk shrines of local acclaim. There are also many such localities, including folk shrines and indigenous churches, throughout Latin America, North America and Africa (Aguilar Ros, 2017; Dafuleya *et al.*, 2017; du Plooy, 2017; Klimova, 2011; Kruger & Saayman, 2016; Steil, 2017).

Today, most Protestant, Catholic, Orthodox and other churches encourage their members to visit church headquarters; historic sites associated with the growth and development of the church; shrines around the world; places where the ancient apostles taught, lived and were

Figure 1.2 The parish church of St Michael, Poland, is an example of a folk shrine, although it became a World Heritage Site in 2003 (Photo: D. Timothy)

martyred; and biblical sites in the Holy Land and Mediterranean region. However, for the most part these visits are not essential for salvation, but they bestow personal blessings; they increase faith, effect spiritual transformations, render their prayers more fervent, heal the body and soul and reinforce the tourists' witness of God. The visits also build solidarity with other Christians.

The tourism industry is beginning to take greater notice of the importance and potentially lucrative niche of religious tourism. A scan of the internet reveals thousands of tour companies in North America, Europe and the Pacific that now specialize in Christian travel in all its forms. In collaboration with church organizations, the new travel industry idea of faith-based tourism is much more inclusive than the traditional views of pilgrimage, noted above, as conceived by faith organizations, anthropologists, cultural geographers, historians and religious studies experts.

While Christian religious tourism encompasses traditional pilgrimage, it also entails travel to sacred and historic sites, missionary travel, religious conferences, retreats and camps, volunteer vacations and attending conventions, meetings and special events. Although bankrupt in early 2011, the World Religious Travel Association functioned in the early 2000s as an industry clearinghouse for marketing and data dissemination related to all forms of religious tourism, with a particular emphasis on Christian travel. Kevin Wright, the president of the association, and many other industry leaders have argued that religious tourism is, and should be, much more inclusive than the constricted version of pilgrimage that has dominated the practice of faith-based travel for centuries. The contemporary notion of faith travel also includes package tours, cruises, resort stays, safaris, weekend getaways and other leisure vacations when these are done in a spirit of fellowship with other Christians of the same denomination, even when the destination itself holds little relevance to official pilgrimage or is not considered sacred in the traditional sense (Wright, 2008).

The inclusion of cruises, safaris and coach tours in the Christian travel product reflects what Turner (1973) and Turner and Turner (1978) refer to as *communitas*, where religious voyagers come together with other pilgrims in spiritual fellowship, where class and the other social influences of everyday life become irrelevant to their hyper-real spiritual experiences in the temporary spaces of otherness (Di Giovine, 2011; Olsen & Timothy, 2006). Turner suggests that without the normal concerns of the outside world, inner meditation and soul searching are easier for pilgrims. Thus, while a Caribbean cruise or package tour of China might have little relevance to sacred space from a geographical perspective, from a psychological perspective, the *communitas* achieved by being surrounded with like-minded Christians allows people to build an affinity of faith with their co-religionists, and thus the trip becomes a sacred experience.

The growing religious tourism sector of the travel industries has adopted a broader and more inclusive vision of faith-based travel. A multitude of tour companies, travel agents and Christian organizations have jumped on this lucrative bandwagon to offer traditional pilgrimage packages, as well as more contemporary experiences, such as pageants, historic site visits and fellowship cruises and safaris. The model of contemporary Christian travel introduced by Ron (2009) employs a similar broad and encompassing view of Christian tourism (Figure 1.3). The model derives from two primary assumptions. First, pilgrimage and tourism are not located at opposite ends of a continuum, as Smith (1992) has suggested. Instead, pilgrimage is one of many different types of tourism – tourism that is motivated by religious or spiritual stimuli. Second, pilgrimage and religious tourism are not synonymous; rather, pilgrimage is only one form of a broader spectrum of religious tourism, but it tends to be the most pious manifestation of this.

Based on these ideas, Ron suggested two broad types of Christian travel, namely pilgrimage and other forms. In Christianity, there tends to be three categories of pilgrimage destinations: sites associated with the New Testament, Old Testament sites and other scripture-based places and non-scripture sacred locations. Visits to these locations are often motivated by deep spiritual desires for self-improvement and worship, and are often the outward manifestations or physical culmination of an inward journey that began long before the pilgrim boarded an airplane.

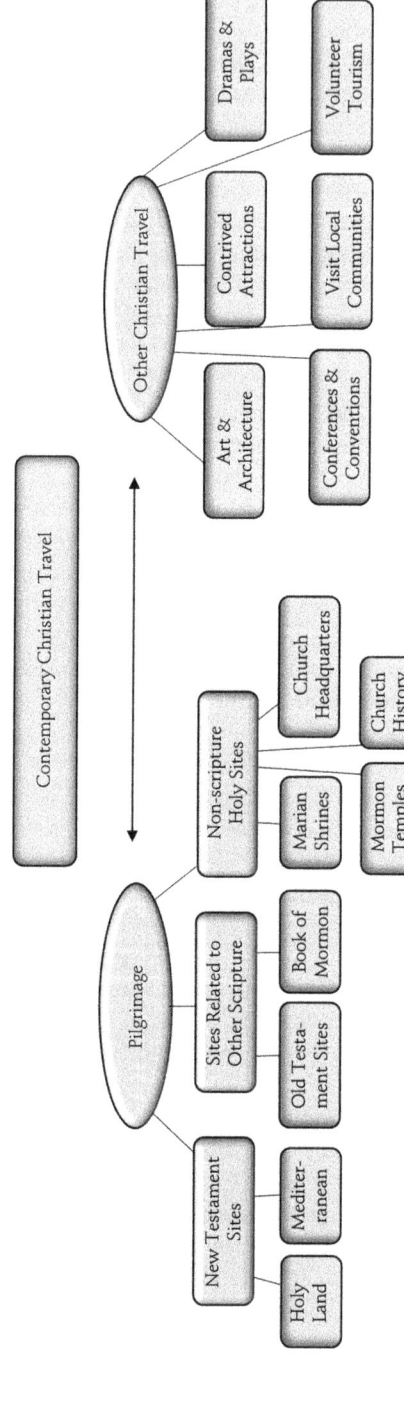

Figure 1.3 A typology of contemporary Christian travel (Source: Modified after Ron, 2009)

New Testament sites can be further divided into locations in the Holy Land (i.e. Israel, Palestine and Jordan) and those throughout the eastern Mediterranean (e.g. Turkey, Greece, Cyprus, Italy). The sites in the eastern Mediterranean relate more to the lives of Jesus' apostles and their missionary work than directly to Jesus himself. Places such as Ephasus and Antalya (Turkey), Rome (Italy) and Athens, Patmos and Thessaloniki (Greece) are examples of important pilgrimage destinations because of the events that occurred there in the lives and ministries of the ancient apostles (Egresi *et al.*, 2012b; Öter & Çetinkaya, 2016).

Other scripture-based visits include places noted in the Old Testament. Old Testament sites are found in Iraq, Syria, Lebanon, Egypt, Jordan, Israel and Palestine and include places of important events or areas where certain characters lived. To distinguish between Old and New Testament sites is essential, since some faiths emphasize the Jewish roots of Christianity (e.g. Christian Zionists), while others focus pilgrimage tours only on New Testament sites. The Qumran site in Israel, where the Dead Sea Scrolls were discovered in the mid-20th century, would also fit this category. Visits to the archaeological site of Qumran are often done in conjunction with other package tours near the Dead Sea. This classification of 'other' scripture also includes the Book of Mormon, which is considered sacred writ along with the Bible for members of the Church of Jesus Christ of Latter-day Saints (LDS Church or Mormon Church) and several other Restorationist groups. Most of the events in the Book of Mormon were believed to have taken place in Latin America. In common with other Christians, Mormons frequently travel to the Holy Land to experience biblical sites, but LDS tour groups also regularly visit ancient sites in Central America as potential locations of events in the Book of Mormon (Hudman & Jackson, 1992; Olsen, 2006b).

Non-scripture-based pilgrimage sites include Marian shrines, church headquarters, LDS temples, saints' shrines and tombs, and church history locations. Several Marian shrines have become very important pilgrimage destinations, such as those in Medjugorje, Fatima and Lourdes, where the Virgin Mary or her likeness is said to have appeared. Church headquarters are important attractions for pilgrims as well. Methodists visiting some of the administrative buildings of the United Methodist Church in Nashville, Tennessee, might have pilgrim-like experiences by meeting staff or seeing various administrative quarters. LDS Church members travel to temples all over the world, as these are considered the holiest place on earth for that denomination. Various shrines and tombs are located all over the world and become important pilgrimage destinations, such as St Patrick's tomb in Downpatrick, Northern Ireland, for Irish Catholics and St Olav's Way and Nidaros Cathedral, the burial place of St Olaf, for Norwegian Lutherans and Catholics. Church historic sites include Assisi, Italy, for Roman Catholics, and Lutherstadt Wittenberg, Germany, for Lutherans.

Ron's (2009) 'other' category of Christian travel, aside from pilgrimage, involves six subtypes of attractions and activities: art and architecture, contrived attractions, conferences and conventions, pageants and drama presentations, volunteer opportunities and visiting local communities. Most of these destinations and experiences are not associated with sanctioned holy sites, but they do involve some element of religion and/or spirituality. This second general category tends to relate more to Protestant travel, but assuredly also involves Catholic and Orthodox church members as well. Many Protestant denominations spurn the traditional notion of pilgrimage to blessed places, because of their common belief that God or the influence of God can be felt anywhere at any time; it is not limited to specific locations. This has resulted in the development of other religious travel experiences that cannot be classified as 'pilgrimage' *per se*.

Christian sites of art and architecture have long provided the backdrop for most cultural tourism in Europe and much of it in Latin America as well. The Cathedral of Notre Dame (Paris), Canterbury Cathedral (England), Derby Cathedral (England) and a multitude of other medieval churches are visited by many tourists, some more religious than others, because of their aesthetic and historical appeal (Francis *et al.*, 2010a, 2010b; Gutic *et al.*, 2010; Hughes *et al.*, 2013; Jackson & Hudman, 1995; Marine-Roig, 2015; Morpeth, 2011; Williams *et al.*, 2007; Wiltshier, 2015; Wiltshier & Clarke, 2012).

Ron's (2009) notion of contrived attractions includes Christian-themed environments, such as the Holy Land Experience in Orlando, Florida (USA); Fields of the Wood Bible Park in Murphy, North Carolina (USA); the Ark Encounter in Kentucky (USA); Nazareth Village in Nazareth, Israel; Christ the Redeemer Statue in Rio de Janeiro, Brazil; Christ of the Ozarks statue in Eureka Springs, Arkansas (USA); and Tierra Santa theme park in Argentina (Ron & Feldman, 2009; Shoval, 2000). There are also purpose-built attractions in the Holy Land that offer biblical meals to foreign tourists (Ron & Timothy, 2013).

Conferences, retreats and conventions are one of the most pervasive categories of religious tourism in Christianity. Church conferences, such as the Southern Baptist Convention's annual conference/convention, held at a different US location each year, draws thousands of Southern Baptists from around North America. The Semiannual General Conference of the LDS Church in Salt Lake City is attended by more than 100,000 people every six months, who come from all corners of the globe. Every three years, representatives from the Pentecostal World Fellowship (2011) gather in different worldwide locations to support each other in prayer, discuss matters of evangelism, promote Christian fellowship, administer relief to the destitute and defend faith and social justice. Youth revivals and motivational meetings (e.g. World Youth Day) are becoming increasingly important throughout the Christian world.

Christian drama includes passion plays and pageants. Passion plays depict the life and death of Jesus Christ. These are important in the Roman Catholic Church as part of Lent. The famous Passion Play at Oberammergau, Germany, which is held every 10 years, has become a standard attraction for many package tours of Europe, even non-religious tours, while many congregations travel together from North America and other parts of Europe to experience the play (Wetmore, 2017). The production typically draws between 450,000 and 550,000 spectators. Other places have begun to offer their own versions of the Passion, such as the impressive annual The Great Passion Play in Eureka Springs, Arkansas, USA. The LDS Church puts on several pageants every year throughout the United States. One of the largest is the Jesus the Christ Easter pageant in Mesa, Arizona, which is conducted in English and Spanish and involves approximately 500 volunteer cast members and some 400 volunteer support staff made up of Latter-day Saints and members of other Christian faiths. The pageant is attended by some 100,000–150,000 spectators during a 10-day period every spring (Adair, 2016; Business Wire, 2005).

Volunteer vacations have become very popular in recent years, and this form of tourism resonates with people who are willing to give of their time and means to do something good for society or the environment. Christian travel also involves a great deal of volunteer tourism, which manifests in three primary ways. First are humanitarian trips that help the world's needy by teaching them survival skills (e.g. gardening, water purification, home construction) or helping dig wells to provide remote villages with clean drinking water. In many cases, it also entails traveling to disaster zones to help recovery efforts and comfort the destitute. Second, Christians travel on short-term 'mini-missions' or 'missions light' to help spread the gospel of Jesus Christ. On these missions, which may last a week or several months, Bible instruction usually accompanies the humanitarian aspects of volunteerism (Brown & Morrison, 2003; Gulatt-Whiteman, 2004). Finally, some Christians have a penchant for volunteering at holy places, such as the Garden Tomb in Jerusalem, which many Protestants believe was the final resting place of Jesus prior to his resurrection. The attraction relies a great deal on volunteer workers from abroad who serve freely at the site for a few or several weeks at a time; their pay is the spiritual growth they experience and the opportunity to serve at such an important locale.

The final type of 'other' Christian travel, according to Ron (2009), is visiting local communities. This may overlap somewhat with the mini-missions noted above, but it may also be a means of demonstrating solidarity with remote Christians, some of whom feel persecuted because of their religious affiliation. 'Living Stones' tours to Israel and Palestine to visit Christian congregations (Sizer, 1999) are one example. Another is solidarity tours to Israel among fundamentalist Christian congregations whose visit is partly politically motivated by standing with the cause of

Israel. Other Christian groups are more sympathetic to the Palestinian cause and participate in solidarity tours to the West Bank and Gaza Strip in support of peace between Israel and Palestine, or to show their sympathy to the Palestinian cause (Brin, 2006; Higgins-Desbiolles & Russell-Mundine, 2008; Kassis *et al.*, 2016).

This Book

This book adopts a similar approach to that of Ron (2009) and Wright (2008) in emphasizing pilgrimage and other elements of Christian tourism in the modern world. It emphasizes Christian travel as part of the larger tourism system and examines Christians' travel activities in sacred space and time – pilgrimage and for other fellowship purposes. Chapter 2 highlights the religious travel patterns and preferences of various Christian denominations. While it is not exhaustive in its coverage of various sects of Christianity, it uses several examples to illustrate pilgrimage and non-pilgrimage travel from a range of sectoral perspectives, as well as geographic patterns of production and consumption in this travel sector.

The third chapter underscores how religion has become a tourism commodity and the ways in which faith-based travel is produced by destinations and service providers and commercialized to become a consumable product for Christian tourists. Chapter 4 spins off from Chapter 3 to provide an overview of the means and ways in which destinations, organizations and service providers market their unique religious products to a growing consumer market.

Chapter 5 examines the phenomenon of volunteer tourism as a commodified and well-marketed form of Christian tourism, and highlights its unique Christian characteristics. The chapter identifies several types of Christian volunteer tourism, including short-term missions, long-term missions, working at biblical archaeology sites, 'solidarity tourism' and staffing various sacred and church history sites around the world. It reflects on the Christian notions of humanitarian work, serving others in the name of Christ, and visiting local communities.

Chapter 6 follows the volunteer chapter because themed environments in the Christian context rely heavily on volunteer staff. A wide range of contrived themed environments are described and analyzed as part of the world's faithscapes and religious tourist attractions. In Chapter 7, pilgrimage routes and religious heritage trails are examined as important tourism products that connect Christians with sacred spaces, such as shrines and spiritual centers. The forms, functions and origins of these spiritual pathways are examined, together with their management and implications for the religious landscapes of Christian destinations. The next chapter focuses on religious events, which include conferences, conventions, special world events, pageants and other dramatic presentations. The final chapter provides some conceptual insights into what has been presented throughout the book and identifies potential areas for future research.

These chapters were designed to highlight the multitudinous patterns, destinations, attractions and activities involved in contemporary Christian travel. They encompass the broader notion of pilgrimage as both a traditional pious activity of the faithful and an enjoyable and meaningful tourism experience of devoted Christians today. They especially take into account the foundational elements of the attractiveness of places according to Christian thinking – spirit of place, scriptural connections, art and architecture, contrived/themed environments, programmed events, volunteer travel opportunities and visiting local communities by way of solidarity tourism and mission work. It is our hope that this volume will stimulate additional thinking into how the gospel of Jesus Christ and the places associated with his life and ministry, as well as those of his apostles and Holy Writ, have become commoditized, while simultaneously providing spiritual enrichment and satisfying travel experiences.

2 Evolving Patterns of Christian Travel: Denominational and Geographical Perspectives

Introduction

There is considerable variation between Christian denominations, not just doctrinally speaking, but also in terms of their travel preferences, behaviors, pilgrim narratives and cultural performances (Bajc, 2006; Bowman, 2000; Guter, 2004; Liebelt, 2010). The Holy Land is the central focus of travel on a global scale for all Christian denominations. However, various churches also have faith-specific destinations to which their adherents travel regularly and with considerable devotion. Some of these are international in scale, such as Medjugorje and Lourdes, which draw millions of Roman Catholics from around the world each year. Christian pilgrimage destinations in some countries, however, have a more domestic market reach and have significant nationalistic undertones, such as those associated with the life of St Olaf in Norway and St Patrick in Ireland.

Likewise, various Protestant groups have their own sacred sites, which few other Christians visit, except perhaps as curiosity-seekers. Examples of these include various church history locations and holy sites presumed to be associated with different scriptural experiences. For example, Latter-day Saint tourists commonly travel to church history sites in New York, Missouri and Ohio, and Russian and Greek Orthodox adherents travel to many church-specific sites in Eastern Europe and Greece, most of which would not exert a natural religious appeal to adherents of other Christian faiths.

Efforts are also under way, however, to effect changes in current markets, including attracting more Christian denominations to locales that traditionally have been the focus of individual denominations, such as attempts to bring Lutherans and Methodists to Rome, and Christians in general to places such as Malta, or in other words, converting sectoral destinations to multisectoral destinations.

This chapter describes several denominations and their unique travel patterns, and it highlights the patterns and trends associated with the common core of Christian travel, namely Jerusalem and the broader

Holy Land. It also examines the geographical broadening of the 'Holy Land' concept and the erosion of place-based pilgrimages toward a modern-day emphasis on pilgrimage/sacred experiences. In the end, the chapter looks at the role that geography and geopolitics, or political instability, plays in diverting traditional markets (e.g. Christians traveling to the Holy Land) to other alternative destinations, such as Greece, Turkey, Cyprus and Italy – all locations of important events associated with early Christianity.

Sectoral and Multisectoral Destinations

As observed by several researchers (Brent Plate, 2009; Bywater, 1994; Ron, 2009) and noted already in Chapter 1, Christian travel is a massive phenomenon. K.J. Wright, past president of the World Religious Travel Association (WRTA), estimated that more than 300 million people travel annually for religious and pilgrimage reasons (Steinmetz, 2009), although the World Tourism Organization (UNWTO, 2011) recently estimated this number to be approximately 600 million each year. Many of these people are Christians traveling for religious purposes, and one of several possible ways to organize our understanding of this vast phenomenon is by making a distinction between individual denominations and multidenominational destinations.

In his or her lifetime, a Christian is likely to visit a number of sacred sites that differ categorically; some will be visited mainly by adherents of a single denomination, while others will be visited by Christians of many different churches and a few sites will be visited by non-Christian tourists as well. An example of the first category of sites is Far West, Missouri (Hamer, 2008) – an important church history site for Latter-day Saints, but it is very unlikely to attract members of other Christian denominations. On the other hand, one is likely to see many diverse Christians at Jerusalem's holy Christian sites (e.g. the Church of the Holy Sepulcher), as well as a wide variety of non-Christian tourists, because such sites are synonymous with the general heritage of the city (Guter & Feldman, 2006; Olsen & Ron, 2013).

This phenomenon can be understood in the terminology of the American anthropologist Robert Redfield (1956) concerning 'great traditions' and 'little traditions', which according to Allison (1997), is the distinction between the higher, elite levels of a civilization (great tradition) and the folk or popular levels (little tradition). According to this analogy, and from the perspective of Christianity as a whole, Far West, Missouri, would be a site of little tradition, whereas the Church of the Holy Sepulcher would be an example of a great tradition.

The distinction between sectoral and multisectoral destinations is not always fixed and unchanging. Denomination-specific sites can become more central and more visited by members of other denominations as well. Rome, for example, has always been associated as a Catholic destination, but it is becoming increasingly popular among Protestants because of its association with some of the early apostles. According to Hartwig (2006),

> Don avoided traveling to Rome for most of his life. He was raised a Pentecostal and had, like many in his generation, assumed Rome was hopelessly corrupted by Catholic culture and cultic devotion to the Pope. A year later, after visiting Rome he says: 'I feel cheated! ... Rome is full of early Christian artifacts and historical sites. It is my heritage, too, and all these years people have steered me away from this incredible resource for learning about the earliest generation of Christians! Rome belongs to me, too! (Hartwig, 2006: np)

Lourdes is another example of this tendency. The famous Marian shrine near the French Pyrenees has been attracting increasing numbers of non-Catholic pilgrims in recent decades (Kselman, 2001). Cranston (1958), a Protestant visitor to Lourdes six decades ago, wrote about the healing powers of the place, and Lambouras (1997), a member of the Russian Patriarchal Cathedral Parish at Ennismore Gardens in London, writes that

> not being a member of the Roman Catholic Church, I felt under no obligation or inclination to give them much thought. But learning that an Orthodox priest had been on pilgrimage to Lourdes, and that the wife of another Orthodox priest organized an annual visit by a group of Orthodox women to Lourdes, my interest was aroused, and I began to feel a strong compulsion to take a closer look at the Marian apparitions and their shrines. (Lambouras, 1997: 1)

There are at least two possible explanations for this phenomenon of single-denomination destinations becoming multisectoral in their appeal. The first was provided by Turner, who referred to peripheral Catholic sites in Mexico that are becoming more mainstream (Figure 2.1). According to Turner (1973),

> If we take this view that pilgrimages sometimes generate cities and consolidate regions, we need not abandon the view that they are sometimes also the ritualized vestiges of former sociopolitical systems... Former centrality has become peripherality, but peripherality may then become the setting for new centrality as waves of pilgrims invade and many settle near the peripheral shrines. (Turner, 1973: 229)

In other words, through original, unisectoral pilgrimage, places may become well known and developed, which then translates into a process

Figure 2.1 Mexican pilgrims arriving at Our Lady of Guadalupe shrine in Mexico City – now an extremely mainstream Catholic destination (Photo: D. Timothy)

of becoming more mainstream and celebrated more broadly. Through this process of centralization, a single denomination site begins to draw visitors, even some pilgrims, from other Christian sects.

The second possible explanation is the ecumenical spirit of contemporary Christianity. During the last few decades, Christianity for the most part has become more inter-Christian in its dialogue and approach. The Roman Catholic Church did not formally recognize the existence of the ecumenical movement until 1960, when it established the Secretariat for Promoting Christian Unity. Soon after, Protestant and Eastern Orthodox observers were invited to the Second Vatican Council (1962–1965). The Decree on Ecumenism (1964) declared by that council encouraged new dialogues between Protestant and Orthodox churches (Kishkovsky, 2010). In 1969, Pope Paul VI visited the headquarters of the World Council of Churches in Geneva, and in 1999 John Paul II became the first pope to visit Orthodox nations (Mcelveen, 2010).

In 1973, the Eastern Orthodox Church published 'Guidelines for Orthodox Christians in Ecumenical Relations' (Stephanopoulos, 1973), and on a more grassroots level, the North Carolina Council of Churches came out with the following pastoral reflections:

> Have you ever wondered what Jesus thinks is most important? ... There is a fourth and final thing that Jesus considers among the most important of all. It is that his followers be one as he and the Father are one. Why

is this on such a short list of things that are most important to Jesus?' (Mcelveen, 2010: 54)

Travel Patterns of Eastern Christianity

Eastern Christianity is divided into a number of families of churches, of which the better known are the Eastern Orthodox Church and the Oriental Orthodox Churches. The churches of Eastern Christianity are distinctive in that the main families of churches are organized into self-governing jurisdictions along national, ethnic and/or linguistic lines.

The Eastern Orthodox Church is a Christian body whose adherents are largely based in Russia, Greece, Eastern Europe and the Middle East, with a growing presence in the Western world. Oriental Orthodox Churches is a modern name for the denominations that rejected the Christological teaching of the Definition of Chalcedon in 451 CE, and include the Armenian, Coptic, Ethiopian and Syrian Orthodox faiths (Livingstone, 2000).

The contemporary travel patterns of Eastern Christianity are under-researched compared to the masses of writings on Catholic and Protestant travel. Additionally, there is a significant gap between the scarcity of research literature and the abundance of non-academic information available in tour operator-focused promotional websites, in blogs, in travel literature and various social media. Several Eastern denominations are not represented at all in the academic research literature, and some are more represented than others.

Eastern Orthodox travel

Eastern Orthodox Church members are avid pilgrims (Bowman, 2000; Terzidou *et al.*, 2017; Triantafillidou *et al.*, 2010). Their most popular religious destinations are Jerusalem, Bethlehem, Istanbul (formerly Constantinople), Mount Sinai, Antioch, Meteora and Mount Athos. They are a pervasive group in the Holy Land, and they visit many different areas in Greece, Turkey and Cyprus that have played an important role in the development of the Orthodox faiths (Figure 2.2).

Constantinople (today's Istanbul) was the former capital of the Byzantine Empire, and the seat of one of the ancient patriarchates. It is the religious center of the Greek Orthodox Church and home to some of the world's oldest churches, including the Hagia Sophia, a former cathedral (now a mosque) and burial place of many ancient patriarchs of the Eastern Orthodox Church (McGuckin, 2010). The Ecumenical Patriarch of Istanbul is generally considered the spiritual leader of the Orthodox Christian churches.

Mount Athos, also known as the Holy Mountain, is an extremely important destination for Eastern Orthodox Christians (Andriotis, 2009; Gothóni, 1993, 1994; Gothóni & Speake, 2008; Kotsi, 1999, 2003, 2007;

Figure 2.2 Church of Saint Lazarus in Larnaca, Cyprus – the final resting place of Lazarus (Photo: D. Timothy)

Sherrard, 1977; Speake, 2005) as is the important shrine of Meteora (Maddrell *et al.*, 2015). The Mount Athos peninsula in Greece has been a bastion of Christianity for approximately 1800 years. The area is home to more than 2000 monks from all over the Eastern Orthodox world (e.g. Russia, Romania, Moldova, Serbia, Bulgaria and Georgia) who live a monastic life of worship. The area is home to exemplary architecture, massive collections of religious art, artifacts, icons and books and was inscribed as a UNESCO World Heritage Site in 1988 (Alexopoulos, 2013).

Although it is an important religious destination, visitation at Mount Athos is governed by strict behavioral guidelines, and several unique regulations pertain to visiting Mount Athos (Della Dora, 2012; Dubisch, 1990, 1995, 2009). Foremost among these is that women are prohibited from entering. While controversial in many respects, the monastic order has been able to maintain this regulation since its founding centuries ago. Secondly, male visitors can enter only with a valid visitors permit, and non-Greeks are required to possess a passport. Third, pilgrims under the age of 18 cannot stay overnight, and finally only 100 Orthodox pilgrims and 10 non-Orthodox visitors are allowed to enter each day.

Saint Catherine's Monastery in Sinai, Egypt, was established during the 6th century CE and is widely regarded as one of the oldest functioning Christian monasteries in the world. It is controlled by the Eastern Orthodox Church known as the Church of Sinai and is a World Heritage Site.

It purports to include the world's oldest continually operating library, housing many ancient books and records, and is a salient pilgrimage destination for Eastern Orthodox pilgrims (Hobbs, 1992; Shackley, 1998, 2001).

In addition to these pilgrimage locations of general Eastern Orthodox interest, many Eastern countries are home to their own 'little traditions' (Redfield, 1956) that appeal to a more state-specific Orthodox audience (Bakalova, 2002; Burtea, 2009; Chiş & Ţîrca, 2009; Jackowski & Marciniak, 2000; Metreveli & Timothy, 2010; Przybył, 2002; Stănciulescu & Ţîrca, 2010; Stoykova, 2009; Ţîrca & Stănciulescu, 2009; Ţîrca et al., 2010), although many of them are also visited by church members from other countries.

Russian Orthodox pilgrimages were popular before the establishment of communism (Nakamura, 1988; Vernitski, 2003); these were largely quelled during the communist period owing to the official state dogma of atheism and the establishment of state controls against religious observance, including pilgrimage travel. In the post-communist era, there has been a revival of religious tourism, especially to the Holy Land (Roitershtein, 2009). Domestically, several monasteries in Russia have once again become popular attractions for Orthodox Russians, including the Diveyevo, Pokrovksy and Valaam monasteries, as well as the Peschchorka shrine (Kormina, 2004).

The Finnish Orthodox post-Second World War landscape is quite unique in the heavy involvement of monasteries in the tourism industry (Mikula, 2013). The New Valamo (New Valaam) monastery was built in Heinävesi, Finland, in 1940 as a refuge for nearly 200 monks who were evacuated from their monastery in a region (Valaam) that was Finland at the time but occupied by the Soviet Union during the Winter War in 1939. New Valamo, the only men's monastery belonging to the Finnish Orthodox Church, has 'become a major ecumenical centre as well as a tourist site. It is an object of pilgrimage not only for Orthodox believers but for Lutherans as well' (Raivo, 2002: 21) (Figure 2.3).

Members of the Greek Orthodox Church undertake pilgrimages to the Convent of the Dormition of the Virgin near Thessaloniki (Rahkala, 2010a, 2010b) and to the island of Tinos (Aslan & Andriotis, 2010; Terzidou, 2010; Terzidou et al., 2008), which is known for 1200 white chapels and the famous church of Panagia Evanglistria. The church was built to house an icon that was found in 1823 by a local nun, who dreamed about the Virgin Mary who informed her about the icon and revealed its location. The gold-plated icon, which is believed to have worked miracles, was found around the same time the modern Greek state was created. As a result, Our Lady of Tinos was proclaimed the patron saint of Greece. The church is the most popular Christian pilgrimage site in Greece (Aslan & Andriotis, 2010). Churches on several of the other

Figure 2.3 The still functioning New Valamo Finnish Orthodox Monastery is a well-known tourist retreat (Photo: D. Timothy)

islands in the Greek archipelago are venerated as holy pilgrimage destinations (Kamenidou & Vourou, 2015).

Oriental Orthodox travel

Much has been written on the history and theology of the Coptic Orthodox Church, which is centered in Cairo, Egypt. The main authority on Coptic pilgrimage practices is Meinardus (2002, 2007), who elaborates on the difference of meaning attributed to pilgrimage by the Copts:

> In the Western world, pilgrimages became associated with the doctrine of forgiveness of sins and the acquisition of indulgences. For the Copts, by contrast, pilgrimage is a visible demonstration of Christian faith in a non-Christian environment. The pilgrimage is the Coptic expression and desire to be close to Christ, the Holy Virgin Mary, and the saints. (Meinardus, 2007: 3)

Although the Holy Land is a potential (and nearby) sacred destination for the Copts, few ever visit because of political tensions and hotly contested territorial claims against other Christian sects within the Church of the Holy Sepulcher (Cohen, 2008; Cohen-Hattab & Shoval, 2015; Timothy & Emmett, 2014). Consequently, Coptic pilgrimages are currently limited to visiting tombs of martyrs in the Nile Delta and the Nile Valley (Meinardus, 2007).

In common with the Copts, much has been written about the Ethiopian Orthodox history and theology, but very little has been said about their pilgrimage practices. Kaplan (2011), however, claims that pilgrimage in Ethiopia,

> ...has not yet been the subject of systematic study ... The specific rituals performed at pilgrimage and the catchment areas from which they draw participants have not been adequately documented. Finally, the vast theoretical literature regarding pilgrimage has not been rigorously applied to Ethiopian cases. (Kaplan, 2011: 153)

According to Kaplan (2011: 154), for Ethiopian Orthodox Christians the highest form of pilgrimage is the journey to Jerusalem at Easter, but they also undertake regular pilgrimages to Däbrä Kol in Eritrea, in honor of one of their saints who is entombed there. The site has a spring, which probably predates the saint, but is said to have miraculously begun to flow when he was murdered by rebels.

In summary, there are three main types of religious travel practices prevalent in contemporary Eastern Christianity. The first entails travel to sacred places of international acclaim and interdenominational significance, such as the Holy Land and Turkey. The second type includes travel to domestic sectorial attractions, such as monasteries, nunneries, burial places and sites affiliated with icons or other objects considered to be carriers of miraculous power. Third are visits to non-Eastern Christian destinations that are more closely associated with the Western Orthodox diaspora (Ron, 2010a).

Catholic Patterns of Travel

Current Catholic travel patterns revolve firmly around acts of pilgrimage and the physical journey involved, in contrast to the Eastern Orthodox, who focus more on the destination – the shrines and their relics and healing powers (Maddrell & Della Dora, 2013; Della Dora *et al.*, 2015). According to Cunningham and Egan (1996),

> To say that the Christian life has a direction is another way of saying something strongly emphasized at the Second Vatican Council: the Christian people are a pilgrim people, and our life, with all its burdens and joys, has a direction that begins in God and ends when all things are summed up in Christ. (Cunningham & Egan, 1996: 10)

The research literature on Catholic travel patterns is vast, and there are several ways of classifying it (Korov, 2014; Liutikas, 2018; Vilaça, 2010). The categories of general Catholic travel, sites of the martyrs, In the

Footsteps of Jesus, the Holy See and tourism, Marian pilgrimage and other themes and destinations are described below.

General Catholic travel

In common with other churches, general Catholic travel involves visiting sacred sites in the Holy Land either as an act of intellectual learning or as an act of faith. From the Catholic perspective, Todd (1984: 43) suggests that 'a place is holy by virtue of the individual's response to it'. In the *Catholic Encyclopedia*, Jarrett (1911) explained Catholic pilgrimages from antiquity to the modern day, with a strong regional emphasis on European pilgrimages. Gayá (2002: 12) reflects on Catholic pilgrimages from the perspective of pastoral theology and elaborates on the Catholic definition of pilgrimage, which is '… a cultural expression that must be undertaken in faithfulness to tradition, with intense religious feeling and as a realization of their Paschal existence'. According to Vukonić (2006: 237), there are three forms of religious tourism within Roman Catholicism: pilgrimage, large-scale gatherings on the occasion of significant religious dates and anniversaries, and general visitations to important religious places and buildings.

Sites of the martyrs

Catholics are especially zealous in visiting locations associated with the martyrdoms and burials of the ancient apostles to commemorate their lives and role in establishing the early church. While Catholics visit the Vatican City owing to its role as the headquarters of the Church and seat of the Holy See, the microstate's main attraction is St Peter's Basilica, the largest Catholic church in the world and the site of St Peter's execution and burial (Timothy, 2001). The Vatican City and its St Peter's Basilica is the most famous site of apostolic martyrdom and burial and is visited by millions of Catholics each year (Kim & Kim, in press; Vukonić, 2006). Not far from the Vatican's borders is the location of St Paul's tomb inside the Basilica of Saint Paul Outside the Walls in Rome proper. These two locations, together with Mamertine Prison (Figure 2.4), where Paul was imprisoned for preaching the gospel in Rome, and several other sites, are salient destinations for Catholic religious tourists in Rome (Josan, 2009; Schmisek, 2017).

Santiago de Compostela, a city in Spain's Galicia region, has received the most research attention by religious tourism scholars of any apostle-related pilgrimage location in Europe (e.g. Frey, 1998; Herrero, 2008; Mashhadigholam Rojo, 2007; Morpeth, 2007; Roseman, 2004; Roseman & Fife, 2008; Santos, 2002; Scheer, 2007; Tilson, 2005; Watson, 2006), although the majority of the studies have focused on the pilgrimage trail leading to the city rather than the city itself as a destination. Santiago is believed to host the burial site of St James, and it has been

Figure 2.4 Mamertine Prison in Rome is where St Peter and St Paul were believed to have been imprisoned during their ministry (Photo: D. Timothy)

one of the most visited shrine cities in the Catholic world since the 9th century CE.

In the Footsteps of Jesus

For Catholics, 'In the Footsteps of Jesus' is a popular pilgrimage theme in the Holy Land, which geographically includes Israel, Palestine and Jordan, and corresponds with the time of Jesus and the locations mentioned in the gospels of Matthew, Mark, Luke and John (Ron, 2009: 291). According to Lux (2010),

> When one brings to mind the land where the great events of our redemption took place … there is a sense of the presence of these events and an experience of Christ's presence brought about by the land. … The most

intense sense of presence, of course, is making a pilgrimage to the Holy Land, visiting and praying at the sites where Jesus lived and walked and the early church took root. (Lux, 2010: 6)

Lux (2010: 60) further suggests that Catholics' relationship with the Holy Land and Christ is 'As Christ is the sacrament of our encounter with God, the Holy Land is a sacrament of our encounter with Christ'. The importance of the Holy Land pilgrimage to Catholics is also expressed in several spiritual guidebooks (e.g. Hagstrom & Vaisvilaite, 1999; Hoade, 1984).

For Catholics, the most essential modern-day pilgrim to the Holy Land is the Pope. There have been four consecutive papal pilgrimages to the Holy Land so far: Paul VI in 1964, John Paul II in 2000, Benedict XVI in 2009 and Francis in 2014. According to O'Mahony (2010), it is now Vatican policy that each pope goes on a pilgrimage to the Holy Land. For Catholics the world over, this imbues the Holy Land with additional light and blessings, and invigorates their collective desire to visit (Bajc, 2011; Biema *et al.*, 2000; Horoszewicz, 2002; O'Mahony, 2005). Papal visits to Jordan and Palestine also 'legitimize' the geographic extent of the broader Holy Land (Katz, 2003).

The Holy See and tourism

In the past few decades, the world has witnessed the fundamental development of a coherent Catholic policy that promotes tourism in general and religious tourism in particular, to such an extent that a 'Catholic travel dogma' can be identified. Olsen (2008: 30) acknowledges a formal theological perspective on tourism in the Roman Catholic Church, which had been formulated during and after the Second Vatican Council (1962–1965) in official church documents such as 'The Church and Tourism: Serving People on Their Travels for Recreation' and in 'Guidelines for the Pastoral Care of Tourism'. One of the results of the post-Second World War growth of tourism was that Popes Pius XII (1939–1958), John XXIII (1958–1963) and Paul VI (1963–1978) started speaking about tourism on a regular basis (Dziubiński, 2009: 254).

John Paul II (1978–2005) did much in formulating the theoretical vision of tourism from the perspectives of priests, theologians, philosophers and ethicists. He saw man as a *homo viator* (person on a journey) (Dziubiński, 2009: 256), and expressed his views on the Christian values of tourism in plethoric documents and speeches. Pope John Paul II saw '...tourism not only as an important social event but also as a spiritual experience, both theological and moral. ...For a Christian, tourism is a way of approaching God...' (Ostrowski, 1997: 152). But the late John Paul II was also an enthusiastic environmentalist. In 1982, he nominated St Francis to be the patron saint of environmentalists. One of the outcomes of this environmental sainthood was the organization of an international seminar in 1982 called *Terra Mater* (Mother Earth) in Gubbio, Italy, which resulted in the *Carta Gubbio* (Gubbio Charter) that encouraged bicycle and walking pilgrimages as more ecologically friendly options over motor vehicles (Ptaszycka-Jackowska, 2000: 86).

The Catholic development of tourism continued with Pope Benedict XVI, the successor to John Paul II. Like his predecessor, Benedict XVI spoke of travel as a way to build a better world based on the principles of solidarity and respect for the needs of all (Dziubiński, 2009: 255). Pope Francis has continued this line of discourse since the beginning of his papacy in 2013, combining an environmental ethic with a human development ethos regarding tourism. Under his direction, to commemorate 2017's World Tourism Day, the Vatican released a statement that encourages the development of tourism in sustainable ways for the betterment of humankind. According to the statement:

> …we Christians want to offer our contribution so that tourism can assist in the development of peoples, especially the most disadvantaged…. The Church is making its own contributions, launching initiatives that really place tourism in the service of the integral development of the person. This is why we talk about tourism with a human touch, which is based on projects of community tourism, cooperation, solidarity, and an appreciation of the great artistic heritage. (Turkson, 2017: np)

The statement also implies that humankind should be good stewards of the earth, and travel to appreciate God's creations and the world's great works of art.

The implications of this pro-tourism stance by recent Catholic leaders are many. These include the Vatican-owned tour company (Opera Romana Pellegrinaggi), which offers both pilgrimage journeys and secular holiday trips, and a hotel in Jerusalem (the Notre Dame Hotel). The Church has also developed sacred site management strategies that comply largely with John Paul II's (2002) views on ecotourism and sustainable development and Pope Francis's current emphasis on travel for the good of the individual soul, as well as an emphasis on monastic hospitality (O'Gorman, 2006; O'Gorman & MacPhee, 2006; O'Mahony & Bowe, 2006).

Marian pilgrimages

Marian shrines are memorials or sanctuaries that mark the locales of an apparition or miracle credited to the Virgin Mary. Many such shrines exist throughout the world and have become important pilgrimage destinations. Marian pilgrimage is a vast subject in Catholicism and is widely spread throughout the Catholic world (Krebs, 2017; Olsen, 2017).

Most scholarly studies of Marian pilgrimage travel can be classified into concept-oriented studies, comparative regional cases and local, single-site case studies. Most concept-oriented studies focus on Marian apparitions and how these have translated into major pilgrimage destinations (Bobbitt, 2008; Hermkens *et al.*, 2009; Horsfall, 2000; Krebs, 2017; Ventresca, 2003; Zimdars-Swartz, 1991). Comparative case studies have examined spatial, emotional and experiential differences among sites and visitors at various European and American Marian shrines (Ambrósio & Pereira, 2007; Blewett, 2004; Nolan & Nolan, 1989, 1992).

Single-site cases have been well documented by academic researchers, focusing largely on descriptive assessments of services for tourists/pilgrims, the sorts of souvenirs offered, visitor profiles and management challenges (Harpur, 2002; Jackowski & Smith, 1992; Jansen & Kühl, 2008; Lehrhaupt, 1991; Post *et al.*, 1998; Pusztai, 2004; Sallnow, 2000; Turner & Turner, 1978).

The most famous and visited Marian shrines in Catholicism are in Europe. These include Lourdes, France (Eade, 1992, 2000; Gesler, 1996; Higgins & Hamilton, 2016; Rinschede, 1986), Fatima, Portugal (de Pinho & de Pinho, 2007; Santos, 2003, 2009), Medjugorje, Bosnia and Herzegovina (Krešić *et al.*, 2013; Liutikas, 2015a; Skrbiš, 2007; Vukonić, 1992, 1996), Knock, Ireland (Krebs, 2017; Shackley, 2006b) and Marija Bistrica, Croatia (Pavicic *et al.*, 2007). While lesser known, there are also Marian shrines in the Americas and Asia (Frenz, 2008; Pagliaroli, 2004; Sallnow, 2000; Stirrat, 2000; Tweed, 1997; Williams, 2010).

Protestant Travel Patterns

The origins of Protestantism were based on a protest against the Catholic notion of pilgrimage, which emphasized indulgences and priestly mediation. Martin Luther went on a pilgrimage to Rome in 1510 and regarded the system of indulgences he faced there as a form of idolatry (Coleman & Elsner, 1995). In his view, '…the way to God and the Promised Land went through the mind and the heart, not through countries and cities' (Christensson, 2010: 58). According to Ron and Feldman (2009),

> in contrast to the phenomenon of the 'holy site', which affirms the essential heterogeneity of space (Eliade, 1959), in Protestant theology, space was homogeneous, as '…the whole earth is full of His glory' (Isaiah 6:3). (Ron & Feldman, 2009: 203)

According to this view, because God and Christ are transcendent and omnipresent, no place can be holier than another. This view is well expressed by John Milton, who in his poem, *Paradise Lost*, referred to pilgrimage as the paradise of fools: 'Here Pilgrims roam, that stray'd so far to seek in Golgotha him dead, who lives in Heav'n' (Milton, 1836: 98, cited in Zwi Werblowsky, 1983). Calvin was also against pilgrimage, and regarded the veneration of relics through pilgrimage a 'vain speculation' and a challenge to the exclusive view of the Bible as the only foundation of truth (Moore, 2003: 70).

Because of the Reformation, most Protestants had avoided pilgrimages for centuries, and it was not until the acquisition of the Garden Tomb in Jerusalem in 1894 (Walker, 1999: 128) that Protestants began to show an interest in creating their own version of sacred space. Today, Protestants do visit Christian sacred sites, but many continue to demonstrate an aversion to the term 'pilgrim', as it seems to be too Catholic (Todd, 1984; Tomlin, 2004). Likewise, many contemporary scholars prefer to refer to Protestant visitation of sacred sites as acts of religious tourism rather than pilgrimage (e.g. Collins-Kreiner *et al.*, 2006; Fleischer, 2000; Smith, 1992). According to Tomlin (2004: 110), 'Protestants do not go on Pilgrimages – at least that is the common perception… In fact, many Protestants do go on pilgrimage, although they do not tend to call it that' (Tomlin, 2004: 110).

In the Footsteps of Jesus

The Holy Land is the pivot of today's long-distance Protestant travel. Although difficult to measure precisely, it is common knowledge among tour operators that Protestants and Jews generate many repeat visits to Israel and the Holy Land. Most Protestant tours and tourists are comparable to other Christian denominations.

There appears to be a stronger affinity among Protestant groups for uncluttered landscapes and natural areas, compared to the overabundant shrinescapes and churchscapes associated with the Catholic and Orthodox churches in the Holy Land (Collins-Kreiner *et al.*, 2006; Feldman, 2007; Feldman & Ron, 2011; Lock, 2003; Ron, 2010b; Ron & Feldman, 2009). In fact, most Protestants, including evangelicals, find the extravagant décor in Holy Land shrines and churches to be rather off-putting and spiritually distracting (Collins-Kreiner & Kliot, 2000; Ron, 2010b; Ron & Feldman, 2009). Most studies have found that Protestants overall prefer to see more authentic, less-developed sites and scientifically accurate representations of sacred spaces and narratives (Belhassen, 2009; Belhassen *et al.*, 2008; Belhassen & Santos, 2006).

The evangelizing journeys of Paul

Greece and Turkey are often referred to in a Christian context as the second Holy Land, or as an extension of the Holy Land (Güçlü, 1998), due to their richness in the roots of Christianity. Pauline sites are especially important to Protestants because of the Apostle Paul's emphasis on outreach and missionary work, which are also prevalent beliefs and practices among mainline Protestants and evangelicals (Han, 2008; Walton, 2000). Trips to Greece and Turkey are often referred to in the industry as 'In the Footsteps of Paul' journeys (Duncan, 2009; Dunn, 2006; Finegan, 1981), which clearly define the regional and thematic differences between these destinations and the better-known and established 'In the Footsteps of Jesus' journeys in the Holy Land. The importance of Paul as an inspiration for modern-day pilgrimages cannot be overstated (Motyer, 2004; Ron, 2009). The New Testament accounts of his missionary journeys in present-day Cyprus, Greece, Italy, Lebanon, Macedonia, Malta, Syria and Turkey have inspired a growing sub-sector of religious tourism in the Mediterranean.

Protestant alternatives to pilgrimage

The Protestant theological opposition to pilgrimage did not extinguish the desire for spiritual and faith-based travel among Protestants. As a matter of fact, many Protestants are frequent faith-based travelers, and Holy Land tour operators base much of their business on repeat Protestant visitors to Israel (Hodgson, 2008). In this context, Fuchs and Reichel (2011) found that nearly half (42%) of the tourists in their study were repeat visitors to Israel, many of whom were religiously motivated to visit. In his field notes, Ron (2011) recorded the following experience:

> I remember once on the Temple Mount while guiding an American Mormon group, I saw an elderly American tour leader. His group was obviously Protestant, most likely Evangelical, and he said to my 64 year old tour leader: 'Hey brother, how many times have you been to the Holy Land?' 'This is my 25th visit' replied my tour leader; 'this is my 42nd visit! Hallelujah!' replied the evangelical tour leader. (Ron, 2011: np)

Ron (2009: 292–293) discusses several non-pilgrimage travel activities prevalent among Protestants, which include visits to Christian sites of art and architecture; visits to contrived attractions, also known as themed environments, or Christian theme sites; attending Christian conferences and conventions; Christian dramatic presentations; Christian volunteer tourism; and visiting local communities in the context of solidarity tours. Several Protestant groups visit local communities in a show of solidarity toward Christian Palestinians, whom the outsiders believe are oppressed by the Israeli state and can benefit from contact with the outside world (Feldman, 2011; Shapiro, 2008). Some of these forms will be elaborated on in the chapters that follow.

Common to some of these travel practices is the notion of visiting an 'ordinary' place for sacred purposes (e.g. humanitarian aid), instead of traveling to a traditional sacred locale. Tomlin (2004) suggests that

Protestant pilgrimage should be regarded as a metaphor for everyday Christian life,

> ...as pilgrimage gives it shape and direction, and orients it decisively towards its future rather than its present, the destination rather than travelling for its own sake. It is perhaps a metaphor which needs to be rediscovered in a post-modern age which has lost any sense of purpose or destination to life, and where Christian existence is liable to take its lead from the surrounding culture rather than its Biblical roots. A Church living in a culture which does not see any direction in the future, but instead celebrates the aimlessness of wandering, needs good Christian imagery which reminds it again and again of its true calling to live in anticipation and hope, not complacency and contentment. (Tomlin, 2004: 123)

Latter-day Saint Patterns of Travel

LDS Church leaders on travel, tourism and pilgrimage

The Church of Jesus Christ of Latter-day Saints has no formal pilgrimage practices or a 'theology of tourism' (Cohen, 2004: 148). However, LDS Church leaders and members recognize sacred spaces and have long held that certain places are more holy or sacred than others. Leaders of the Church of Jesus Christ of Latter-day Saints maintain that the church's historical and sacred sites cannot be compared to those of other faiths, which are often associated with the forgiveness of sins or miraculous healings (Mitchell, 2003). These personal events are not expected to occur at LDS sacred sites; instead, they can occur anywhere at any time through proper personal repentance, priesthood blessings and righteous living (Hudman & Jackson, 1992). According to Bruce R. McConkie, a well-known LDS leader and theologian, 'Neither shrines nor pilgrimages are a part of true worship as practiced by the true saints... [T]here is no thought that some special virtue will attach to worship by performing [pilgrimage to sacred sites]' (McConkie, 1966: 574, cited in Olsen, 2006b).

Despite the lack of a coherent theology of pilgrimage or tourism in general, church leaders have long encouraged informal pilgrimage-like journeys to temples and places related to church history and heritage (Olsen, 2006b). This is perhaps because so much of Latter-day Saint theology derives from its history (Head, 2006; Mitchell, 2003). According to Madsen (2003),

> Church leaders evidently feel that the Church needs more than just theology and history to maintain cohesion and unity, it needs a geography as well; sacred space that all Mormons – whether in Utah or Uganda – can feel a part of, thus rooting the religion in place. (Madsen, 2003: 252)

According to Laga (2010), the development of Mormon historical sites was strongly encouraged by Gordon B. Hinckley (church president 1995–2008), who led many of the church's efforts to acquire and restore land, homes, barns, stores and other heritage buildings as a means of protecting the church's tangible heritage and as a tool for helping members build their faith through a collective memory (Laga, 2010).

The LDS Church invests many resources in developing and maintaining heritage sites and visitor centers, among which the best-known are probably Temple Square in Salt Lake City, Utah, the historic city of Nauvoo, Illinois, and the town of Palmyra, New York. According to Olsen (2009: 133), this initiated tourism development takes place because tourism is regarded as a missionary tool, and is used by the church to accomplish some of its proselytizing and ministerial goals.

Bible land tours

Visiting the Holy Land is considered by Latter-day Saints to be a pivotal goal and the journey of a lifetime. The numbers of LDS visitors to the Holy Land are relatively small compared to other Christian tourists, which reflects the fact that there are only some 16 million Latter-day Saints worldwide. Nonetheless, they are an important travel market segment in the Bible lands, and they travel for the same purposes as other denominations – to walk where Jesus walked, to feel the spirit of the Holy Land and to experience the geographies of the Bible (Guter, 1997, 2000, 2006). The importance of the Holy Land to Mormons is evident in the large number of tours developed and sold through church-related media and private institutions (Hudman & Jackson, 1992). According to Olsen (2006b: 262), 'The importance of the Holy Land is deep and can be seen in the establishment of a physical presence in Jerusalem via the church-owned Brigham Young University (BYU) Jerusalem Center for Near Eastern Studies'.

In addition to traditional Christian places, Latter-day Saints visit a few other uniquely LDS sites in the Holy Land that few other denominations would care to visit. Foremost among these is the BYU Jerusalem Center, which was built as a satellite campus for Brigham Young University, the church-owned university, where pupils can study Middle East history, biblical history, Hebrew and Arabic (Olsen & Guelke, 2004b). Some Latter-day Saint tours also include brief stops at the Orson Hyde Memorial Garden on the Mount of Olives in Jerusalem, where in 1841 the early church leader dedicated Palestine for the gathering of Israel; the Orson Hyde Square in Netanya; the Temple Institute in Jerusalem; the graves in Haifa of LDS missionaries who died in the late 19th century; and the Lehi Cave in the Judean Shephelah, which some scholars believe is connected to the first family discussed in the Book of Mormon (Chadwick, 2009; Ron, 2011).

Book of Mormon tours

Mormons are avid Bible readers and believe the Bible to be the literal word of God. Unlike other Christians, however, Latter-day Saints have an additional Holy Writ, the Book of Mormon, which describes sacred events among residents of the Americas between 600 BCE and 100 CE. Although the locations of these events are not clearly demarcated in the book, there is a unique LDS tourism product that focuses on 'Book of Mormon lands', which are believed to be where some of the ancient Maya, Inca and Aztec ruins in the Americas are located (Hudman & Jackson, 1992; Olsen, 2006b). In addition to a growing Book of Mormon lands travel industry, several guidebooks have been published to help potential visitors interpret what they see (e.g. Johnson *et al.*, 2008).

Church history tours

As already noted, much LDS doctrine and many of its practices are rooted in its history and geography. Mormon history and geography are inextricably interlocked with doctrine and spiritual learning (Madsen, 2006; Morehead, 2008). In the words of Mitchell (2003), LDS Church members

> study Church history alongside the study of the Church texts, the *Book of Mormon* and the *Doctrine and Covenants*, being taught these history lessons on Sundays, by Sunday School teachers, rather than history teachers or scholars. In these lessons, the emphasis is often on the spiritual lessons to be learned from history. (Mitchell, 2003: 140)

Learning about church history is an important spiritual activity that increases solidarity within the church and helps reinforce members' faith (Anderson, 1980; Campo, 1998; Mitchell, 2001; Olsen & Timothy, 2002). Visiting historic sites is perceived as a form of serious learning and a manifestation of devotion. As mentioned above, church leaders strongly encourage the acquisition and restoration of Mormon representational landscapes (Ron, 2002) where they frequently establish visitor centers to interpret church history and historic sites, to help protect sacred places, to promote a positive image in the regions where they are located, to build faith among LDS visitors and to evangelize among non-LDS tourists (Mitchell, 2003; Olsen, 2012b, 2013; Olsen & Timothy, 2018).

Latter-day Saints visit their historic sites individually or on organized tours. The most popular locales in the United States include Temple Square in Salt Lake City, Utah; Nauvoo, Illinois; Palmyra, New York; Kirtland, Ohio; the Joseph Smith Memorial Farm in Vermont; and various locations along the westward Mormon Trail in Iowa, Nebraska and Wyoming (Brayley, 2010; Bremer, 2000; Davis & Austin, 2002; Erekson, 2005; Hudman & Jackson, 1992; Smelser, 2009). In addition to the

United States, many other countries in North and South America, Asia, Europe, Africa and the Pacific Islands also feature LDS memorials and historic sites that commemorate the local establishment of the church, important events, famous people or sacred locales (Head, 2006; Timothy & Schmidt, 2011) and appeal to a more local LDS audience.

Other patterns of LDS travel

For Latter-day Saints, the temple is the ultimate sacred space (Finlayson & Mesev, 2014; Madsen, 2003), and according to Hudman and Jackson (1992: 113), the sanctity of temples is both part of official doctrine and of the perception of church members. Visiting a nearby temple is rarely perceived as an act of tourism, but rather a routinized ritual, which involves sacred rites and ordinances. On the other hand, some Mormons 'collect' temple visits and try to visit as many of the current 159 operating temples worldwide as possible (Olsen, 2006b). Visiting remote temples is frequently combined with 'ordinary' travel for non-religious reasons.

Genealogy tourism has become one of the fastest-growing sub-segments of heritage tourism, and a subject of growing academic research (e.g. Higginbotham, 2012; Meethan, 2004; Santos & Yan, 2010; Timothy, 2008). In the Church of Jesus Christ of Latter-day Saints context, however, it is also a manifestation of religiously motivated travel. For Mormons, learning about one's ancestors and connecting someone to his or her forebears is a religious obligation through temple rites, such as proxy baptisms on behalf of the dead and the joining (sealing) of families as far back as possible. Thus, the pursuit of genealogy is semi-obligatory (Otterstrom, 2008), which often translates into family history travel where people desire to visit their ancestral lands, conduct genealogical research in local archives, meet distant relatives and participate in cultural events. The church has also established the world's largest genealogical library in Salt Lake City, which attracts millions of visitors every year from around the world (Olsen & Timothy, 2018) (Figure 2.5).

The Evolution of Christian Travel

Over the centuries, the geography of Christian travel has changed enormously since the early believers traveled on pilgrimages to the land of Jesus. These changes can be summed up in at least three main ways: from Holy Land to holy lands; from sacred space to sacred activities; and the globalization of Christian travel.

From Holy Land to holy lands

The term 'Holy Land' was most likely introduced by an early Christian writer, Justin Martyr, around the year 160 CE (St Justin Martyr, 2003). In the early days of Christianity, there was only one Holy Land,

Figure 2.5 The Family History Library in Salt Lake City, Utah (Photo: D. Timothy)

comprising the territories and regions where Jesus was born, lived and died. In contemporary geopolitical and religious terms, it refers to overlapping parts of Israel, Palestine and Jordan.

Some 1700 years later, Christians visit sacred sites on nearly every continent and in many countries. Ron (2009) outlines the geography of contemporary Christian pilgrimage, which includes three groups of destinations, namely New Testament locales, sites associated with other sacred scriptures and non-scriptural holy places. Locations in the first category are found in many Mediterranean countries, including Cyprus, Greece, Israel, Italy, Lebanon, Macedonia, Malta, Palestine, Syria and Turkey. Most sites in the second group are in Israel, Egypt, Palestine, Jordan and Latin America. Elements of the third group can be found almost anywhere, but overwhelmingly in Europe and Latin America (Nolan & Nolan, 1989; Park, 1994; Turner, 1973; Turner & Turner, 1978). Devotional travel has expanded the original concept of the Holy Land into a much wider range of 'holy lands'.

From sacred spaces to sacred activities

Christian travel is dynamic. Increasing numbers and types of Christian tourism are becoming commonplace outside the definitional confines of traditional pilgrimage. There has been a paradigmatic shift from only venerating localities and sites, to enriching travelers' spiritual lives through deeper engagement in activities and experiences that may not necessarily be identified with any specific location or sacred space. Examples include Christian voluntourism, especially humanitarian aid and other forms of short-term missions (STMs), attending Christian cultural performances and gatherings, taking part in historical re-enactments and visiting biblical-themed environments. Such activities are perceived as sacred and significant.

There are at least three possible explanations for this trend. First is the Protestant reluctance to undertake traditional pilgrimages. According to this viewpoint, this reluctance has translated into activities rather than places, although this paradigm change encompasses non-Protestants as well (Cleary, 2009; Livermore, 2008; Wuthnow, 2009).

A second explanation has to do with the distinction between 'old tourism' and 'new tourism' (Mowforth & Munt, 2003; Poon, 1994, 2003). New tourism, among other differences, is more activity oriented (Poon, 1993), includes new forms of tourism, seeks more meaningful experiences and activities and is more aware of its impacts on the destination. 'New tourists', or 'post-tourists', are motivated by a desire to be different than the traditional mass tourists who often do more social, cultural and ecological harm than good (Feifer, 1985; McCabe, 2015; Singh, 2004). This, consequently, manifests in new forms of tourist consumption (Gottdiener, 2000; Shaw & Williams, 2002).

The third plausible explanation is the concept of economy of experience, which was examined by Pine and Gilmore in 1998. Accordingly, developed economies have already passed through three stages – agrarian, industrial and service – and are now focusing on the fourth stage: the experience economy (Pine & Gilmore, 1998). This idea was developed further (Pine & Gilmore, 1999), and has since been widely adapted to various tourism settings (Chang, 2018; Charters *et al.*, 2009; Hayes & MacLeod, 2007; Sørensen & Sundbo, 2008).

The globalization of Christian travel

In most cases, today's Christian traveler is no longer one who pinches pennies to afford a once-in-a-lifetime journey. Many Christians worldwide have become more affluent and globally minded, and spend a large portion of their spiritual energy and financial means on religion-oriented tourism. This tendency is enhanced by Christian leaders who are literally 'frequent flyers in the name of Christ'. For example, Kaiser (2003) describes the phenomenon of Pope John Paul II's frequent travels:

> In a meeting this past June in the Vatican's Clementine Hall with people who have been most involved in his travels over the years, the pope explained why he has been such a frequent flyer: 'Right from the day I was elected as Bishop of Rome, October 16, 1978, with special intensity and urgency I heard the echo of Jesus' command: "Go into all the world

and preach the Gospel to all of creation" – to tell everyone that the Church loves them, that the pope loves them and likewise to receive from them the encouragement and example of their goodness, of their faith'. (Kaiser, 2003: np)

Globalization may be regarded as 'the compression of the world and the intensification of consciousness of the world as a whole' (Robertson, 1992: 8). In a Christian context, the globalization of religious travel can also be understood in relation to the concepts of pilgrimage mobilities and transnationalism. According to Bajc *et al.* (2007: 321), today's research on pilgrimage focuses more on movement and mobilities than on the Christian destination, which is reflective of the deeper experiences sought nowadays by spiritually oriented travelers. Bajc *et al.* (2007) suggest that 'centering' in the pilgrimage sense should be

perceived as a verb rather than a noun. In these terms, the 'centre out there' [Turner, 1973] cannot be taken for granted, as tends to be the case with early studies on pilgrimage. Rather, the 'centre' must be seen as constantly translated to new places, at different scales, and with often unanticipated social consequences. (Bajc *et al.*, 2007: 328)

Christian transnationalism was considered in depth by Wuthnow and Offutt (2008). They provide three examples that are relevant to this discussion on the globalization of Christian travel. The first is the use of missionaries and other 'professional and other full-time religious workers who go from one country to live and work in another country…' (Wuthnow & Offutt, 2008: 216). Their second example is the use of foreign religious workers, which can easily be linked to the short-term mission phenomenon, and the third is the development of pilgrimages, which 'represent another critical component of transnational religious activity' (Wuthnow & Offutt, 2008: 220).

Geopolitical Instability and the Mediterraneanization of Christian Travel

From a tourism perspective, the Holy Land tends to connote two main characteristics: sanctity to Christianity and political instability. The overlap of these two features has been challenging to the tourism industry, and has consequently led the industry to evaluate and react. This section elaborates on these two processes.

Political instability in the Holy Land and Christian travel

Political instability includes contentions of many sorts, including terrorism, wars, coups, riots and political protests, social unrest and strikes. The Middle East in general, and the Holy Land in particular, have long been regarded as centers of political instability. Collins-Kreiner *et al.* (2006) examined the implications of political crises on Christian travel to Israel. According to the owner of a major Holy Land tour operator, the important issue is not only the political unrest itself, but also the fact that the ongoing conflict has continuously shorter 'in-between' rest periods (Abu Dayyeh, 2005). When taking into account the events of unrest in the broader Middle East, including the Gulf War (1991), Iraq War (2003–present) and the Arab Spring uprising in several countries (2011), the region looks even less stable (Butler, in press).

The industry's response: Exit or adapt?

The second intifada (2000–2004) caused some major changes for Christian tourism. The long duration and the very broad spatial distribution of the unrest resulted in an appropriate response by the industry. Many tour operators dropped the Holy Land from their list of destinations, some hotels were converted to other non-tourism uses and tour guides and bus drivers sought other professions. Contrarily, some tour operators decided to adapt to the changing geopolitical environment by rediscovering and promoting alternative Christian destinations (Bartholomew & Llewelyn, 2004). In this context, it is worthwhile quoting a letter sent by Hani Abu Dayyeh to Holy Land tour operators his company works with:

> As we are now just getting out of the worst case for a drop of tourism to the Holy Land, it is worth it to take a moment to just think, before we will plunge in marketing, promoting and selling the Holy Land primarily and with a complete disregard or ignoring the other destinations within the Lands of the Bible… We really cannot afford the luxury of depending solely on the market for the Holy Land and allow the other destinations to slip by the wayside… Perhaps in the new reality of our days, we should have alternative 'stand-alone' destinations or at least 'stand by' destinations. We must be cognisant of the fact that we should give our clients credible biblical alternatives and focus our marketing and promotion money on what I consider two other major destinations besides the Holy Land… [The Seven Churches of Revelation in Turkey and Rome] (Abu Dayyeh, 2005: np)

This adaptive approach has become prevalent, and after the successful implementation of the Mediterraneanization of Christian travel, came the second stage – that of the globalization of Christian travel. The first stage included two sub-stages: converting sectoral destinations to multisectoral destinations (e.g. Rome for Protestants) and developing new Mediterranean Christian destinations such as Malta and Sicily (Hodgson, 2008).

The globalization of Christian travel includes new destinations such as Russia, China and India (Hodgson, 2008), and according to another tour operator, his company has developed tours to alternative destinations like Hawaii, South Africa, the British Isles and Alaska. When conditions get rough around the Holy Land, clients are usually advised to alter their destinations, while still traveling in a Christian social environment (Tyndall, 2011).

Conclusion

Beyond their common affection for the Holy Land, the varying theologies and doctrines between Christian churches result in distinct travel patterns, touristic behaviors, sacrosanct spaces and spiritual manifestations. Most, if not all, Christian denominations have a strong affinity for travel to the Holy Land – a geographical construct that is continuing to expand beyond the borders of Israel and Palestine to include other New Testament localities in Cyprus, Turkey, Lebanon and Greece, as well as Old Testament sites in Egypt and Jordan (Farra-Haddad, 2015). The Holy Land notion is also enlarging figuratively with additional Mediterranean places associated with the Bible being venerated for their important roles in the ministries of the ancient apostles and their martyrdoms. Even within the Holy Land, different sects of Christianity esteem diverse locales and landscapes, emphasizing their varying preferences for simplicity, extravagance or exceptionality. However, geographies of demand have seen both spontaneous and deliberate changes in recent decades with increasing numbers of uni-denominational destinations and attractions becoming more desirable to a multisectoral market.

In addition to traditional faith-based connections to physical space through pilgrimage, modern emotional geographies also point to a growing desire among most Christians to undertake symbolic pilgrimages that have less to do with location and more to do with experience. This concept, which reflects Feifer's (1985) notion of the 'post-tourist' or Poon's (1993) 'new tourist', both of whom seek deeper and more fulfilling experiences beyond the titillation and fakery commonly associated with traditional mass tourism, reflects the abstract sense that wherever a believer travels can become a 'holy land' for him or her based upon the experience and its outcomes.

3 Commoditizing Holy Places and Commercializing Sacred Experiences

Introduction

As noted elsewhere in this book, the original precept of Christian pilgrimage entailed humbling oneself as part of a sanctification process. In this regard, as Chapter 7 later notes, the lived encounters (with deity, self, other pilgrims or nature) on the pilgrim trail were essentially as important, if not more so, than reaching the destination itself owing to the process of self-consecration attributed to the hardships associated with walking the route (Turner, 1973; Whalen, 2011).

An important principle reflected in the pilgrimages of Christians, and those of some other faiths as well, is the notion of solidarity and equality. The impartiality with which God treats his children played out in the *communitas* that evolved through pilgrimage experiences, that everyone was equal in the eyes of deity. With the melding of these two conceptions – equality and the sanctification of self through pilgrimage – religiously motivated travel was generally self-disciplined and austere. Pilgrims spent as little money as possible and were fixed on reaching their destination in order to purify themselves, purge iniquity from their lives and demonstrate devotion to deity.

Until relatively recently, pilgrimage travel was so spartan that it was ignored as a potential source of economic development by pilgrimage destinations. Little thought was given to serving the needs of pilgrims beyond inexpensive or free hostels, non-motorized transportation, a few memento vendors and small-scale food providers. During the past century, however, the tides have turned. Sacred destinations now realize the increasing pecuniary potential of religious tourism to create jobs, raise tax revenues, increase regional incomes and encourage outside investment in tourism and hospitality services (Collins-Kreiner *et al.*, 2006; Shackley, 2006a; Vijayanand, 2013). Religious tourism is also now seen more commonly as a way of diversifying or resuscitating struggling economies (Olsen, 2003), and religious tourism and pilgrimage are seen as big business in many popular destinations (Collins-Kreiner, 2010b; Rotherham, 2007).

Increasing numbers of entrepreneurs and destination management organizations (DMOs) are breaking from the spartan traditions of pilgrimage by offering more leisure services to pilgrims, providing high-end accommodation, arranging luxury transportation options, establishing fast-food outlets and posh restaurants, selling local and imported souvenirs and creating tour packages that include pilgrimage and non-pilgrimage activities in a single itinerary. While the emergence of non-pilgrimage forms of tourism (e.g. general heritage tourism) in traditional pilgrim destinations is partly responsible for these changes, the increasing sophistication of the modern pilgrim, the gradual modulation of pilgrims' travel expectations and the diminishing need for austerity in the modern pilgrimage have led overwhelmingly to increased demand for more comfortable, packaged and leisure-oriented religious experiences (Olsen & Timothy, 2006; Tirca & Stanciulescu, 2011; Vukonić, 1996).

Although some religions attempt to maintain the simplicity and egalitarianism associated with traditional pilgrimages, even these are changing little by little, or in some cases astonishingly fast. Qurashi (2017) describes the commercialization process that is currently unfolding in Mecca, Saudi Arabia, in relation to the hajj and umrah pilgrimages. Tour operators and other vendors now sell a wide range of classes of hajj experiences (Timothy & Iverson, 2006). According to Qurashi (2017), poor pilgrims are being pushed out of Mecca, as access to the holy city is being granted increasingly through pre-purchased packages that are sold as three-star to five-star experiences. Owing largely to Saudi Arabia's management of the city and international investments, Mecca is now home to major hotels and resorts such as Hilton, Marriott, Sheraton, Le Meridien, Raffles, Hyatt Regency and Swissôtel. As well, to the dismay of many devotees, several sacred heritage sites in the vicinity of the Grand Mosque have been and are planned to be razed to make way for greater commercial development and expansions to the mosque to accommodate increasing numbers of pilgrims.

Although this intensity of commodification of the sacred, which al-Saadi (2014) terms the 'Vegasization' of Mecca, has generally not occurred at Christian pilgrimage sites, the commodification of Christian holy sites is ubiquitous even if at a small scale. During the past quarter century, many efforts have been made to capitalize on the lucrative Christian travel market by diversifying the product beyond the traditional pilgrim rituals and acts of devotion. DMOs, tour companies, transportation operators, guides and other service providers now offer a wide range of Christian travel products. These include, but are not limited to, themed cruises, package tours to traditional pilgrimage locales, package tours to non-traditional destinations, theme parks (discussed in Chapter 6) and the mass production and sale of souvenirs, both traditional religious keepsakes and contemporary kitsch.

This chapter examines the ways in which religious sites, pilgrimage experiences and sacred souvenirs are commercialized and commodified into consumable tourism products. In particular, it focuses on the important economic role that Christian tourism plays in many worldwide destinations and examines the commoditization of Holy Writ, the life of Christ and the ministry of the apostles through the development of theme parks, tours and cruises, organized events and souvenirs. The chapter concludes with a discussion of the general reactions of religious observers and scholars to the commercialization of the gospel.

Tourism, Economic Development and Commodifying the Sacred

The foremost reason that communities, regions and countries desire to develop and promote tourism is its economic development potential. Tourism is considered a labor-intensive service industry that has a considerable capacity to create local jobs, increase tax revenues, stimulate entrepreneurial activity, reduce poverty and help supplant or complement diminishing primary and secondary industries, such as mining, agriculture and manufacturing (Conlin & Jolliffe, 2011; Dwyer *et al.*, 2010; Hall, 2007; Ioannides, 2003; Mathieson & Wall, 1982; Sznajder *et al.*, 2009; Xie, 2015). As tourism grows, destination communities may benefit in indirect ways as well. For example, evidence suggests that tourism affects residents' quality of life significantly not only through increased employment but also through improved access to services (e.g. health care, education, recreational opportunities) (Uysal *et al.*, 2016) and better quality infrastructure (Ioannides, 2003). Another indirect benefit is increased levels of empowerment and self-determination (Scheyvens, 1999; Timothy, 1999, 2007), particularly among indigenous peoples, women and immigrants (Apostolopoulos *et al.*, 2001; Johnston, 2003). Religious tourism, like other forms of tourism, is considered a tool for realizing these benefits for the spiritual destination. With this recognition comes varying levels of commercialization and commoditization of the sacred.

The commodification of religious symbols, ceremonies, spaces and artifacts is not endemic to Christianity (Hernandez-Ramdwar, 2013; Kartal *et al.*, 2015; Shenhav-Keller, 1993; Shi, 2007, 2011; Stausberg, 2011; Suntikul & Butler, 2018; Vijayanand, 2013), as the example of Islamic pilgrimage to Mecca noted earlier illustrates. Furthermore, since the cultural practices and traditions associated with Buddhism are among the most salient attractions for tourists in South and Southeast Asia, in countries such as Myanmar, Tibet and Bhutan for example, Buddhism is deliberately commoditized for tourism and sold as an important part of the national product (Hall, 2006a; Kitiarsa, 2010; Nyaupane & Timothy, 2010).

In common with holy sites of other faiths, most Christian destinations realize the economic potential of pilgrimage and have intentionally developed commercially as a way to capture tourist spending (Shackley, 2001; Wharton, 2006; Wiltshier & Clarke, 2012). This is not a new phenomenon. While the over-commercialization we see today in religious destinations was not a salient part of medieval Christian pilgrimages, the desire among pilgrims to bring home mementos from their journeys, including fragments of the *terra sancta*, and their need to lodge and dine during their journeys brought about earlier forms of commodification. Through the years, commercialization of pilgrimages became the norm once individual entrepreneurs, destinations and organizations began to realize pilgrimage's economic promise (Shoval, 2000) (Figure 3.1).

Even during early Christian pilgrimages, services developed to attend to the needs of religious journeyers. Along pilgrimage routes, hostels, refuges, inns, churches and eateries were constructed for pilgrims' temporal and spiritual nourishment as they traveled to the holy shrines of Rome and Santiago (Houlihan, 2000; Timothy & Teye, 2009). These eventually evolved into restaurants, cafes, hotels, bed and breakfasts, souvenir shops, museums and health spas along well-established pilgrim trails in Europe (Cropera, 2007; Kaufman, 2005; Scandolara, 2008; Timothy &

Figure 3.1 The extreme commercialization of Lourdes, France, is part of its tourist appeal (Photo: D. Timothy)

Teye, 2009). One of the earliest pilgrim guidebooks, known as *Codex Calixtinus* or *Liber Sancti Jacobi*, written in approximately 1139, was utilized by the Cluniacs as a 'marketing document' to promote the pilgrimage to Santiago. In the words of Houlihan (2000: 21), the Codex was a 'sort of medieval Michelin' that provided sagacious advice regarding 'where to go and what to watch out for… where not to drink the water, and of ferrymen, toll-collectors and innkeepers out to rip off the unsuspecting pilgrim'.

Today, religion has been accused of being a commercial enterprise – profit over prophet (James, 2010; McAlexander *et al.*, 2014; Nichols, 2008). For example, in the words of Daswani (2013: 250), 'Pentecostalism was no longer a calling from God that provided divine direction, but a commercialization of Christianity that allowed you to become a new person through paying for a few courses in theological college'. In some Christian sects, monetary payments for forgiveness in lieu of more arduous propitiations have become normative, and televangelists frequently petition believers for money in exchange for their prayers (James, 2010). These examples and the requirement to pay for church-supervised weddings, funerals and baptisms in many Christian denominations, as well as requiring entrance fees to access historic churches, has led some observers to lament the contemporary requirement to 'pay to pray' (Olsen & Guelke, 2004a; Voase, 2007; Willis, 1994), especially when visitors perceive it to be their heritage. In a scathing critique of such practices, Einstein (2008: 170) laments that 'Jesus did not have an intricate corporate structure, nor did he provide his faith only to those who could pay for it'.

Christian merchandising and product sales have become a sign of more materialistic times with the proliferation of Christian music, books, radio and television shows, televangelism, mass advertising, biblical theme parks, faith-promoting motion pictures, virtual pilgrimages, t-shirts, bumper stickers and websites (Daswani, 2013; Einstein, 2008; Goh, 2014; James, 2010). An important part of this growing trend in commercial Christianity is the development of various travel-related experiences and products, including theme parks, organized tours and cruises, religious events and sacred souvenirs. There are other sorts of commercial products, but these four are the focus of the rest of this chapter.

Theme parks

While biblical theme parks are discussed in greater depth in Chapter 6, they are also worth mentioning briefly in this chapter on commoditizing Christianity. One of the most opportune examples of these sorts of attractions is the Ark Encounter, a life-sized replica of Noah's Ark built after its description in the book of Genesis, which opened in the US state of Kentucky in July 2016. The 155-meter-long, US$100 million ark was constructed by a Christian group to reaffirm their belief in the biblical account of Noah and the flood, and to provide the Christian message to visitors. Inside the ship are displays and exhibits that show what life might have been like aboard the ark, including animal replicas in cages and stalls (Lovan, 2016). The ark is the centerpiece of the Ark Encounter theme park, which also includes restaurants, zip line rides, a small zoo and other recreational activities.

The organization's sister attraction is the Creation Museum, located 72 km from the ark, the grounds of which are also home to a zip line, petting zoo, souvenir shop, restaurants, a mining sluice setup and botanical gardens (Answers in Genesis, 2016). Preceding the Ark Encounter, an evangelical Christian theme park known as Noah's Ark was built in Hong Kong in 2009 (Goh, 2014). Its aim is to provide a Christian learning environment where the creationist view is advocated and Christian principles endorsed for visitors. While many of these Christian theme parks function as non-profit organizations, they are simultaneously commercial ventures that employ nearby residents and appeal to both devout Christians and other curious visitors.

Organized tours and cruises

While many pilgrims traveled in groups in early Christianity (Elsner & Rutherford, 2005), the best example of modern-day commercial pilgrimages began in the 1860s when Thomas Cook & Son (now the Thomas Cook Group) began offering popular pilgrimage travel packages to Palestine and Egypt for British citizens who desired to visit the Holy Land (Larsen, 2000). Since that time, pilgrimage tours have become extremely popular throughout the world. Increasing numbers of travel agencies, tour operators, church groups, faith leaders, volunteer groups, community centers, DMOs and other private and public organizations are offering religious travel packages (Feldman, 2007; Ron & Feldman, 2009; Rotherham, 2007; Shoval, 2000).

While many individuals still make their own way to pilgrimage destinations and arrange their own itineraries, increasingly, religious tourists are relying on pre-packaged pilgrimages that provide all-inclusive travel experiences that incorporate pre-arranged transportation, lodgings, meals, guided tours and prayer sessions. Many tours aim to bypass the traditional pilgrim trails in order to arrive directly at the shrine or pilgrimage center. Most Christian package tourists are willing to give up much of their independence for the sake of group security and fellowship (Ron & Feldman, 2009).

With the growth of direct internet travel sales, travel agencies and tour operators have had to adapt in recent years to a tourism system wherein service providers (e.g. airlines, hotels, car rentals) no longer pay commissions. One way of adapting has been agencies learning to specialize in certain destinations and travel products, and satisfying the needs of particular market segments. In recent years, many travel companies in the home places of the travelers have hired religious tourism specialists to arrange pilgrimage itineraries and cater to the needs of Christian travelers. Likewise, many religious destinations have established tour companies and travel agents to provide on-site services for incoming groups. Every year, the Opera Romana Pellegrinaggi, a Vatican-sponsored pilgrimage tour company operated by the vicariate of Rome organizes a wide range of package tours to various parts of the world. In 2015, the agency offered 62 separate tours under various biblical, ministerial and heritage themes (Table 3.1).

Beyond arranging air and ground transportation, lodging and guided tours, several pilgrim tour companies are now offering highly specialized pilgrimage products. One such product, biblical meals, is an important element of a growing number of tour packages. Among many Christian tourists to the Holy Land, there is a deep-seated desire to know Jesus and his early disciples more personally. This increasingly manifests in visitors being interested in learning about the everyday life of early Christians and Jesus, including holiday traditions and the food they ate. The Bible mentions many different alimentary products (e.g. figs, honey, lamb, oil, flour, fish and loaves) and gustatory experiences (e.g. manna from heaven, quails for the Israelites, the Last Supper and Jesus turning water into wine). The Bible also uses food frequently as a metaphor for God's

Table 3.1 A sample of Catholic tours sold by Opera Romana Pellegrinaggi, 2015

Theme	Examples of tours	Length	Price/person (euros)
Biblical itineraries	• Holy Land and Samaria • Jordan • Turkey and Cyprus	8 days 6 days 10 days	1190.00 1300.00 1480.00
Marian itineraries	• Lourdes by ship • Fatima and Lisbon • Santiago de Compostela, Porto and Braga	8 days 3 days 5 days	855.00 550.00 870.00
Religious and cultural itineraries	• Montenegro and Bosnia, with Medjugorje • Tallinn, Helsinki and St Petersburg • Uzbekistan	6 days 7 days 8 days	1250.00 1810.00 1880.00
Missionary itineraries	• Mexico and Our Lady of Guadalupe • Sri Lanka • Argentina and Patagonia	11 days 10 days 13 days	2980.00 2660.00 3980.00
Christian itineraries in Italy	• Turin and the Shroud • The Basilicas • Assisi, Gubbio and Loreto	3 days 5 days 3 days	405.00 570.00 330.00
Christian itineraries in Rome	• The Basilica of St Peter and the tombs of the popes • The Vatican museums and the Sistine Chapel • In Rome with Pope Francis	2 hours 2–8 hours 1–2 days	14.00 27.50 30.00–90.00

Source: Opera Romana Pellegrinaggi (2015).

dealings with humankind (e.g. Canaan as the Land of Milk and Honey) (Ron & Timothy, 2013).

Many Holy Land tours now offer at least one biblical meal to illustrate how and what the ancient Canaanites and Israelites ate. These usually take place at certain venues that specialize in biblical foods and provide scripture-based narratives to help interpret the meal in terms of physical setting, dishes, dress, language, content and performance. Some Holy Land tour operators offer Last Supper re-enactments, which are particularly popular among American evangelicals (Ron & Timothy, 2013). Additionally, organizations in North America and Europe offer church groups at home Passover meals that may satiate their desire to visit the Holy Land to some degree. These celebrations of biblical food in the Holy Land or at home act as 'conveyers of spiritual strength and religious devotion' (Timothy & Ron, 2013: 102) and may enhance one's spiritual connections to God.

Another interesting perspective related to biblical food is a growing number of botanical gardens that focus on plants, fruits and vegetables of the Bible. Dozens of books have been published to assist Christians in growing biblical fruits and vegetables in their home gardens. However, several 'biblical gardens' have been established in Europe, Israel, Asia and North America that devote their botanical landscapes to the more than 125 plants mentioned in the Bible, and many of these have become attractions for tourists.

Cruises resemble most land-based tour packages in that they are all-inclusive and provide opportunities to visit several individual destinations. Tour operators and cruise companies began presenting Christian cruises only a few decades ago. These are now another important pilgrimage product that allows tourists to combine the pleasures of cruising with spiritual growth through visits to sites associated with the ancient apostles (Gross & Lück, 2012; Timothy, 2011). Many organizations offer combined land and cruise packages, or cruise-only packages that trace the missionary routes of the apostles, primarily Paul and John. Pilgrim Tours (2016) sells products such as 'Footsteps of Paul & John' land and sea products that focus overwhelmingly on Turkey, Greece, Cyprus and Italy, where much of the gospel was preached in ancient days and recorded in the New Testament. Genesis Tours (2016: np) sells a similar experience where cruisers can enjoy Greece, Italy, Malta and the Holy Land with renowned Bible scholars. Bible classes are taught on board, and pilgrims 'pray in some of the Bible's most prominent sites as we enjoy fellowship and make new friends'.

Latter-day Saints (LDS) also avidly participate in the same New Testament-oriented Mediterranean cruises. But because of their belief in the Book of Mormon as another testament of Christ, they also participate in Book of Mormon cruises, although these are less commonly consumed among LDS tourists than other packages and cruises are. Most LDS scholars believe the locations described in the Book of Mormon to be in Central and South America (Hauck & Hansen, 1988; Sorenson, 1985). Several tour operators sell Book of Mormon tours that focus on Belize, Guatemala, Mexico and Honduras (Hudman & Jackson, 1992; Olsen, 2006b), while Caribbean cruises that stop in Mexico and Belize are becoming more popular as sea-based counterparts. Once in port, LDS groups are taken by coach from the harbor to tour the inland ruins of the ancient Maya and other indigenous groups, where these sites are interpreted within the framework of LDS doctrine and Book of Mormon geography.

A variety of Christian cruises are also offered to places that are not traditionally associated with scriptural accounts or church history. For example, many Christian cruises to China and Southeast Asia are available. These tend to extol the virtues of a growing Christian community in non-traditional Christian places and occasionally offer on-shore visits to churches, orphanages and missions. The main goals of these and cruises to Scandinavia, the Caribbean and South America, however, are to nurture Christian fellowship, or *communitas*, particularly within a given denomination. Cruises sold specifically to Jehovah's Witnesses, for example, provide the following selling point: 'Each evening separate dining room tables will be reserved in the main dining room for our group of Jehovah's Witnesses so you can get acquainted with other Friends from around the country' (Bethel Tour Vacations, 2016: np). Other goals of Christian cruises are to learn about disparate parts of the world from a religious perspective (e.g. the Creation) or to provide matchmaking opportunities for single travelers.

Almost all of these Christian cruises have several things in common. First, a well-known evangelical, Latter-day Saint, Catholic or mainline Protestant scholar or celebrity accompanies the group to offer church-specific instruction from Holy Writ and to add celebrity appeal to the experience. Second, they all emphasize spiritual development and religious fellowship as two important byproducts of the cruise. Third, they offer prayer meetings on the ship and at historic sites, instructional seminars onboard, wholesome entertainment and spiritually uplifting music onboard or at the archaeological sites they visit.

Religious events

Events are an important part of the Christian faith and many are commemorated in a variety of ways. Chapter 8 covers Christian events in considerable detail, but they are also noted in this chapter on commodification.

The years 1999 and 2000 were considered sacred by many Christians; 1999 was a time to prepare for the new millennium, which corresponded with the 2000th anniversary of the birth of Jesus Christ. Pope John Paul

II declared 2000 the year of the 'Great Jubilee' and undertook his own pilgrimage to the Holy Land in March of that year. He visited several sacred sites in Israel, Palestine and Jordan, which venerated the Holy Land even further for Roman Catholics. The Pope's Jubilee visit as part of the millennium celebrations resulted in a significant growth of Holy Land tourism in 2000 and the years that followed.

In 1999, as the world prepared for the new millennium, Christian destinations throughout the world geared up for a growing influx of tourists. Notable among these destinations were Israel and Palestine. Israel's Ministry of Tourism anticipated large waves of Christian tourists who would come to celebrate not only the 2000th birthday of their Savior but also to welcome the new millennium, which many believed would usher in the return of Jesus to gather his righteous followers. Millions of people prepared both for doomsday and for the rapture.

From the destinations' perspective, to prepare for the anticipated event, infrastructure upgrades were made. Thousands more hotel rooms were built, and a number of cities with historic importance to Christians were gentrified (Olsen & Timothy, 1999). While plans in Israel (e.g. Nazareth 2000) and in Palestine (e.g. Bethlehem 2000) were geared toward urban renewal, at their core was the desire to attract and service the needs of millennial tourists – both worshippers and doomsday expectants – which they succeeded in doing (Al-Rimmawi & Butcher, 2015; Cohen-Hattab, 2013; Cohen-Hattab & Shoval, 2007; Gelbman & Laven, 2016; Kliot & Collins-Kreiner, 2003). The event caused Palestine's tourism numbers to soar from 200,000 in 1998 to 330,000 in 2000 (Isaac, 2010). Israel's tourist numbers grew from 2.28 million in 1999 to 2.67 million in 2000 (Kliot & Collins-Kreiner, 2003). Although arrivals to both destinations plunged toward the end of 2000 with the commencement of the second intifada (Palestinian uprising against Israel), the impact of the commencement of the third millennium after Christ was clear.

In addition to historic city renewal efforts, more direct commercial endeavors were undertaken. Vineyards in Galilee unveiled several new commemorative 2000 wines in the region where Jesus turned water into wine and spent most of his ministry (Olsen & Timothy, 1999). Additional savior-centered millennium tours were planned and sold to adulate Jesus' ministry and commemorate his birth.

Another important event in Christian history was the baptism of Jesus by John the Baptist in the Jordan River. While the exact location of this event remains unknown, evidence suggests it took place at or near the current commemorated locale near the Dead Sea and Jericho – Qaser el-Yahud (on the Israeli side) and Bethany Beyond the Jordan (on the Jordanian side). This location became a popular pilgrimage destination centuries ago, as substantiated by some of the remaining archaeological evidence on the Jordanian side (Mustafa, 2014; Waheeb, 2008).

In 1967, following the Six-Day War, Israel occupied the West Bank of the Jordan, including Qaser el-Yahud, which remained closed under strict military control for more than 40 years. During this time, to satiate the needs of Christian visitors, Israel's Ministry of Tourism opened the Yardenit baptismal site in 1981 in the Galilee region as a proxy locale, where Christian tourists could see the Jordan River, dip their toes in it, collect holy water from the river or be baptized during their Holy Land pilgrimages. Following the 1994 peace treaty between Jordan and Israel, excavations on the Jordanian side in 1996–1998 led to many archaeological findings that helped substantiate that this was the traditional location of John the Baptist's ministry and the baptism of Jesus as commemorated by early pilgrims. In 2002, Jordan opened its side of the river to tourists (Haddad *et al.*, 2009; Mustafa, 2014; Shunnaq *et al.*, 2008). Israel followed suit opening its side to tourists in 2011 under the administration of the Israeli military, the Ministry of Tourism and the Israel Nature and Parks Authority. The entire area on the Jordanian side was designated a UNESCO World Heritage Site in 2015. While both baptismal sites lie only a few meters apart, the international boundary runs between them, and visitors are not permitted to cross the border at that locale (Figure 3.2).

Figure 3.2 Christian travelers being baptized in the Jordan River at the Qaser el-Yahud site. Note that the string of floating bubbles marks the international border (Photo: D. Timothy)

One of the eminent events in Christianity, the baptism of Christ, is widely celebrated at the Jordan River. The Yardenit site in the north has a strong commercial environment, largely because a kibbutz operates the site as an income source. The Qaser el-Yahud site is less developed from a commercial standpoint, largely because it is operated by the Israel Nature and Parks Authority and lies within a high-security border zone. Nonetheless, both sites are anxiously visited by numerous tour groups, and being baptized at either Yardenit or Qaser el-Yahud is a highlight of many people's journey. This experience, which emulates the event involving Jesus and John the Baptist two millennia ago, is a major selling point for many Holy Land tours that capitalize on it.

Souvenirs

Bringing home a memento of one's journey is an intrinsic human desire. Almost all tourists depart their destination with tangible objects to remind them of their journeys and to commemorate their experiences. In abstract terms, souvenirs may be intangible such as memories, friendships and increased faith, but in most instances they are objects that 'serve as tangible markers of an otherwise intangible and ephemeral experience' (Swanson & Timothy, 2012: 490).

There is an entire sub-industry or set of industries around souvenir production, and souvenirs are one of the biggest expenditure items among all types of tourists, including pilgrims (Reader, 2014; Timothy, 2005). In common with other elements of commoditized pilgrimage, the economic value of souvenirs in religious destinations is immense (Fleischer, 2000; Shackley, 2004, 2006b). Spiritual travelers are extreme souvenir consumers. This phenomenon is not new. As already noted, ancient pilgrims desired to take home tangible mementos of their hallowed experiences and sacred destinations. Many of the earliest souvenirs were shells, jewelry, stones, soil, leaves, water, archaeological relics and metal badges (Houlihan, 2000).

Eventually, destination residents began crafting mementos specifically for pilgrims as a way of forfending looting and pilfering (Evans, 1998). Soon after, destination residents identified an opportunity to capitalize on pilgrims' wishes for tangible artifacts to 'prove' they had been at a holy site (Evans, 1998; Swanson & Timothy, 2012).

As early as the 11th century, the Way of St James began to experience commercial souvenir development. Royalty and regional leaders encouraged French crafters and vendors to settle and sell along the route, 'so much so that the most popular route across Spain became known as the *Camino Francés*' (Houlihan, 2000: 19). Owing to these and other economic and commercial enterprises, the Camino eventually became a 'cultural artery' for the diffusion of handicraft and artisan skills, as well as architectural and intellectual ideas (Houlihan, 2000: 20).

Olivewood crafts have dominated the Holy Land souvenir market since the 4th century CE following the construction of the Church of the Nativity. Owing to the significance of olive trees in the biblical narrative and ministry of Jesus, olivewood souvenirs have long been a favorite of Christian pilgrims (Figure 3.3). As part of the nascent movement of pilgrimages to the Holy Land, artisans arrived from Europe, settled in Bethlehem and began the olivewood industry (Salman, 2006). During the 16th and 17th centuries, Greek Orthodox monks and Italian craftspeople on pilgrimage taught many of Bethlehem's inhabitants the art of woodcarving. As early as the 1600s, sacred olivewood handicrafts were regularly exported from the Holy Land for overseas consumption. By the mid-17th century, the Franciscans had already established a well-oiled export enterprise in Bethlehem. Goods were sent to Acre via Jerusalem and shipped to major ports in Europe where they were distributed throughout Catholic Europe. In particular, demand among the faithful was for olivewood rosaries, crosses and other religious icons that were blessed by priests at holy sites before being exported to Europe (Norris, 2013).

This art form continues to be one of Bethlehem and the West Bank's most profitable tourism products made by the region's Palestinian Christian population (Bethlehem Christian Families Mission, 2010). Export of these spiritual expressions made from the wood of the Bible continues today, and these items are offered to consumers at Christian shops

Figure 3.3 Olivewood carvings in Bethlehem, Palestine, are among the most favored Holy Land souvenirs (Photo: D. Timothy)

throughout the world. Furthermore, almost all souvenir shops in Israel and Palestine are lined with olivewood depictions of the nativity, crosses, rosaries, picture frames and Christmas ornaments.

While souvenirs have many different functions, they are foremost, triggers of memory every time they are seen, used, touched, worn or discussed (Collins-Kreiner & Zins, 2011; Kaufman, 2005; Timothy, 2005).

> While the souvenir is removed physically from the sacred experience of travel, it stands in proxy for the extraordinary once the tourist returns to his or her ordinary environment. Souvenirs allow people to move symbolically between the mundane, ordinary and profane bounds of home, and the extraordinary 'sacred' places and 'other' times associated with their travels. The souvenir thus becomes much greater than its physical form; it represents the whole of the experience. (Swanson & Timothy, 2012: 492)

This is reflected well in the souvenir sophistication process described by Smith and Olson (2001). They suggest that first-time visitors to a place are inclined to purchase inexpensive, trite and kitschy mementos that are embossed with the name of the site visited. Usually, these objects are mass-produced in faraway places, with little connection to the sites they are meant to commemorate. With subsequent visits, tourists become more sophisticated in terms of what they know about the destination and what they expect to derive from their experiences. Through this sophistication process, tourists begin to acquire more meaningful souvenirs that are increasingly 'authentic' and which reflect a better sense of place by depicting what is more indicative of the destination; they also tend to buy fewer souvenirs with each consecutive visit (Collins-Kreiner & Zins, 2011; Smith & Olson, 2001). Many Christian pilgrims undergo a similar transformation, wherein they buy cheap, imported souvenirs with embossed names of the places they visit. Subsequent visits to venerated locales probably result in higher-quality purchases of items that have deeper spiritual meanings, and some may forego tangible souvenirs altogether, focusing instead on gaining intangible 'souvenirs' of the soul.

Souvenirs have immense social value for tourist consumers (Paraskevaidis & Andriotis, 2015). They may have an even deeper meaning for pilgrims and other religious tourists as they sometimes represent a bridge between the sacred space and time of the pilgrimage and the secular space and time of home. In the words of Houlihan (2000: 22), 'the added frisson to be gained from closeness to the real object or from standing at the scene of some historical event can give these objects and places a numinous power not dissimilar from that attributed by the pilgrim to the relics of martyrs'.

Most pilgrims 'need to bring things home with them from the sacred, extraordinary time or space, for home is equated with ordinary, mundane times and space... the non-ordinary experience... is by nature ephemeral, but they can hold on to a tangible piece of it, an object that came from it' (Gordon, 1986: 136). For many religious travelers, sacred souvenirs develop even deeper meanings following a journey and as years go by (Kaell, 2012). They become honored showpieces that demarcate the inspirational experiences of a pilgrimage and become infused with divine qualities (Kaell, 2014). For some Christian pilgrims, the souvenir and its point of purchase are as important as the site visited – sometimes even more so. 'When the pilgrimage entitles the pilgrim to an upgraded social or religious status, it is very important that the pilgrim bring home some visible proof' of their having been there (Stausberg, 2011: 210).

Many mementos are purchased as gifts for people who were unable to undertake the journey themselves. A participant in one pilgrimage study noted, '... I also think that bringing back a small souvenir for people from a holy pilgrimage site can mean the world to the person, allows them to feel a part of that pilgrimage themselves and allows them to know they are thought about and loved' (Higgins & Hamilton, 2011: 266). One American participant in Kaell's (2012) study held deep spiritual reasons for visiting the Holy Land. Yet, much of her time was used in shopping for gifts for people at home. In Jerusalem, she even missed out on visits to some important sites, including the Church of the Holy Sepulcher, because she was too busy shopping at the souvenir market. For this particular tourist, shopping and missing certain site visits were difficult but a necessary part of the pilgrimage: distributing gifts to friends and family members after her return (Kaell, 2012: 134). Through the process of gifting Holy Land souvenirs, returned travelers affirm their own identities as believers, while simultaneously 'fulfilling what they believe is their special responsibility to bolster collective faith, particularly in the family' (Kaell, 2012: 134). Even the strategic placement of pilgrimage mementos in the home may be an extension of the dutiful pilgrim, so that the objects can best be noticed and admired by family members and visitors (Peters, 2011), thereby bearing testimony to the pilgrim's faith.

Today, religious tourists consume an eclectic mix of religious and secular souvenirs (Figure 3.4). However, Shackley (2006b: 97–98) specifically noted four different types of keepsakes sold to tourists at Catholic destinations. First are destination-specific souvenirs. These include general items (e.g. coffee mugs, tea towels and t-shirts) and stereotypical items that depict popular images of the country or broader region being visited. Examples include small shamrocks or leprechauns sold in Knock, Ireland. Second are knick-knacks particular to the destination and its sacred center. These might include a wide range of merchandise, such as guidebooks, statues and figurines, photo frames and albums, refrigerator magnets, pens and pencils, book bags and walking sticks. Third are items associated with funerals and dying (e.g. grave markers, urns, plaques,

Figure 3.4 Shops in Medjugorje sell an eclectic range of religious and non-religious souvenirs (Photo: D. Timothy)

wreaths). The fourth type of pilgrimage memento is worship-related items, including rosaries, prayer books, bible verses, religious metals, crosses and other such items. Beyond Catholicism, to this list could be added denomination-specific items, such as carvings of religious figures, replicas of objects mentioned in Holy Writ and various food and wine items.

A final twist on the commodification of religious souvenirs is the acculturation and cultural adaptation processes frequently undertaken by souvenir sellers in certain places in order to sell more goods. For example, in Jerusalem, many Arab Muslim souvenir vendors are known to take on the persona of the tourists. They often 'become Christians' figuratively of course, as a way of relating to their potential customers. They are especially adept at learning various denominations' church-based spoken vernacular and feigning their Christ-centered discipleship. This helps them relate better to the pilgrims, pierce their souls and negotiate better sales.

As part of this donning the tourists' religious identity, many merchants spend considerable time and effort learning a variety of foreign languages to make stronger impressions (Bowman, 1989). In an early 20th-century account of his travels to Lourdes, one Irish pilgrim commented on his amazement at hearing a French shop owner use the Irish Gaelic term *slán leat* (goodbye) as he was leaving (O'Flanagan, 1928); it certainly flagged the attention of that pilgrim and drew him back in.

According to Bowman's (1989) observations, Jerusalem's tourist merchants pride themselves on their

> chameleon-like qualities, being able to shift languages, religions, politics and even their national identities to suit what they perceived to be the tastes of potential customers. Most of the merchants... were capable of speaking five to six languages with surprising proficiency. Muslim merchants could be good Christians for Christian tourists and pilgrims, and many Muslims and Christians played at being Jews for foreigners delighted with the success of the state of Israel. (Bowman, 1989: 82)

The same is still true today in Jerusalem and elsewhere.

A geography of religious souvenirs

These manifestations of commodified mementos result in unique geographies of Christian souvenirs in pilgrimage destinations. The authors' observations at Lourdes and in Jerusalem suggest that vendors further from the holy attraction tend to sell fairly generic Christian souvenirs, such as crucifix pendants and postcards of the Pope or general holy sites. The closer one gets to the grotto at Lourdes or the Church of the Holy Sepulcher in Jerusalem, the more worship-related the objects become (e.g. holy water or empty bottles for tourists to fill), candles and icons. Shackley (2006b: 97) explains a set of spatially distinct retail zones at Knock, Ireland, which can also be found at most other Catholic shrines. Inside the shrine or sacred site itself, attendants or other caretakers sell certain authorized, inexpensive and spiritually significant items, including postcards, music, posters, candles, books and icons (Kotsi, 2007, 2012). These are typically sold by the church or other religious organization, with the proceeds used to help maintain the site and pay the salaries of non-volunteer workers. Outside the grounds of the shrine, but as near to it as possible, is a secondary retail zone characterized by privately owned shops selling religious memorabilia and non-religious souvenirs (Klarin, 2014; Woodward, 2004). 'These offer an eclectic mixture of wares with retailing and other service functions often muddled together, so that a coffee shop may also be a souvenir stand and flower shop' (Shackley, 2006b: 97). According to Shackley's observations, these concentrated shopping zones may develop organically as religious tourism grows (usually in older destinations) or, as in the case of Knock, they may be intentionally developed as part of the tourism business district (Getz, 1993) planning efforts by the host community.

This physical division between the sacred (the holy site, shrine, church or monument) and the profane (the commercial zone and townscape outside the shrine) is well demarcated in many destinations (Shackley, 2006b). At Lourdes, for instance, there is a clear division between the commercialized/profane area where shops, hotels and restaurants are found, and the hallowed zone where the grotto, spring and churches are located. Figure 3.5 clearly shows the demarcated border between the sacred and the profane in Lourdes symbolized by the gate and fence. Of this boundary between the irreligious and the sacrosanct in Lourdes, one participant in Higgins and Hamilton's (2011: 265) study noted,

> the grotto…is like another world, the grotto and the basilica is like another place completely, the minute you go through the gates it is the strangest thing, but it is almost like a presence enters you, and it stays with you throughout the domain… They have managed to keep the bustle and tack of the commercial site of Lourdes away from the domain. (Higgins & Hamilton, 2011: 265)

Items for sale inside the shrine are sometimes seen as the most sacred. For this reason, identical objects will often be purchased there rather than from vendors located outside the shrine area. 'The further one gets from the shrine, the less holy the object, hence the fact that shops at airports or towns near[by]… sell only routine local souvenirs, not items intrinsically connected with the shrine' (Shackley, 2006b: 102).

At a smaller scale, even in-shop spatialities exist. At Lourdes, Medjugorje, Santiago de Compostela, Fatima and Knock, the commercialization of holy souvenirs caters exclusively to the needs of Roman Catholics.

Figure 3.5 The gate demarcates the border between the sacred and the profane at Lourdes (Photo: D. Timothy)

However, in the Holy Land, where there are pilgrims from many diverse Christian churches, even within some individual stores and handicraft showrooms, unique spatial patterns are evident. In many large shops in Israel and Palestine, for example, there are sections or entire rooms for Roman Catholics, Russian Orthodox, Greek Orthodox, Latter-day Saints and North American and European Protestants. In response to this, merchants are adept at identifying which Christian groups are visiting on which days. Sometimes, tour leaders call ahead to inform shopkeepers of their intentions, but many shopkeepers are skilled enough to observe and listen for clues that will help determine which Christian denomination is shopping at any given time.

Some of these socio-spatial patterns can be explained in part at least through differing theologies. Kaell (2012: 136) argues that Protestants and Catholics, for example, view tangible objects and their place meanings differently. Protestants have historically had a tendency to see the hand of God in the Holy Land more clearly in nature, so they have tended to buy souvenirs with landscape images and nature-oriented emblems. 'For Protestants, a pressed flower imbued with divine presence is a vital addition to a mass-made commodity like a bookmark' (Kaell, 2012: 140). Catholics on the other hand, are more inclined to purchase souvenirs that focus on the saints or the Virgin Mary – things that reflect their emphasis on Marian apparitions, the interceding power of saints and the blessings of priests. 'Catholics are less dependent on natural items since a priest's blessing also serves to invest commercial souvenirs with presence' (Kaell, 2012: 140). Today, Catholics are disposed to buying olivewood souvenirs of rosaries and images of Mary. Ultra-conservative evangelicals, on the other hand, have a tendency to purchase Jewish symbols (in solidarity with Israel) and items bearing biblical verses (Kaell, 2012, 2013).

Reactions to Commercialized Pilgrimage

A prevailing sentiment among critics is that the touristification or commoditization of religious travel experiences is inevitably negative, and that commercialization is incompatible with the spirit, which Higgins and Hamilton (2011: 265) refer to as the sacred being 'contaminated by commercialization'. The commodification of religious relics, icons and memorabilia into mass-produced consumables has, in many observers' minds, cheapened not only the pilgrimage but also religious icons, souvenirs and events (Di Giovine, 2012; Egresi *et al.*, 2012a; Griffin, 2012; Higgins & Hamilton, 2011; Vukonić, 2002; Zaidman, 2003) into religious kitsch analogous to the 'tourist trash' or 'airport art' so commonly available in tourist destinations everywhere (Olsen & Timothy, 2006). Likewise, Olsen (2012a) pointed out that the excessive commodification of the sacred can result in unsatisfactory travel experiences and in fact may end up in conflict and spaces of contestation. Others suggest that such developments may undermine the authenticity of religious destinations and diminish the genuine pilgrim experience (Sharpley, 2009).

Truth be told, it takes money to operate religious organizations, evangelize, minister, maintain shrines and sacred sites, and advocate for the greater good of society. This is especially so in contemporary times when there is so much competition for people's time, devotion and finances. Thus, not only have the behaviors of the pilgrims themselves changed over the centuries through faster-paced lifestyles and more dependence on modern conveniences (e.g. air travel, mobile phones, comfortable lodging), but so have the religious organizations that manage sacred sites, and the destinations that host them as they realize the fiscal value of religious tourism. Schott (2008) and Shackley (2002, 2006a) contend that because pilgrimage has been subsumed into the global tourism system, it does not mean that sacred sites and religious travel experiences are no longer genuine expressions of faith. On the contrary, such changes have functioned to democratize religious tourism in a way that enables more devotees to travel than ever before.

Most tourists who seek spiritual growth and divine communion are able to see past the mercantile landscapes of holy destinations and realize the need for economic growth, employment and retail development in the destination. According to one Catholic pilgrim at Lourdes, the pervasive retail landscape can unintentionally contribute to a more penetrating pilgrim experience.

> I believe that you just have to cling to your faith and ignore all the tackiness, and all the nonsensical things that happen around you whilst on your pilgrimage. I suppose you could say that is a new form of penance in modern day pilgrimage that you have to eradicate from your mind, all the irrelevant things happening around you. (Quoted in Higgins & Hamilton, 2011: 265)

In the context of commercial souvenirs,

> divine presence bridges the potential gap between commodity and gift. This is particularly important for 21st century American pilgrims who, despite vendors' assurances, know that the inexpensive items they buy as undirected gifts are sometimes made in China. Although they are not generally bothered by this – after all, some acknowledge that it is this reason they can afford to buy so many gifts – they rely even more strongly on divine presence to make sure that a bookmark is not just another Chinese product but a Holy Land souvenir. (Kaell, 2012: 141)

While the pilgrim 'kitsch' and overdeveloped touristic infrastructure may be a distraction for some people, most still value the importance of being in a sacred place and are able to overlook these distractions.

Conclusion

Religious destinations have long understood the important role of tourism, whether religious pilgrimage or cultural tourism, in their economic growth. Today, many Christian organizations and sacred sites now realize that to remain financially viable, they need to acknowledge tourism, whereas they were loath to do so before. Christian destinations have learned to maximize earnings from limited resources and from a form of travel (e.g. pilgrimage) that for centuries comprised a non-spending market (Olsen, 2006a; Wiltshier, 2011; Wiltshier & Clarke, 2012). However, the face of religious travel has changed from the austerity and piousness associated with medieval to late modern Christian pilgrimages (Turner, 1973) to one that involves more leisure activities of a traditional 'touristic' nature.

The lines between tourism and pilgrimage have blurred considerably over the past century (Collins-Kreiner, 2010b), with the tourism industry, public officials, tour operators and DMOs in most cases no longer distinguishing between the two but rather acknowledging that pilgrimage is, in one way or another, a form of religious tourism. With the commercialization of the gospel into theme parks and other themed environments, cruises and package tours, planned events and souvenirs, the line between the sacred and the profane has become even thinner and blurrier. While the commoditization of the sacred in some observers' thinking demonstrates a deep degree if impiety, many Christian travelers have adapted to these changes. They suggest that commercial interests are needed today to support the broader evangelical message, that commercialization is a sign of the modern times and that one can ignore the commodified elements of the journey if they choose to do so. Every major faith tradition on earth today is facing the same threat of commoditization. In Christianity, however, it appears to be an increasingly acceptable outcome of the increased globalization of human mobility, including dutiful pilgrimages and pleasure travel.

4 Promoting Christian Tourism

Introduction

As Chapter 3 emphasized, religious tourism is big business, and although many 'traditional' pilgrims spend relatively little money on their journeys, this is changing drastically, and the overall economic impact of pilgrimage-based tourism throughout the world is immense (Egresi et al., 2014; Vukonić, 2002). With this realization, religious tourism has become the focus of much promotional attention by destinations, tour operators, travel agencies and other service providers.

The promotion of religious travel is done primarily in the same ways and using the same methods as all other forms of tourism. Its main goal is to promote places, increase visitor numbers and augment regional and business income through tourist expenditures. It is important for destinations to satisfy the needs of visitors and to meet their expectations. This is particularly true in Christian destinations. Because Christian pilgrimages or religiously motivated travel in general are not obligatory as they are in some other faiths, people have the option whether or not to visit a place, how long they will stay or how frequently they will visit. Although most shrines and churches care little about attracting more visitors, except for the purpose of ecumenical outreach and spreading spiritual enlightenment, the destinations where these sites are located care a great deal about attracting more visitor attention and meeting visitors' travel requirements. Thus, Christian destinations and commercial attractions must compete for the increasingly lucrative visitor market. In doing so, they too must satisfy Christian travelers' needs and desires by providing unique and memorable experiences that help visitors feel the spirit while simultaneously learning something new and enjoying their stay (Richards & Fernandes, 2011).

This chapter carries on from the commodification discussion before it to examine the promotional activities associated with Christian travel. It first examines the main stakeholders that promote, market and produce religious travel experiences, such as destinations and their management organizations, tour operators and travel agencies, faith organizations and other service providers. It also describes some of the marketing tools used by the faith travel industry to reach a broader market, and the ways in which Christian destinations typically help create satisfied customers. The chapter concludes with a discussion about the role of Christian sacred spaces as place brands and iconic tourism images.

Marketing Christian Travel

Like all other forms of tourism, Christian travel has a long marketing and promotional history (Bar & Cohen-Hattab, 2003). Even during Roman and medieval times, evidence of early commercialization has been documented, from crafters selling icons and religious handicrafts, to people letting out rooms for money in their private homes along routes and in sacred destinations, and to certain organizations arranging group packaged pilgrimage trips to shrines in Europe and Jerusalem (Hunt, 1984; Jacobs, 2002; Stemberger, 2000; Wilkinson, 1977). Thomas Cook's 19th-century marketing efforts noted in Chapter 3 are an example of early commercial efforts to market packaged Christian pilgrimages. Throughout history, evidence shows that many intermediaries have been involved in facilitating Christian-focused travel and encouraging it – early manifestations of religious tourism marketing efforts (Belhassen, 2007; Cohen-Hattab, 2004; Kaell, 2010; Timothy & Daher, 2009; Vogel, 1993).

Besides the travelers themselves, there are at least four sets of interested parties, or stakeholders, in the promotional aspects of Christian tourism: destinations, faith organizations, tour companies and travel agencies, and other service providers. Each one of these has a distinct role to play in promoting and marketing contemporary Christian travel.

Destinations and destination management organizations (DMOs)

Christian destinations today are looking beyond their altruistic role of providing spiritual experiences in sacred space to encompass a socio-economic role for the community at large. Today, it is virtually impossible to find pilgrimage destinations that focus solely on traditional pilgrimage functions. Rather, it has become more common for pilgrimage locales to market themselves as religious tourist destinations or even broader cultural destinations, as a means of economic development (Battour et al., 2010; Grondys et al., 2014; Olsen, 2006a, 2011, 2014; Richards & Fernandes, 2011; Simone-Charteris & Boyd, 2010; Stefko et al., 2013; Vukonić, 1992, 2002). These promotional activities usually become the responsibility of DMOs, whose job is to promote awareness, entice visitors and manage the destination product in order to satisfy the needs of tourist consumers (Figure 4.1).

Archaeological sites and archaeologists realize that tourism is necessary to fund their projects and justify their existence in many

Figure 4.1 Tourists can buy Christian-themed bus tours of Rome on coaches such as the one shown (Photo: D. Timothy)

cases, particularly with public agencies and bodies. In the same way, traditional Christian destinations now realize the need to expand their market beyond the traditional style of pilgrims to encompass a broader tourist niche, particularly younger and more affluent markets (Russell, 1999).

As noted elsewhere in this book, even non-traditional destinations are beginning to cater to the solidarity and kinship desires of Christians. Destinations whose primary attractions are religious in nature must nowadays consider the need to provide regional income, tax revenue and employment in all services that are needed to support pilgrimage travel. And, while pilgrims and other religious tourists, as well as the organizations to which they belong, might see themselves as being separate from tourists, most destinations care little about this distinction, since all visitors, regardless of motives and purposes, bring tourist expenditures and utilize local services.

Christian tourists are the largest market segment for Israel (Gelbman & Collins-Kreiner, 2013), and the country has worked tirelessly to market itself as the best and most important Christian destination in the world (Ariel, 2006). Although, like most well-known religious destinations, the Holy Land's unique selling proposition is its religious heritage and its salient biblical role among Christians (Suleiman & Mohamed, 2011). Since the Holy Land is innately an important destination for Christians, fewer marketing efforts are as essential for Israel and Palestine as perhaps they are for secondary destinations.

Religious destinations and specific attractions constantly seek ways of improving their ability to meet the needs of pilgrims, other religious tourists and non-religious tourists and increase all visitors' satisfaction levels. Religious heritage sites are nearly always a part of the broader tourism product of regions and destinations and must be part of national, regional and local tourism strategies in ways that create complementary relationships between Christian heritage and other tourist attractions and services (Fernandes *et al.*, 2015).

For example, much of the rich heritage of Catalonia, which is promoted and marketed as one of the region's primary tourism assets, is its Christian heritage – monasteries, churches, cathedrals, cemeteries, religious celebrations and faith-based gastronomy (Aulet & Hakobyan, 2011; Aulet *et al.*, 2017; Vidal *et al.*, 2013). The countries of Georgia and Armenia, as well as parts of the UK (e.g. Wales and rural England), are similar to Catalonia in that much of their tourism is based upon an ancient Christian landscape that features vast quantities of churches, monasteries and similar sacred spaces that attract not only pilgrims but many other types of tourists as well (Busby, 2002; Metreveli & Timothy, 2010; Thomas, 2016). Georgia and Armenia claim to be the world's first Christianized countries, and both emphasize this fact in their tourism promotional efforts. The majority of the heritage attractions in both countries are of Christian origin and provide the essence of cultural tourism in the two nations (Fernandes, 2011; Timothy, 2014). This is common in many parts of Europe, where the church long provided the best impetus for preserving built heritage, and therefore it is the religious heritage in connection with that of the ruling elites that has been best preserved and forms the foundations of many countries' and regions' cultural resources (Ambaw, 2015; Bideci & Albayrak, 2016; Brice *et al.*, 2003; Jackson & Hudman, 1995; Liutikas, 2015b; Shackley, 2006a; Winter & Gasson, 1996).

In common with marketing planning for all other forms of tourism in destinations, it is crucial that all stakeholders have a voice in decision-making (Timothy, 1999). This is especially critical in the context of religious tourism (Pavicic *et al.*, 2007), because so many of the issues surrounding faith, spirituality, sacred space and contestation are associated with religious tourism destinations. One element of this is collaborative planning. Church–state partnerships are crucial in developing successful religious tourism (Tilson, 2005). Santiago de Compostela, Spain, is one of the best success stories where the Catholic Church has worked hand in hand with the government of the autonomous community of Galicia in marketing and promoting Santiago as both a pilgrimage destination and a major cultural destination for the benefit of that corner of Spain (Olsen, 2014; Santos, 2002; Tilson, 2005).

Tour operators and travel agencies

Thousands of tour operators and travel agencies throughout the world specialize in pilgrimages and religious tours (Morrison, 2014; Triantafillidou *et al.*, 2010). Some of their commercial products (e.g. packaged pilgrimages and Christian cruises) were discussed at length in Chapter 3. However, given the importance of tour companies and travel agencies in the Christian travel market, expanding that discussion in this chapter is worthwhile.

To meet the needs of specific church groups, entire denominations or individuals, thousands of Christian tour companies and travel agencies worldwide work to organize packaged products and experiences that will help build participants' faith and testimonies, create fellowship and solidarity among members of certain faith groups and provide mingling opportunities for Christian singles or family groups. They do this primarily by putting together travel products to locations of interest to various Christian denominations or specialty groups. They negotiate air and land transportation, lodgings, guest speakers, visits to museums and sacred sites, biblical meals, social gatherings, genealogy excursions and other such faith-based services and activities, so that everything that Christian travelers need is organized and paid in advance, which allows participants to enjoy the spiritual elements of the journey in a carefree setting.

Faith Journeys, based in Tempe, Arizona, for example, caters to two broad market segments – Catholics and Protestants – although the agency can customize travel for any faith organization. Pre-programmed Catholic tour options focus on the Holy Land, Italy, France, Central and Eastern Europe, Spain and Portugal, Ireland and the UK, Greece and Turkey, and Mexico. Their Catholic tours in Eastern Europe include themes of social transformation, faith-building, music and miracles, healing and the footsteps of Saint Paul. Several thematic tours of Italy, the Vatican City, France, Spain and Portugal are available, focusing on Roman Catholic shrines and sacred sites in those countries, as well as journeys through the UK, Ireland, Greece, Turkey and Mexico. Several themed Holy Land tours are also available, including 'Women of Valor', which focuses on the women of the Bible; youth spiritual adventures in the Holy Land; singles Holy Land tours; the Exodus journey focusing on sites in Egypt, Jordan and Israel; and 'Follow in the Steps of Jesus Christ' tours. The company's Protestant tours include many similar products (e.g. singles and youth tours), but they also provide Reformation tours, such as 'In the Footsteps of Martin Luther' and the 'Reformation Tour of Germany', as well as journeys that focus on other known reformers such as John Knox, John Calvin, John Wesley and Ulrich Zwingli (Faith Journeys, 2017).

Christian tour companies come in many forms. Sizer (1999) described four main types of Christian tour operators that do business in the Holy

Land. The first are secular companies that provide what are essentially packaged holidays or vacation experiences with perhaps a few religious sites included for religiosity's sake. Many of their products are recreational in nature, nature oriented or focused on Israel's other, less Christian-oriented sites. The second type are companies that offer spiritual experiences and Bible-based tours where travelers can walk in the footsteps of the Savior and learn biblical lessons in the places where they happened. Zionist-type tour agencies are the third sort identified by Sizer. While most Christian visitors to the Holy Land and their organizers would likely argue that their pilgrimages are apolitical (Olsen, in press), this could not be further from the truth with regard to the elements of pro-Israel or pro-Palestine sentiment that pervade many tour itineraries in the region (Belhassen, 2009; Bowman, 1992; Brin, 2006; Isaac, 2013; Moufakkir, 2010; Sharif, 1976; Timothy & Emmett, 2014; Troen & Rabineau, 2014). This third type tends to concentrate on the Jewish dimensions of Christianity and promote solidarity with Israel, focusing on the foundation of the state and its biblical divination. Finally, there is a small network of agencies that actively urge contact with Palestinian Christians, which are commonly known in local lexicon as 'Living Stones' (see Chapter 5). Although the term 'Living Stones' is the official name of a British non-governmental organization (NGO), it is now commonly used to refer to Christian Palestinians (Feldman, 2011; Sizer, 1999; Timothy & Olsen, 2006). These visits typically take Christian tourists beyond the *de facto* borders of Israel into the Palestinian-controlled territories (e.g. Bethlehem, Hebron and Nablus) to meet with Arab Christians who have been cut off from access to Israel, the churches of Jerusalem and other holy Christian sites, in the same way other Palestinians are restricted in their mobility. Israel does not differentiate between Arab Muslims and Arab Christians in its policies toward the Palestinians (Raheb, 2002). Many tour company efforts are geared toward building camaraderie with the plight of Palestine's fellow Christians and the hardships they suffer under Israeli occupation (Isaac, 2016; Keating, 2007; Troen & Rabineau, 2014).

Religious organizations

The third group of promotional stakeholders is comprised of religious organizations, such as churches, congregations, study groups and scripture societies, which desire to organize religious travel experiences for their members. Many faith groups within Christianity promote pilgrimage or other sorts of devotional tours as a means of developing individuals' faith in Christ and building testimonies (Belhassen, 2009; Olsen & Timothy, 2006; Reader, 2014). From a ministerial perspective, these experiences are regarded as opportunities to build intragroup solidarity, whether or not they take place in sacred locales (Ron & Feldman,

2009). From an ecumenical perspective, pan-Christian harmony is also encouraged through ecumenical tours, such as the group experiences in non-Christian destinations (e.g. China) mentioned earlier and the solidary visits to Arab Christians in the Holy Land, also discussed previously.

Many famous Christian evangelists and locally known ministers participate in tours of the Holy Land and other Christian destinations as group escorts or guides (Feldman, 2007). Many organize pilgrimage tours for their own congregations only, while others open up their groups for broader consumption as a way of meeting minimum group size requirements. In this effort, they become part of the tourism product as they travel with their congregants, guiding and interpreting the biblical significance of the sites in their itineraries (Ambrósio & Santos, 2012). They usually work in close collaboration with tour operators in the destination to organize travel logistics, while the ministerial escorts provide the spiritual enlightenment and personal connectedness that so many Christians desire. For some religious organizations, these tours are a source of income to assist their ministries financially, while for others it is another way of shepherding their flock. Regardless of the organizational purpose, religiously motivated travel is an important element of many Christians' devotion to the Lord and to their church society.

Service providers

The fourth stakeholder comprises the multitude of other service providers that work with tour agencies to provide experiences for Christian consumers. These include, but are not limited to, coach services, hotels, airlines, cruise companies, restaurants and tour guides. Most of these tertiary providers market their products through travel agencies and tour operators rather than directly to tourists, although there are Christian-specific services (e.g. biblical meal providers) that might advertise to individual travelers in addition to tour groups.

The best-researched service provider in the Christian context is tour guides. Tour guides have many roles to play: storyteller, political messenger, safety officer, interpreter, entertainer, linguist, company representative, content expert, educator and crowd manager, to name but a few (Weiler & Black, 2015). Nowhere is this truer than within the Christian travel industry, especially in the Holy Land.

Relatively few Christian travelers in the Holy Land visit as individuals; the majority come on organized tour packages for convenience, deeper engagement with the spirit of the place and fellowship with co-religionists, and for security reasons. Relatively few guides in Israel are Christians, although there are some Arab Christian guides within Israel and in Palestine. In Israel, they are primarily Jews who have learned to navigate the Christian Bible, emphasize the biblical accounts and places most pertinent to different sects and understand the gospel-speak of the various denominations with which they work. In fact, some guides prefer working with certain Christian church members over others; they look differently at the behaviors, activities and interests of different Christian groups (Gelbman & Collins-Kreiner, 2013). Likewise, certain groups prefer different kinds of guides. Catholics tend to prefer Palestinian Christian guides where possible, while most Protestants prefer Jewish guides instead of Muslim, Catholic or Christian Orthodox Arabs (Feldman, 2007: 356).

In their role as sociopolitical emissaries and storytellers, many guides' narrations 'promote particular political views of the Israeli–Palestinian conflict, and lend them authority by saturating them with particular Christian meanings and associations' (Feldman, 2011: 62; see also Hercbergs, 2012). Nonetheless, the Jewish Israeli guides and the tour leaders together become co-producers of the Bible Land storyline. Good guides will, by interpreting the Bible, 'grant significance to visitors' movement that constitutes the visitors as pilgrims' even when the guide himself or herself is a 'reluctant witness' to the gospel truths contained in the Bible (Feldman, 2007: 351).

Marketing Mechanisms

Like all other forms of tourism, Christian travel requires intentional marketing efforts to increase visitation and sales. Nowadays, this even includes traditional pilgrimages, not just packaged tours, cruises and theme parks, being marketed for larger consumption. However, as Chapter 2 clearly noted, different denominations have different destination or attraction preferences, which obviously affects an individual's personal connection to a specific site or region (Poria *et al.*, 2003), which influences his or her travel preferences. This has significant marketing implications.

Pilgrims are perhaps one of the most difficult niches to influence through marketing campaigns (Richards & Fernandes, 2011). This is so for a couple of reasons. First, most Catholics or Orthodox Christians who want to travel on pilgrimage have already planned to undertake the journey. Convincing them to do a pilgrimage is not the issue, but perhaps their destination choice is; however, many traditional pilgrimage destinations are reluctant to compete against one another for visitors' attention, as this might appear to be too commercial. Second, in many cases, no matter how much effort is devoted to influencing their consumer travel decisions, members of certain denominations will likely not be persuaded to visit sites associated with other denominations. For instance, convincing American Southern Baptists or members of various Pentecostal churches to visit Roman Catholic destinations, such as Medjugorje or Lourdes or Latter-day Saints (LDS) church history sites, would be a nearly impossible task. As a result, destination marketing specialists have learned to invest their resources wisely in campaigns that will have the most impact – not persuading people to travel but persuading them which shrine to visit.

Print is still important in the religious tourism sector. Guidebooks and pilgrim maps published by church presses or private church-affiliated organizations have a long history in the Christian travel industry. In spite of the ever-increasing efficiency and efficacy of the internet, physical guidebooks are still popular marketing tools and information sources (Beck, 2017; Collins-Kreiner, 1997; Dyer & Hatteberg, 2014; Wright, 2008). Many destinations, church organizations, private authors and ministries continue to publish guidebooks that help Christian tourists plan, visit, find places to stay, identify sites to see, dine, hire guides and use local transportation. Most printed ads tend to be published in church-specific magazines, newspapers and catalogues and focus on the sites and activities that are most attractive to their members. Advertisements for archaeological digs and some other themed environment volunteer opportunities usually aim at a broader Christian audience.

The internet is the most obvious and widespread means of promoting Christian travel. This takes many different forms including site-specific websites, DMO marketing websites, travel blogs and various social media platforms. The importance of social media in tourism promotional efforts cannot be overstated. Social media functions as a promotional tool in two primary ways. First, the media provide online platforms for travelers to share their experiences and offer recommendations. User-generated information is now vast and widespread, and many people utilize it as the basis for many of their travel decisions (Zhou *et al.*, 2017). Millions of internet users share their vacation photographs, stories about their trips, reviews of attractions and hotels and their satisfaction or dissatisfaction with their destinations on platforms such as Facebook, Twitter, YouTube and Pinterest, including travel-specific sites such as TripAdvisor (Garay Tamajón & Cànoves Valiente, 2017).

The second use of social media is attractions and destinations promoting their appeal to a larger potential market than could ever have been done through traditional print media (Yoo & Lee, 2015). This is considered a low-cost marketing tool, and it also allows operators to refute unfair reviews they might perceive from user-generated content or to correct erroneous online statements. Social media-based information is so pervasive that it allows all Christian service providers to gain additional exposure with relatively little effort and may be considered by some to be a less-commercial way of spreading the message.

Social media is extremely relevant in the context of religious travel. In common with all other sorts of heritage destinations, the widespread use of social media is becoming more commonplace in religious tourism settings (Nilsson & Tesfahuney, 2016). Churches, cathedrals, shrines and other Christian heritage sites are among the most commonly rated, liked and shared resources in destinations. Billions of comments, experiences, likes and dislikes have been shared for the whole world to see. People's decisions to visit certain places, stay in specific lodging facilities or dine in restaurants are strongly influenced by the ratings and commentaries they see on travel-oriented social media.

Mega-events are commonly used as major tourist draws and to broaden a destination's visibility. High-profile sporting events are one of the most prominent examples of this. The same is true for religious tourism. As Chapters 3 and 8 explain, destinations and Christian organizations actively use Christian events as a means of increasing arrivals and spreading the word. The events associated with the millennial change at the end of 1999 were remarkable. This event was used industriously by both Israel and Palestine to draw attention to the second millennium commemoration of the birth of Jesus and the potential cataclysmic events that might happen then. Both Palestine and Israel actively used this as a strong marketing mechanism to draw Christians from all over the world (Olsen & Timothy, 1999).

Christian mega-events are held throughout the world, and while church organizers are most concerned with their evangelizing and organizational purposes, the destinations where they are held are primarily interested in generating increased tourist expenditures (Laing & Frost, 2016). On many occasions, the government of Zimbabwe has encouraged the organization of large-scale Pentecostal events that involve healing meetings, sermons and miracle seeking, as a way of stimulating tourism in that country. Chibaya (2017) discussed this phenomenon and noted that Methodist, Jehovah's Witness and Pentecostal conventions in Harare regularly result in full hotel occupancy, busy restaurants and increased rentals of buses and motorcoaches. Many destinations have considered the value of religious meetings, just as they consider mega-sporting events or cultural festivals.

Creating Satisfied Christian Travelers

One of the most salient marketing goals of DMOs, tour companies and other service providers is to deliver satisfying experiences for their customers (Rivera *et al.*, 2009; Smolčić Jurdana & Soldić Frleta, 2017). This is seen as a way of exacting increased expenditures, spreading positive word of mouth and increasing the chances of a return visit. Dissatisfying experiences, however, have the opposite effect and the disappointment experienced by tourists may have long-term implications for the destination and its service providers (Alegre & Garau, 2010; Michalkó *et al.*, 2015).

Quality customer service

From a destination marketing perspective, it is vital to consider the quality of the religious experience and the satisfaction of the religious consumer. Even though tradition implies, and some modern observers suggest, that true pilgrims are more willing to withstand a degree of hardship in their travels than leisure travelers are because of the power of propitiation such travails might entail, good customer service is extremely important. Just like other travelers, religious tourists desire good customer service, reasonable lodgings and food standards, trouble-free transportation and good guiding (Ron, 2018; Triantafillidou *et al.*, 2010; Weidenfeld & Ron, 2008). In fact, the comfort and ease of Christian pilgrimages are now marketed as highlights of most package tours (Triantafillidou *et al.*, 2010).

Research suggests that reliability, responsiveness, tangibility, assurance and empathy are among the most important qualities that comprise a pleasant pilgrimage (Eid, 2012). These are essentially the same qualities required in more general travel experiences. In the specific realm of Christian tourism, however, well-trained guides are essential in helping provide satisfying encounters (Feldman, 2007), especially knowledge of the Bible and linguistic abilities in the context of Holy Land tours (Feldman, 2014). In some cases, good acting abilities are needed as Jewish Israeli guides become temporary and 'reluctant witness[es] to scriptural truth... facilitated by historically transmitted practices of viewing, classifying history, and Orientalizing shared by Protestants and Zionists' (Feldman, 2007: 351) as they co-produce with Protestant pastors a 'mutually satisfying performance that transforms the often-contested terrain of Israel-Palestine into Bible Land'.

Marketing for religious needs in tourism

There is a growing realization that adherents to certain faiths require specific services and products during their pilgrimages or during other holiday experiences. Most research on this topic has focused on the needs of Muslim tourists for halal food and sharia-compliant lodgings and services (Battour *et al.*, 2010, 2011; El-Gohary, 2016; Hassan & Hall, 2003; Henderson, 2016; Mohsin *et al.*, 2016; Mohsin & Ryan, in press; Ron, 2018; Timothy & Ron, 2016; Weidenfeld & Ron, 2008). These include gender-segregated recreational facilities, available prayer rooms, posted prayer times, Qurans and prayer rugs in rooms, qiblats (Mecca directional markers), halal-certified kitchens, alcohol-free menus and Muslim staff (Timothy & Ron, 2016).

Less research has been done on the needs of Jewish tourists, although several scholars have examined kosher laws and the rules of *kashruth* while traveling and the desire for Orthodox Jews to seek out Sabbath-compliant hotels (e.g. Cahaner & Mansfeld, 2012; Cohen Ioannides & Ioannides, 2006; Corsale, 2017; Dinis & Krakover, 2016; Jochnowitz, 2004; Krakover, 2017; Rotkovitz, 2004).

Even less research has been done on the specific needs of Christian travelers, probably because most Christians have fewer dietary, lodging and Sabbath restrictions than Jews or Muslims do (Fleischer & Nitzav, 1995; Timothy & Ron, 2016). Nonetheless, members of some churches do in fact adhere to strict dietary and/or behavioral rules that include their actions during vacation time or spiritual travel. For example, some churches encourage their members to refrain from excessive drinking and certain foods. While less pervasive now than in the past, many traditional Catholics continue to refrain from eating meat on Fridays (Dugan, 1994), and the Seventh-day Adventist Church strongly discourages using tobacco and alcohol, and subscribes to a healthy eating standard, including veganism whenever possible (Brown, 2015; Dugan, 1994). The LDS Church prohibits drinking alcohol, coffee and caffeinated tea and using tobacco; church members are also encouraged to eat meat 'sparingly' (Albala, 2011; Brown, 2015; Reeve, 2010). These examples illustrate the unique dietary needs of some Christians while traveling and might be something DMOs and services providers might consider in their planning efforts.

Beyond food, Weidenfeld (2006) recommends that Christian destinations should be willing to do things that make visitors feel more at ease and as though their needs are cared for. Examples include hiring Christian employees at hotels as a way of being able to relate better to the tourists' experiences, providing information about various faith-related events and institutions in the area and furnishing Bibles in hotel rooms. One Christian tour company in Israel that specializes in Latter-day Saint pilgrimages caters to the unique needs of this particular denomination: 'In addition to the "guide"…, you are being guided by the only LDS tour operators in Israel. That makes the whole experience even better, because LDS standards apply in the entire event. You get experienced drivers who have never smoked; the bus has never been smoked in. The hotels have higher religious standards, and their restaurants observe the Jewish "Word of Wisdom", kosher. And… the Sabbath is sacred, there's no touring schedule on Saturday, the LDS Sabbath in Israel' (Israel Revealed, 2017: np).

Authentic experiences

One of the most important aspects of tourism, particularly within the realm of cultural heritage and religious travel, is the notion of authenticity. As this chapter suggests, for many people, having experiences they deem to be authentic makes their involvement more satisfying and enjoyable. Andriotis (2009) identified several different manifestations of religious authenticity among people visiting the Greek Orthodox shrine of Mount Athos. Spiritual authenticity is a felt spiritual magnetism, which impresses upon visitors to pray and undertake religious activities and devotion. Cultural authenticity is manifested through art, history and architecture. Environmental authenticity involves solitude and tranquility, as well as alignment with nature. Secular authenticity seekers do not desire a normative 'tourist' experience. Instead, they want the old-fashioned pilgrimage settings and traditional practices.

Andriotis' spiritual authenticity is manifested in many ways. For example, for most Christians, 'feeling the spirit' is the strongest element of an authentic encounter with the sacred. Engagement with the divine may be defined by emotive sensations or impressions in the mind or in the soul, often resulting in the shedding of tears, feelings of awe and inspiration, the swelling of faith, the burning of testimony and being touched by the spirit in other ways. These are the authentic encounters many pilgrims seek (Olsen, 2012a; Ross, 2014) and may derive from reading scriptures, hearing stories, listening to inspiring sermons, singing hymns of praise, contemplating Christ and his ministry or visiting sacrosanct places. A combination of these in sacred space epitomizes the authentic experiences many people seek. Tour guides play an important role in promoting these sorts of experiences; good guides can evoke emotions and personalize the sacred to individuals in a tour group. While the educative and scientific values of religious places may also inspire, they usually take second place to the experiences that are less describable, less tangible, more personal and more profound.

The comradery and kinship, or a oneness in Christ that people feel with their group members also often translates into a sense of spiritual authenticity. Contrarily, people who consider themselves to be pilgrims in the strictest sense of the word might have what they perceive to be less authentic experiences when they find themselves surrounded by non-pilgrim visitors who may detract from the spirit (Terzidou *et al*., 2008).

As regards existential and cultural authenticity, a Christian visiting a Buddhist temple in Thailand might not be as moved spiritually as his or her accompanying Thai friend is, regardless of whether the site is aesthetically pleasing, historically important or archaeologically authentic. Thus, from the perspective of existential authenticity, proximity to deity, spiritual inspiration and religious importance of place are all markers of authenticity for religious tourists, and in most cases religious travelers do seek authentic experiences, however those are defined (Belhassen *et al*., 2008; Blackwell, 2007; Pusztai, 2004; Simone-Charteris & Boyd, 2010; Vukonić, 1992).

Perhaps more than any other type of tourist, the Christian traveler is inclined to be a 'literalist' – someone who expresses the desire to see, touch or stand upon the 'exact' spot where something momentous occurred (Collins-Kreiner & Kliot, 2000). This lends another element of environmental authenticity to the Christian travel experience. Walking in the footsteps of Christ may be taken literally to mean finding the stones or bedrock the Savior physically walked on during his earthly ministry, being re-baptized in the precise location where Jesus was baptized in the

Jordan River or touching the very same walls of the Mamertine Prison in Rome where the Apostle Paul was incarcerated before his execution. While relatively few such locations have been identified as being genuine, historically accurate and known in the truest sense of the word, there are locations in Rome, Jerusalem, Capernaum and Nazareth that are verifiable from the correct time period and in locations that would have almost assuredly been visited by Jesus or the apostles.

Some literalists also want to partake of authentic biblical food, which can be purchased in Israel along with a traditional dining experience that reflects many ceremonial customs of ancient Canaan (Ron & Timothy, 2013). Official souvenirs purchased as genuine mementos gain their authoritative authenticity by bearing the images of ancient apostles or the Pope, or by having been blessed by a priest (Kaell, 2014; Vukonić, 2006). Material objects picked up from sacred locales, including rocks, leaves, branches or seashells, are innately imbued with divine legitimacy and environmental authenticity by virtue of their being part of the same ancient ecosystem that existed at the time of a sacred event.

Likewise, the images of sacred landscapes depicted by early Christian travel writers have skewed people's perceptions of what the Holy Land and European shrines look like today (Jacobs, 2002). Romanticized representations of sacred places have long been oversold to Christians through the media, brochures, websites and various memorabilia (Long, 2003). This has led to preconceived imaginaries of what the village of Bethlehem or Nazareth should look like. Many people face disappointment when they arrive in these sacred locales to see that they are in fact bustling cities rather than ancient villages and are disappointed by the apparent lack of their anticipated authentic Holy Land (Collins-Kreiner & Kliot, 2000).

In a mixture of spiritual and environmental authenticity, many Christian groups believe their own faith traditions to be more authentic or truer than others (Olsen, 2003). This sometimes translates into people of different denominations visiting the sacred locales of other churches and feeling unsanctified or inauthentic. The flamboyance of many Orthodox and Catholic churches and shrines in the Holy Land, for example, has been known to detract from feelings of authenticity among Protestant Christian pilgrims (Collins-Kreiner & Kliot, 2000).

Finally, related to Andriotis' secular authenticity, many Christian pilgrims want to be alienated from the modern world, especially the tourist world, by being immersed in the traditional spiritual cloak of a sacrosanct place and process (Shapiro, 2008). For example, in many Santiago de Compostela pilgrims' minds, what sets them apart from the 'touristic other' is their arriving at the destination not by coach, airplane or car but via the pilgrimage route. Traveling the camino by bicycle or on foot is valorized because it represents a more authentic pilgrimage (Badone & Roseman, 2004b).

Safety and security

As noted previously, religious tourism and pilgrimage tend to be less elastic than other forms of tourism, meaning that even in the face of economic downturns and political instability, faith travel tends not to decline as quickly as other forms of tourism (Collins-Kreiner, 2010b; Collins-Kreiner *et al.*, 2006). Nonetheless, safe and secure environments are among the most important ways of maintaining a destination's reputation and providing satisfying experiences for religious tourists (Eid, 2012). Even though the Holy Land is the most prominent Christian destination in the world, it is among the most politically volatile, and safety has been a crucial part of developing the Christian tourism product in Palestine, Israel and the broader Holy Land (Suleiman & Mohamed, 2011; Timothy, 2013; Timothy & Daher, 2009).

Most Christian travel happens in organized package tours (Feldman, 2014; Kaell, 2010; Ron & Feldman, 2009; Rotherham, 2007; Shachar & Shoval, 1999; Shoval, 2000). One of the reasons for this is so that the story of Jesus can be brought to life through fellowship, guides and the spirit, which 'give tangible form to the Christian faith' (Bajc, 2006: 101–102). Another primary reason, however, is more pragmatic. Package tours provide a degree of safety, especially with regard to the Israeli–Palestinian conflict, which independent travel cannot provide (Bowman, 1992). According to Feldman (2007: 356), group pilgrims are willing to 'sacrifice part of their independence and adventurousness for the sake of security'.

Branding Christian Heritage

Most places on the tourism map have a 'brand', or an image that depicts the historical or modern essence of the place. Place branding occurs either organically or intentionally. Organic branding, as the name implies, is non-deliberate. It happens over lengthy periods of time as localities (e.g. cities, regions or countries) become known for certain characteristics, such as climate, historic events, living culture, unique food traditions, physical geography and natural environment, religious centrality or a combination of these. This usually happens from years of exposure to outside markets through media reports, educational curricula, literature and television (Hankinson, 2004). Rome is known as the 'eternal city' through its historical position as the center of Europe and 'eternal capital' of the Roman Empire. Today, it is still the eternal city because of the permanence of its intact heritagescapes and its position as one of the most important tourism destinations in the world. The moniker continues to be used today both in popular lexicon and in the city's marketing plans. Similarly, Paris is known as the city of romance owing to its historic architecture, scenic streetscapes, associations with wine and food and the traditional lore associated with amorous spells of romance and falling in love. This glamorized image of France's capital was developed over many years through cinematic expressions, novels, television shows, magazine articles/travel writing and even postcards sent by earlier romance-seeking sojourners.

Intentional place branding occurs when destinations try to communicate an image to existing or potential markets. The brand is normally based on a place's unique characteristics that are already widely known or which a locale might wish to initiate (Campelo, 2017). Sometimes, these efforts include re-branding in situations where a place's image might need to be reinvigorated, such as after a crisis or a lull in visitation (Avraham & Ketter, 2008; Morgan et al., 2011). These purposive branding efforts often include designing and marketing new slogans or brandlines that are meant to identify how destinations wish to be perceived by external consumers.

Both of these means of place brand development are apparent within the context of Christian travel, and they both build upon each other. Hundreds, if not thousands, of religious sites constitute the very foundations of tourism development in many destinations as iconic representations of place through the organic process of pilgrimage and historic importance as portrayed in popular folklore, churchy writ, movies and novels. This frequently provides a competitive advantage for the destination over other alternative destinations (Richards & Fernandes, 2011). For example, Canterbury Cathedral is not only the primate of the Church of England and the larger Anglican movement throughout the world, and a significant pilgrimage center, it is also the foremost anchor tourist attraction in the city. The churches and 'churchscape' of Helsinki are a salient part of that city's tourist attractiveness (Jokela, 2014). St Peter's Basilica is iconic of the Vatican City and an anchor attraction for the city of Rome, in company with the Colosseum and the Roman Forum. Through time and natural processes, Jerusalem has been nicknamed the 'Holy City' owing to its historical connections with Judaism, Islam and Christianity, and its continued prominence as a center of religious influence.

Purposive branding can be seen in several places where Christian heritage dominates the tourism product. The example of Spain's Galicia region with its marketing focus on Santiago de Compostela presented earlier is a noteworthy case in point. Likewise, the town of Medjugorje has grown into a massive tourist destination, and its entire tourism product is based upon the Marian apparitions that occurred there in the 1980s and the shrines that developed in their wake. While pilgrimage visitations began organically in the village during the 1980s, they have grown into mass visits that have reshaped the entire region. The town's branding efforts, as well as those of the national tourism authorities in Sarajevo, focus overwhelming on the Marian shrines and churches of this mass religious tourism destination (Figure 4.2). In the minds of many Catholic pilgrims, Medjugorje is synonymous with Bosnia and Herzegovina (Vukonić, 1992). Similar branding efforts are discernable

Figure 4.2 Medjugorje and its Marian history is a major tourism brand for Bosnia and Herzegovina (Photo: D. Timothy)

in Knock, Ireland, and Fatima, Portugal (de Pinho & de Pinho, 2007; McDermott, 2008).

The world's most popular heritage brand is the World Heritage List (WHL) kept and maintained by the United Nations Scientific, Educational and Cultural Organization (UNESCO). At the time of writing, the list included 1073 World Heritage Sites (WHSs) (832 cultural, 206 natural and 35 mixed) located in 167 countries. UNESCO also maintains a List of Intangible Cultural Heritage. To be considered for the WHL, a site or locale must be deemed to have 'universal' heritage value for all of humankind. Most of the sites and locations on the list are world-class historic attractions, many of which have been significant tourist attractions for decades or centuries. The UNESCO brand is a coveted award in many countries, as there is a common perception that this trademark imbues an objective value and a level of authenticity not possessed by other heritage locales (Adie *et al.*, 2018; Hassan & Rahman, 2015; Poria *et al.*, 2011). There is also a common (mis)perception that being inscribed onto the WHL will inevitably result in increased tourist visitation.

Many of these WHSs represent religious heritage and commemorate the importance of faith in people's lives (Goral, 2011; Irimiás & Michalkó, 2013). A good number of these are Christian pilgrimage destinations, including Canterbury Cathedral (Ballantyne *et al.*, 2016); the Routes of Santiago in France and Spain and the pilgrimage city of Santiago de Compostela (Lois González, 2013); the Church of the Nativity and the

Pilgrimage Route in Bethlehem; and the Wooden Churches of Southern Małopolska, the Pilgrimage Church of St John of Nepomuk, Petäjävesi Old Church, the Pilgrimage Church of Weis and many other monasteries, shrines and sacred locales (Goral, 2011; Meskell, 2015; Murzyn, 2008).

Branding efforts go beyond single sites and destinations. Several long-distance religious routes and pilgrim trails have become focal points in regional destination branding exercises. Christianity-based heritage routes in Catalonia are now the focus of promotional efforts to brand the region as an important cultural destination both for pilgrims and for general tourists (Timothy & Boyd, 2015; Vidal et al., 2013). In a similar fashion, the Cultural Routes Program of Europe uses Via Francigena, Camino de Santiago and other religious trails as branding tools to broaden the program's appeal (Santos, 2002).

Conclusion

Most visitor destinations desire to increase arrivals, and all destinations desire to improve visitor expenditures. A key way of achieving these goals is to ensure customer satisfaction. While Christian travelers are known to be willing to endure a degree of hardship during their journeys, especially those for whom a journey is considered an authentic pilgrimage, they too desire enjoyable and satisfying encounters with the sacred and divine. DMOs, religious societies, tour operators and travel agencies, guides and other service providers are key stakeholders in realizing these goals for Christian travelers and the destinations they visit.

Quality customer service, catering to travelers' religious requirements, providing authentic experiences and ensuring safe and secure encounters are fundamental to delivering rewarding outcomes for pilgrims and other Christian travelers. This has the potential to result in increased expenditures, longer lengths of stay, repeat visits and positive word of mouth through personal contacts and online recommendations.

Organically developed place brands that focus on Christian sites, events and people have a long tradition of creating desirable destinations. Through intentional promotional efforts, however, this has been augmented in recent decades by UNESCO WHLS inscription and purposive efforts by destinations to increase the visibility of their religious heritage and to compete with other sanctified localities.

Christian destinations and travel intermediaries are not too different from those associated with other tourism functions. Their aim is to generate revenue from visitor spending. While many specific holy sites care little about increasing numbers and expenditures, because their focus is on ministering and ecumenical outreach, others have made conscious efforts to develop a tourism industry that includes both dutiful pilgrims and cultural tourists (Liro et al., in press). All visitors require joy in their journeys, whether this is manifested differently among different people or not. Promotional efforts aim to satisfy this basic necessity and buttress each place's spot in the global realm of contemporary Christian travel.

5 Christian Volunteer Tourism: Solidarity, Spreading the Gospel and Humanitarian Service

Introduction

Volunteer tourism is one of the most pervasive and fastest growing forms of contemporary Christian travel and takes a variety of forms (Bandyopadhyay, 2018). Various churches organize 'mini-missions' (also known as short-term missions, or STMs) that allow adherents to spend shorter periods of time, generally one to five weeks, in the mission field assisting in programs that focus primarily on hygiene, agriculture, construction and Bible study or evangelizing. These are becoming an increasingly important form of humanitarian tourism. However, while not typically included in official definitions of 'tourists', long-term missionaries are also travelers who make salient social and economic contributions in their destinations.

There are other forms of Christian volunteer tourism-like journeys that have not been well examined in the literature, such as solidarity visits to Israel or Palestine. These sometimes involve working in a kibbutz, short-term service in the Israeli army or working with Arab Christians in Palestine (Ron & Timothy, 2016). Such efforts are an important element of tourism among evangelical and fundamentalist Christians, particularly from Europe and North America. Other types and situations include volunteering for long- or short-term periods at sacred sites; religious-themed sites; archaeological digs that are relevant to Old and New Testament heritage; and visitor centers or historic sites as guides, maintenance crewmembers or managers.

This chapter provides an overview and typology of many of the volunteer tourism opportunities undertaken by Christians as part of their religious or spiritual practices. It describes STMs, long-term missions (LTMs), solidarity visits, volunteering at biblical archaeology sites and volunteering at Christian tourist attractions, including examples from the Garden Tomb, Nazareth Village, Lourdes and various churches' historic sites. The primary issues and implications of these volunteer opportunities are highlighted.

Volunteer Tourism: A Growing Subsector of the Travel Industry

Volunteer tourism (sometimes referred to as voluntourism or volunteer vacations) is defined by the travel industry as 'voluntary service experiences that include travel to a destination in order to realize one's service intentions. In a more refined and balanced approach, voluntourism is the integrated combination of voluntary service to a destination with the traditional elements of travel and tourism – arts, culture, geography, history, and recreation – while in the destination' (VolunTourism, 2014: np). Volunteer tourists are people 'who for various reasons, volunteer in an organized way to undertake holidays that involve aiding or alleviating the material poverty of some groups in society, the restoration of certain environments, or research into aspects of society or environment' (Wearing, 2001: 1). These definitions reflect several motives, primary among these being altruism, or a desire to give back to society and make a difference in the lives of others. Other motives are more self-oriented – opportunities to become immersed in a different culture, to learn and to develop one's resume with international experience – or social, including family bonding and spending time with friends (Brown, 2005; Carter, 2008; Grabowski, 2013; Lo & Lee, 2011; McGehee, 2014; Sin, 2009; Tomazos & Butler, 2010; Wearing, 2001; Wiltshier, 2014).

The idea of volunteer tourism became popularized by the founding of Volunteer Service Overseas in 1958 by Alec and Mora Dickson, and the later establishment of the US Peace Corp in 1961 during the Kennedy administration. Some, however, argue that the modern concept of volunteer tourism derives from the 1951 foundation of the Volunteer Graduate Scheme, today known as Australian Volunteers International (VolunTourism, 2014). The later establishment of Habitat for Humanity in 1976, fueled this movement even further (Stoddart & Rogerson, 2004). Even before the formation of these organizations, the idea of traveling the world in the service of humankind was manifest in the early missionary efforts of Jesus's apostles throughout the Mediterranean and in the modern era by the vast networks of Christian missionary programs that exist throughout the world.

Volunteer tourism is a growing phenomenon in many parts of the world and involves many different activities related to rural development, construction, clean water provision, hygiene and health care, human rights and social justice, agriculture, archaeology, religion and proselytizing, environmental maintenance, heritage interpretation, youth development and orphanage work, education, technical assistance and many more activities. There is no official data concerning the geographic sources of volunteer tourists on a global scale, but according to Mostafanezhad (2013), the main national origins are Australia, Canada, Denmark, France, Germany, Japan, the Netherlands, New Zealand, Norway, the United Kingdom and the United States. Research shows that people's inclination to undertake service trips is frequently a direct consequence of their personal values and extant patterns of volunteer service at home (Gulatt-Whiteman, 2004; Holmes & Smith, 2009).

Despite the lack of data, there is a discernable 'geography of compassion'. Mostafanezhad (2013) suggests that many volunteer tourists prefer going to a less poverty-stricken developing country first (e.g. Thailand), then on subsequent journeys they are more willing to visit difficult destinations such as many in Africa or South Asia. Popular voluntourism destinations include India, Nepal, Thailand, South Africa, Ghana, Ecuador, Kenya, Costa Rica, Peru, Brazil, several less-developed Pacific islands and Eastern Europe (Carter, 2008; Tomazos & Cooper, 2012). While most volunteer travel occurs in less-affluent countries, it is also prominent in the developed parts of the world. This philanthropic style of tourism is a modern manifestation of the 'new tourism' or 'post-tourism', as described in Chapter 2 wherein people seek deeper and more meaningful experiences (Mustonen, 2006; Spencer, 2008, 2010).

The negative side of volunteer tourism

What makes volunteer tourism so unique is its ostensible altruistic motivations; people use their vacation time and their own means to travel to a given location to engage in work that helps other individuals, communities or the earth (Benson, 2008; Butcher & Smith, 2015; Govender & Rogerson, 2010; McGehee & Santos, 2005; Mostafanezhad, 2014). While volunteer tourism is generally applauded for its efforts to make a positive difference in the world, scholars have begun to point out that not all elements and outcomes of this experience are positive (Coghlan & Gooch, 2011; Guttentag, 2009; Wearing & McGehee, 2013). According to some critics, it appears that volunteer tourism is not too different from other forms of tourism, some of which tend to be quite destructive to destination people, places and environments (McGehee, 2014). In fact, volunteer tourism is swiftly becoming a form of mass tourism with the potential to exact a heavy carbon footprint and social impact, just as general tourism does. Some people see the veneer of volunteer tourism as simply a façade or a packaged commodity to be consumed by the masses (Carter, 2008). In the words of Vodopivec and Jaffe (2011: 111), volunteer tourism is 'a particular, neoliberal form of development practice, in which development is not only privatized but can be packaged as a marketable commodity'.

While some observers tout voluntourism as a tool for building cross-cultural understanding and cultivating peace (Brown, 2005), critics see this type of tourism as a newer form of neocolonialism with several implications (Bandyopadhyay & Patil, 2017; Hall & Tucker, 2004). In this regard, while the activity may ostensibly be helpful for the destination community, volunteer tourism can be quite harmful as it entrenches 'paternalism and inequitable relationships', especially when voluntourists are unaware of the 'underlying power and privilege issues inherent in voluntourism' (McLennan, 2014: 163). Volunteer tourists often see themselves as 'white saviors' for a people who are incapable of surviving in their own home environment. However, this '"helping" the less fortunate… in the global South' exacerbates the divide and 'reproduces them further' (Bandyopadhyay & Patil, 2017: 644).

The consistent presence of volunteer tourists within a region has the potential to create dependency relationships wherein residents never develop beyond the welfare activities of the visitors (Guttentag, 2009; McGehee & Andereck, 2008). Similarly, the visible gap between the haves (volunteers) and the have-nots (local residents) can result in certain levels of animosity on the part of locals or increased intensity of the demonstration effect (Fisher, 2004; Griffin, 2013; Guttentag, 2009). The development of neocolonialist relationships might also result in volunteer tourists and their programs entering a community to make a difference, even when the community does not desire such a change. In fact, many voluntourism decisions may be made by non-profit agencies, government institutions or tour operators without any real input from the community it purports to help (Carter, 2008; Guttentag, 2009).

Volunteer Tourism: A Christian Perspective

Although there are no statistics on the religious affiliation of volunteer tourists, it might be assumed that a significant number of them are Christians, because many come from countries where the majority of the population is Christian and because one of the edicts of Christianity is to serve others, especially those in need. A relevant question therefore is how can the distinction be made between volunteer tourism performed by Christians and Christian volunteer tourism? A Christian doing volunteer work might be involved in any range of activities, such as cleaning up a trail, planting trees to replenish a forest following a fire, cleaning up after a flood or helping on an archaeological dig to satisfy a hobby. Many Christians who are more liberal would be inclined to take advantage of volunteer opportunities related to environmental protection (Timothy, 2013). Christian volunteer tourism, however, may be different in that it has a religious or spiritual bent and would be more likely to be undertaken as part of one's role as a Christian – volunteering in the name of Christ.

Although there is no clear distinction, an evangelical pastor who was interviewed in this context explains,

> …the distinction is that Christian volunteer tourism has a defined mission. The reason for touring is to do the volunteer mission project. The nature of the project would be humanitarian (Good Samaritan), or

teaching, or something with a distinctive 'Christian' philosophy. All the people on the team have one clear goal. They have one mind and one philosophy. It's as much about the 'why' of the project as getting the job done. It is the Christian thing to do! (Pack, 2013: np)

According to Howell (2012: 28), the distinction is in the narratives and '…culturally embedded discourses about otherness, mission, blessing and suffering'. One can also assume that the context matters. A volunteer tourist who serves in the name of Christ and his or her mission trip is organized by a Christian congregation is more likely to be defined as a Christian volunteer tourist.

Types of Christian volunteer travel

Table 5.1 categorizes several main types of Christian volunteer activities. This typology is not as simple as it may seem, because some of the terms have more than one meaning in the context of Christian service. For example, the term 'short-term mission' has a common cultural context of evangelical Americans visiting developing countries, but by definition, every short-term Christian volunteer activity may be an STM. The categorization here distinguishes between various Christian service activities according to the common name of the activity, the actions performed, the main denominations that have adopted these activities, some common geographical locations and the broad tourism context. The examples of denominations in the third column and the tourism contexts in the fifth column are not meant to be comprehensive but rather provide some prominent examples of each. Each of these will be examined in more detail below.

Short-term missions

STMs can be seen as 'short travel experiences for Christian purposes such as charity, service or evangelism' (Howell, 2012: 20). Some definitions emphasize the time span (usually less than two years), whereas others emphasize the relationship to pilgrimage and tourism, or distance STM participants from the normative 'tourist' and his or her leisure activities (Occhipinti, 2016). Howell (2012: 23) suggests that STMs are 'guided by theological commitments and embedded in a wider social context, STM is a type of travel unto itself in which particular guiding narratives shape the experiences of participants'.

The history of modern STMs goes back to the mid-20th century. After the Second World War, many conservative young Christians grew dissatisfied with the established mission agencies. They saw these agencies as insufficient and unable to respond to the new generation's exposure to the world and enthusiasm for foreign travel and culture on the one hand, and the desire to help and make an impact as Christians on

Christian Volunteer Tourism 87

Table 5.1 Types of Christian volunteer travel

Name	Activities	Denomination	Location	Broad tourism context
Short-term missions (STMs)	Very broad: Mercy ships, construction work in less-developed countries, orphanages, teaching the gospel, distributing New Testaments, teaching English	traditional Protestants and evangelical; recently also among Catholics	Global	Sometimes STM activities are combined with ordinary tourism activities
Long-term missions	Christian missions throughout the world involving entire families and helping to establish a gospel presence; tendency to work in less-developed countries; may involve staffing visitor centers	evangelicals, Mormons, Protestants	Africa, Asia, Latin America	Statistically not a form of tourism; a stand-alone activity, although many undertake tourist-like activities while in their mission fields
Solidarity visits in the name of Christ	Meet with local Christian and non-Christian communities	traditional Protestants and evangelicals	Africa, Southeast Asia, Israel, Palestine	In Israel and Palestine, solidarity visits often have a political agenda
Archaeological site volunteers	Assist in digging, organizing and cataloguing artifacts	Protestants, Catholics, Orthodox, other Christian groups, non-Christian volunteers	Israel, broader Holy Land, Mediterranean	Either a stand-alone activity, educational experience or as part of a tour package
Volunteers at Christian sites				
Garden Tomb	Guiding pilgrims, administrative work, physical facilities	Protestants	Israel	Most likely a stand-alone activity but may involve other regional journeys and resemble STMs
Nazareth Village	Guiding pilgrims, act in staged settings, administrative work	Protestants	Israel	
Lourdes	Lay helpers (*brandcardiers*), assist disabled pilgrims get in and out of pools, push wheelchairs	Traditionally Catholics	France	
Church history sites	Interpret the site-specific heritage, administration, evangelize, conservation, site maintenance	Mormons and several Protestant groups	North America, Europe	May resemble STMs and may involve other regional travel

the other hand (Howell, 2010). Between 1946 and 1960, the growing fervor for evangelism drew some of these young Christians into missionary service. Two organizations in particular, Youth with a Mission (YWAM) and Operation Mobilization (OM), developed new paradigms of mission work, capitalizing on people's enthusiasm for evangelizing. These organizations developed a limited-term approach to missions that would allow people to evangelize and serve without the long-term commitment involved in so much traditional Christian missionary efforts until that time (Pack, 2008).

This more adaptable approach to Christian volunteerism enables more people to serve during public and religious holiday periods, school breaks and summer holidays. During the past three decades, the world has seen a significant increase in the number of volunteers who are able to devote their short work and school breaks for humanitarian and proselytizing service rather than traditional holiday-making (Han, 2008). The number of STM participants has grown from just a few hundred in the 1960s to many millions today (Howell, 2012; Lough *et al.*, 2014) and typically involves people who actively volunteer in their home communities, are well educated and are active church-goers (Brown & Morrison, 2003; Trinitapoli & Vaisey, 2009).

There is no question that STMs end up being transformative experiences for those who participate. A number of studies have been done on the effects of STM participation on people's post-trip lives. These studies indicate several types of changes, including increased spirituality and/or religiosity, added giving and philanthropy, increased incidents of volunteer service and civic engagement and, in some cases, returning as long-term missionaries.

For most participants, STMs are faith-building experiences that bring people closer to God, develop their testimonies of the gospel and help them re-commit to living faithfully at home. Even for people who are not necessarily religious at home, volunteering abroad can be a spiritually cathartic experience (Hensel, 2012; Zahra, 2006, 2011; Zahra & McIntosh, 2007). Gulatt-Whiteman's (2004) study of participation in a Churches of Christ Latin American Mission in Peru found that spiritual growth was a significant outcome of the experience, at least in the short term. For many, the experience helped them better appreciate the blessings of God in their own lives. The experience led others to pray and attend church more often and be more patient with the people around them. STMs are often encouraged for youth by parents to help affirm their children's blossoming faith. Research shows that participation in mini-missions does indeed help strengthen religious beliefs among adolescents and helps them increase participation in church activities (Beyerlein *et al.*, 2011; Trinitapoli & Vaisey, 2009).

Increased charitable giving to mission organizations, humanitarian agencies or churches has been suggested as another outcome of STMs, together with an increase in civic engagement (Gulatt-Whiteman, 2004; Probasco, 2013). According to research by Beyerlein *et al.* (2011), undertaking STMs significantly increases young people's chances of becoming more deeply engaged in civic activities, including volunteer service at home and elsewhere. According to Lough *et al.* (2014), this comes largely through the cultural and global awareness that STMs engender. Serving in LTMs later in life has been observed as another potential outcome of the engagement that results from STMs (Harris, 2002; Wan & Hartt, 2008).

Very little longitudinal research has been done to understand the long-term implications of STM participation on charitable giving, civic engagement or spiritual development (Probasco, 2013). Thus, it is very difficult to assess how these ephemeral mission experiences might influence people's service and philanthropic activities later in life. Nonetheless, there is some evidence to suggest that such activities in adolescence might affect one's worldview and result in more engagement in a variety of social justice activities and church-oriented service.

Critics of the STM phenomenon argue that by their fleeting nature, STMs may be superficial and futile with neocolonialist undertones, where 'white' Christians from the developed world descend upon the natives in the global South with an attitude of superiority and arrogance, which might compromise indigenous dignity and widen socio-economic inequities (Arya & Nouvet, 2018).

In common with other volunteer tourism activities, STMs have been criticized as partly to blame for growing levels of dependency, which is especially true compared to professional or LTM efforts (Zehner, 2013). As well, they are often seen by local administrators as being too short to make a permanent difference in destination residents' lives. Their results are often a bandage approach rather than a solution, and host communities 'encounter the flow of teams as foreign social products' (Offutt, 2011: 796). This 'ministerial inefficiency' is of increasing concern to many religious organizations in developing countries (Zehner, 2013).

Some observers have noted that STMs may help reduce racism or other prejudices among participants. However, according to the work of Johnson (2014), these service activities can in fact enhance existing prejudices and stereotypes as a result of the short duration of contact and a lack of deeper community immersion.

Long-term missions

Long-term missionaries are sometimes referred to as career missionaries (Bush, 2000), which differentiates them from the other categories of tourism described in this book. Because the World Tourism Organization defines a tourist as someone who travels away from home for at least

24 hours but less than a year, most long-term missionaries do not fall within these definitional parameters, although those who serve less than a year do (Wan & Hartt, 2008). Even long-term missionaries, however, because of their residential or expatriate status, frequently undertake 'touristic' activities in the countries or regions where they serve, including sightseeing, beach-going, shopping and visiting friends and relatives. Thus, while serving in the long term, they become ancillary tourists and the boundaries between their humanitarian or evangelizing work and their recreational pursuits are not always clear.

The advantages of LTMs are clear. They avoid much of the superficiality associated with STMs because they are seen as being more firmly embedded in the local community. Long-term missionaries often learn local languages and are more culturally adapted, and they become key stakeholders in community organizations and quality of life exercises. Many LTM volunteers first served STMs, so that both experiences are linked and often share a personal conversion history (Harris, 2002; Wan & Hartt, 2008). Many short-term missionaries end up serving LTMs as a direct result of their STM experiences (Harris, 2002).

Solidarity visits

According to the United States Conference of Catholic Bishops,

> Solidarity is action on behalf of the one human family, calling us to help overcome the divisions in our world. Solidarity binds the rich to the poor... It calls those who are strong to care for those who are weak and vulnerable across the spectrum of human life. (Quoted in Lamberty, 2012: 181)

Solidarity tourism is a pilgrimage comprised of faith and politics, where one of the main foci is people visiting to demonstrate unity for a political or social justice-related cause (Timothy & Daher, 2009). Solidarity tourism is one of the least understood manifestations of volunteer tourism among Christians. Nevertheless, it is important and growing. Christian solidarity 'tourists' have long visited China, disguised either as sightseeing tourists or English teachers in an effort to evangelize (Ma & Li, 2018). Today, however, an increasing number of Christian tours are offered in China. While their primary purpose is ostensibly to tour the country in company with other Christians in a spirit of fellowship, much of their purpose is also to visit Chinese Christians in a show of solidarity – Christians who are often seen by outsiders as being oppressed by the atheism-oriented communist regime.

There are sundry other examples of Christian solidarity tourism, but nowhere is it more vivid than in Israel and Palestine. While not all solidarity visits to the Holy Land occur in the context of Christianity (Belhassen *et al.*, 2014), solidarity among believers is an important element of this phenomenon and usually favors one ethnic group (i.e. Israelis/Jews or Palestinians/Arabs) over the other (Belhassen & Ebel, 2009; Isaac, 2013; Shapiro, 2010; Sizer, 1999; Troen & Rabineau, 2014) – a partisan difference that is somehow regarded as 'divinely justified' (Feldman, 2011: 62). The guides, more than any other stakeholder, have the power to compose images of 'us' and 'them', those in the right and those in the wrong, divide or unify within the conflicting Holy Land narratives (Bowman, 1992; Feldman, 2016).

Pro-Israel faction

The first faction is comprised of Christians who visit the Holy Land in support of the State of Israel. This market is made up mainly of American evangelicals who see the re-establishment of the Israeli state and the gathering of the Jews from the four corners of the world as fulfillment of an ancient prophecy (Wagner, 2002). In addition to visiting sacred sites associated with the ministry of Christ, many of their itineraries and activities are devoted to demonstrating support for Israel and Zionism (Belhassen, 2009; Belhassen & Ebel, 2009). For many Christians, the land of Israel exudes the presence of Christ; it is the land of the living word of God (Bajc, 2007). These Bible Belt 'Christian Zionists' see modern Israel as

> nothing short of a miracle... Its sheer existence, survival, and advancements are signs of God keeping his past promises... The state also serves as a sign of the times, an arrow pointing toward the future and the second coming of Christ and his millennial reign. Thus, in the Christian Zionist worldview, the state and its political history are explicit manifestations of the divine plan for the world, justifying – if not actually requiring – visits to sites like the Parliament or Har Herzl... At the same time, the visits are about demonstrating solidarity with God's chosen people in God's promised land, by loving whom God loves and providing them with material, emotional, spiritual, and political support. In this Christian Zionists feel themselves to be partnering with God, helping to further his plan. (Shapiro, 2008: 311–312)

The pro-Israel faction was energized in 1971 by the Jerusalem Conference on Biblical Prophecy. Some 1400 Americans attended the conference, which included a special address by David Ben-Gurion. The conference organizers billed the event as a 'ringside seat at the second coming', and most speakers agreed that Israel's existence and recent geographical expansion were all part of God's plan (Weber, 2010). This conference was a formative event that marked the beginning of a wave of evangelical solidarity tours to Israel. American dispensationalists founded travel agencies with loaded names such as 'Bible Prophecy Tours'. One of the most widely publicized solidarity gatherings of evangelicals in Israel is the annual Feast of Tabernacles conference sponsored by the International Christian Embassy of Jerusalem (ICEJ). This gathering is customarily addressed by the Israeli prime minister, and thousands of participants take part in the annual 'Jerusalem Parade' throughout the city and its environs (Clark, 2007; Weber, 2010).

The level of solidarity among some evangelical church members becomes even more poignant during times of geopolitical crises. Research by Collins-Kreiner *et al.* (2006: 36–39, 93, 116) found that during security crises, when Israel is being threatened by its neighbors, the number of 'solidarity pilgrims', including evangelicals from North America, Brazil, South Korea and other countries rises, while arrivals of other tourists decline. The economic importance of this unique market segment can be seen among Arab merchants in East Jerusalem who, in contrast to how they really feel, sell pro-Israel propaganda souvenirs to capitalize on Christian Zionists and other visitors to their city.

A unique type of solidarity 'tourist' is comprised of migrant workers in Israel and other Christians living in the country. Many Christian Israelis (approximately 2% of the country's population) have multi-generational roots in Israel and belong to a wide range of Catholic and Orthodox churches. However, there is a growing presence of recent migrant workers and temporary residents who belong to various Zionist evangelical churches (Kemp & Raijman, 2003). These are passionate visitors to biblical sites during their free time, rendering them 'part-time pilgrims' or 'weekend pilgrims' (Frey, 1998: 20). Many are fervent supporters of Israel, often to the level of hostility toward, and exclusion of, Arab Israelis, even those who belong to traditional Christian churches (Kemp & Raijman, 2003).

Pro-Palestinian faction

Sizer (2003: 254), a well-known critic of Christian Zionism, refers to pro-Israel solidarity tours as 'terror' tours. While extreme, this sentiment is prevalent to varying degrees among many groups that maintain solidarity ties with the Palestinians and their cause in Jerusalem, the West Bank and Gaza (Brin, 2006).

The second type of Christian solidarity tourists in the Holy Land are those who desire to meet the 'Living Stones', which are, as explained earlier, Palestinian Christians who are cut off from the rest of Christianity and Christian holy sites in Israel. They are the living stones of the church as opposed to the dead stones of archaeological sites and ancient churches (Kassis *et al.*, 2016). In addition to visiting sites in Israel of general Christian interest, 'Meet the Stones' pilgrimages provide opportunities to meet, interact and share stories and experiences with the Living

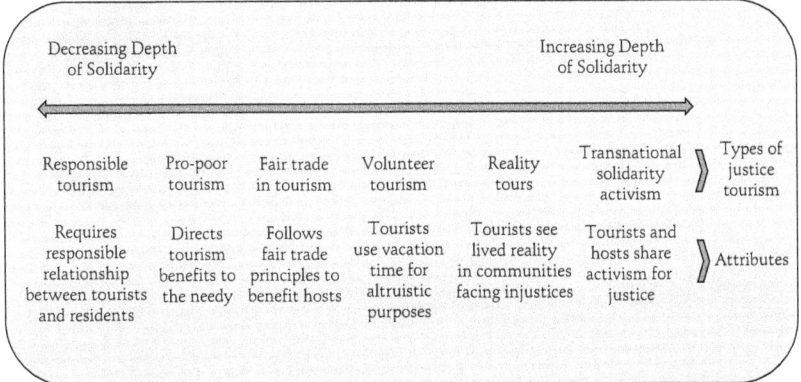

Figure 5.1 A continuum of justice tourism (Source: Redrawn from Higgins-Desbiolles, 2009: 338)

Stones. These tours, according to Keating (2007: 69), '...will offer a different and much more compelling vision than that offered by the Israeli office of tourism'.

Higgins-Desbiolles (2009) regards Palestinian solidarity tours within the broader framework of 'justice tourism'. According to her continuum of justice tourism, where responsible tourism reflects the lowest depth of solidarity, 'reality tours' and 'transnational and solidarity activism' reflect the deepest depth of solidarity (Figure 5.1). Justice tours of Palestine reflect a high level of solidarity among tourists, tour operators and guides, and local Palestinians (Higgins-Desbiolles, 2016; Kassis, 2004, 2015; Kassis *et al.*, 2016).

Not all Christian tourists to Israel fall into these two categories. Plenty of groups remain neutral, learning more about the conflict in general rather than taking sides (Brin, 2006), even if they lean one way or another in their doctrine or dogma approach to the Holy Land (Figure 5.2). Moufakkir (2010) suggests this more neutral manifestation should be titled 'peace tourism' as an antithetical movement toward solidarity tourism which, he argues, perpetuates stereotypes and widens the gaps between aggressors.

Archaeological site volunteers

Volunteer tourism has evolved in several directions and the definition provided earlier of assisting others in need includes individual people, communities, organizations, animals, nature and the broader environment (Markwell, 2015; Measham & Barnett, 2008; Timothy, 2018a, 2018b, 2018c). Most research on volunteer tourism focuses on humanitarian aid; much less has been written about archaeology-based volunteer tourism.

Figure 5.2 An advertised Holy Land tour with obvious solidarity undertones (used with permission)

Archaeology tour companies plan, market and sell hands-on archaeology experiences by the millions every year. The companies liaise with research teams, dig crews, cultural officers and government agencies to determine the workforce needs of archaeological projects. They arrange travel, lodgings and other service requirements for tourists, and provide information about the geographical and historic context of the digging sites. The volunteers receive perfunctory or in-depth training in digging, sifting, cleaning and cataloging artifacts and are usually involved in all of these activities during their encounters (Pfanner, 2011; Shai & Uziel, 2016; Timothy, 2018a, 2018c). Some university archaeology programs and ministries of antiquities advertise for volunteers independently of tour companies.

Many archaeology projects rely overwhelmingly on volunteer labor, either from the local community or from tourists, who may be a mix of 'serious' heritage tourists and 'casual' archaeology dabblers (Timothy, 2011). Many artifacts and scientific knowledge have been discovered through the labor of volunteer tourists; volunteers are crucial to the success of thousands of archaeological programs worldwide (Timothy, 2018c).

One of the earliest cases of using volunteer tourists on a large scale was at the archaeological excavations at Masada, Israel, which took place in the 1960s. According to Yadin (1966: 260), who was the managing archaeologist, most of the volunteers were tourists who were able to select from nine two-week periods between November 1964 and April 1965. The whole project was considered a great success. According to Ben-Yehuda (1995: 56), 'Yadin had at his disposal on any given day about two hundred volunteers who were actually involved in the excavations'. These volunteers came from 33 different countries.

Volunteers not only volunteer their time, but also pay for their experience through a program fee, which normally includes meals and lodgings at a community facility, such as a school, dormitory or community center. They also have to pay their own transportation costs in addition to program fees.

For many Christian volunteers, being close to the earth, working in the soil, touching the remnants of ancient civilizations, especially those mentioned or featured prominently in the Bible, or standing where Jesus or ancient prophets stood, comprise an indelible and unforgettable experience that educates and builds faith. Table 5.2 lists some current and recent Bible-related archaeological digs that are seeking volunteers from around the world. According to one Christian volunteer in the Holy Land, 'The work was no more strenuous than gardening, and I was delighted to be working on the remains from the city that the apostles Peter, Andrew and Philip called home' (quoted in Miller, 2006: 80). Another volunteer archaeology tourist commented that he 'enjoyed the people, the lectures, the work, the traveling, and the time spent alone with God. Would I go back a second time? Would I put up with all the dust, dirt, sweat, heat and no ice! Absolutely!' (quote in Miller, 2006: 84).

For people who have a more casual interest in sacred archaeology but who are unable to spend one to eight weeks on a dig, there are several 'dig for a day' programs at various locations around the world (Ron & Timothy, 2016). Certain tour operators provide three- to four-hour programs

Table 5.2 A sample of Bible-related archaeology sites in the Holy Land and Mediterranean seeking volunteers, 2015–2018

Site name	Country	Biblical significance
Jezreel	Israel	Site of Old Testament events, overlooks the Jezreel Valley, the supposed site of the future and final battle of Armageddon
Azekah	Israel	Fortified city of Judah, mentioned prominently in the Old Testament, overlooks the valley where David slew Goliath
Kursi Beach Excavation	Israel	Place of the New Testament miracle of the demons and the swine, near the shore of the Sea of Galilee
El-Araj	Israel	Possible location of Bethsaida during Jesus's ministry, near the shore of the Sea of Galilee
Mount Zion	Palestine/Israel	Location of many Old and New Testament events in Jerusalem, site and period of the ministry of Jesus
Shiloh Excavation	Palestine	Site of the ancient tabernacle, well-known site of Old Testament sacrifices
Khirbet Safra	Jordan	Ancient crossroads and transportation corridor between Madaba and the Main Hot Springs, overlooking the Dead Sea
Abila of the Decopolis	Jordan	An important city on the ancient strategic route between Nabataea and Damascus, remnants of Byzantine churches and Roman baths
Tall Jalul	Jordan	During the Iron Age, this city was home to Ammonites and Moabites, many biblical references to their rivalries with the ancient Hebrews
Idalion	Cyprus	Bronze Age through Roman era settlement, considerable trade with sites in the Holy Land and Egypt

Source: Associates for Biblical Research (2018), Biblical Archaeology Society (2018).

where people can get their hands dirty, participate in heritage seminars, dig, sift and handle ancient artifacts (Archaeological Seminars Institute, 2006).

Outside the Holy Land, there are also archaeological volunteer opportunities in areas where medieval churches, cemeteries and pilgrimage shrines are being excavated.

Volunteering at Christian sites

Religious institutions in general and Christian organizations in particular, encourage volunteer work at religious centers and sites. Gill (2006: 144) argues that 'when Jesus gathered the twelve disciples, He made a strategic decision to build His kingdom as a volunteer-intensive organization. He could have built His ministry on other options, such as a solo act or a wholly professional staff, but He chose to use volunteers…'. Members of many Christian faiths spend a great deal of time volunteering at historic sites, visitor centers, shrines, churches, events and other sacred places and celebrations (Davidson &

Gitlitz, 2002). They volunteer in many capacities – as groundskeepers, heritage preservationists, language and heritage interpreters, managers, re-enactment actors, guides or caregivers. At the Catholic shrine of Knock, Ireland, 'an army of volunteers – here termed the Knock Shrine Stewards and Handmaids – helps care for pilgrims' (Davidson & Gitlitz, 2002: 317–318).

Most research on Christian volunteer tourism addresses Christian travelers' engagement with local populations and improving residents' quality of life through humanitarian aid. The following sections are somewhat different, however, owing to their focus on people who volunteer at Christian sacred sites, whose motive is often either self-actualization or evangelization. Examples are provided from the Garden Tomb in Jerusalem, Nazareth Village in Nazareth, Lourdes (France) and Latter-day Saints (LDS) church history sites.

Guides at the Garden Tomb

The Garden Tomb is the Protestant alternative to the site of Jesus's crucifixion, burial and resurrection, which is commonly identified with the Church of the Holy Sepulcher among Catholics and Orthodox Christians. The site was purchased in 1894 and is operated by the Garden Tomb (Jerusalem) Association, which is a non-profit organization registered in the United Kingdom. The site is staffed largely by volunteers from many Christian denominations, usually from the United Kingdom and other parts of Europe and is funded by donations, endowments and sponsorships through the Friends of the Garden program (Garden Tomb Jerusalem, 2017).

One of the tasks performed at the site is guiding groups through the garden. Site managers make every effort to ensure that guiding is done exclusively by its own volunteer guides, unless services are needed in a language they cannot provide (Bowman, 2000; Ron, 2009, 2010b; Ron & Feldman, 2009). The majority of the guides are volunteers from overseas who desire to spend an extended period in Jerusalem (Engberg, 2017) (Figure 5.3); many of them have clerical backgrounds. Their primary role is to evangelize, to recount the New Testament account of Jesus's ministry, remind visitors about his death and resurrection, which many believe occurred at that locale, and encourage spiritual moments through their words, actions and teachings:

> The garden tomb itself is actually not the end focus of the polite and friendly guides there, who frequently summarize their presentations with a declaration of belief in Christ rather than confidence in the tomb. It is not uncommon to hear those guides say something along these lines: 'The most significant thing about the Garden Tomb is that it is empty! He is risen! And because of this, we too shall all rise again!' (Chadwick, 2003: 46)

Figure 5.3 A volunteer guide at the Garden Tomb (Photo: D. Timothy)

The guides must be well versed in scripture, people of strong faith and are required to undergo a strict screening and approval process. Like guides everywhere, they can make or break the experience, as the following quotes from the establishment's website indicate:

> Our guide… was so good as he gave the message that Our Lord is Risen He is not here! We so appreciated his boldness in telling the true story of our Lord and keeping to the account found in the Bible. (Visitor from the United States)

> We were given a wonderful introduction to this place that gives one a real sense of peace and tranquility. I would like to commend our guide… he impress [us] to no end, and I would like to thank him for this. (Visitor from South Africa)

Nazareth Village

Established in 2000, Nazareth Village is a commercial biblical-themed environment that was designed to bring 'to life a farm and Galilean village, recreating Nazareth as it was 2,000 years ago. It is a window into the life of Jesus, the city's most famous citizen' (from a site brochure, quoted in Ron, 2010b: 122). Since 2007, the village has regularly received Christian (often Mennonite) volunteers from Western countries (Figure 5.4), who come for a few weeks at a time to staff the set in period costumes (Ron, 2010b; Shackley, 2008).

Figure 5.4 A volunteer worker at Nazareth Village (Photo: D. Timothy)

Although it is not an official sacred site for any denomination, Nazareth Village is well visited and has been integrated into many Christian tourist itineraries. Because many of its staff are volunteers, it has frequently be likened to established holy places, such as the Garden Tomb, which endows Nazareth Village with an aura of spirituality akin to sites of worship, rather than that of a commercial enterprise. Malezhki's (2011) research among American Mennonite and Baptist volunteers at the attraction revealed some interesting spiritual experiences. One Mennonite woman replied, '[I] wanted to do something good for Jesus, my Lord. Share the land of Jesus with my family' (Malezhki, 2011: 89). Another Mennonite voluntourist exclaimed:

> I felt God calling me into missions early in that year. I wasn't sure where I was going, but I just knew He wanted me to go somewhere. Through working with Eastern Mennonite Missions, Nazareth Village opened as an opportunity for volunteering. It seemed like the right fit for me and where God was leading me to. (Malezhki, 2011: 87)

Lourdes

Since Bernadette Soubirous's Marian apparitions in 1858 in the area of today's Lourdes shrine, the city has become a major Roman Catholic pilgrimage destination (Agnew, 2014, 2015; Dahlberg, 2000; Eade, 2000, 2012, 2014; Gesler, 1996; Harris, 2013). The site, situated in the foothills of the Pyrenees in southern France, relies heavily on volunteers. The city is one of the most visited Marian shrines by people with physical disabilities and chronic health problems (Goldingay *et al.*, 2014). Cranston (1958) quoted one pilgrim's explanation for why Lourdes is so popular among the world's disabled. It is not only the belief, hope and desire to be healed, but also:

> Here the able-bodied helpers and others aren't afraid of us. We're not shuffled off and hidden in some corner. Here we're VIPs! We're in the front for every service, we're spoiled rotten. We are looked after, and we're made to feel valued, and not like we're a nuisance. We are part of the group and not left out. (Cranston, 1958: 10)

In fact, a significant number of pilgrims to Lourdes suffer physical frailties and medical maladies. Owing to its mission to serve this special population, many volunteers are needed to help in a wide variety of capacities (Figure 5.5). Agnew (2014: 18) estimated that in 2011, Lourdes received 6.3 million visitors, of whom 87,500 were hospitalier volunteers, who looked after 53,600 sick or disabled pilgrims. As early as the 1950s, Cranston (1958: 7) counted more than 2000 *brandcardiers* (stretcher bearers). While records of the numbers of volunteers at Lourdes are imprecise, some estimates suggest it is more than 100,000 (Spano, 2008). It is clear that the destination is heavily volunteer-dependent on people who

Figure 5.5 Pilgrims with physical disabilities and volunteers at Lourdes, France (Photo: A. Ron)

are typically assigned one of three types of tasks: male helpers (brandcardiers), female helpers (handmaids) or the ladies of the baths (Eade, 1992) and those performing 'rolling duty' – assisting pilgrims with disabilities in hotels and other areas with their wheelchairs (Agnew, 2014).

A popular saying goes that 'Rome is the head of the church, but Lourdes is its heart' (Dahlberg, 2000: 35). Several sources mention the special atmosphere of Lourdes, or the 'spirit of Lourdes', which emphasizes the emotive aspects of being there, perhaps more so than at many other Marian shrines, and the voluntary assistance rendered to the disabled. Volunteer helpers are an important source of information, and as a generalization, they feel blessed by the opportunity to help but often come away from the experience being helped more than they helped (Agnew, 2014: 102). The volunteer atmosphere appears to be contagious, with many labels assigned to the experience such as the 'Lourdes high' or 'serial pilgrims' (Agnew, 2015: 516).

Churches and church history sites

Catholic, Orthodox and Protestant churches all have sites that are famously associated with their religious history. Several Protestant and Restorationist denominations, however, purposefully preserve, interpret and promote visits to locales associated with the development of their churches in various parts of the world, as noted in Chapter 2. Many chapels and historic sites in the American South that are associated with the development of the Baptist or Methodist churches or famous people in America's religious history are frequently marked as important heritage attractions and feature prominently on many tour itineraries (Ahn, 2007; Neal, 2014). A large number of famous Reformation sites and churches in Europe have also been preserved and interpreted as museums and anchor attractions (Jackson & Hudman, 1995). Many of these historic churches and other sites rely overwhelmingly on volunteer workers. Staffing museums and gift shops with volunteers is very common throughout the Christian world.

As described in Chapter 2, the LDS Church actively purchases, restores, protects and opens its historic sites for a variety of reasons. Most of these places are staffed by volunteer missionaries who are 'called' to serve for periods between six months and two years. For the most part, they are charged with maintaining sites, answering visitors' questions about the church and its history, interpreting the secular and spiritual importance of the locales and evangelizing (sharing their testimonies) with both LDS and non-LDS visitors (Olsen & Timothy, 2018).

Conclusion

Volunteer tourism is one of the fastest growing manifestations of tourism today. It is trendy, and many travel consumers see it as a more responsible alternative to the traditions of mass tourism that have developed since the Second World War. Christians are keen volunteers, and the Christian faith provides the conceptual rationale for this growing subsegment of the volunteer tourism sector. Serving the poor and needy, giving of oneself, donating time and means, evangelizing their faith and standing for what they feel is right, are all important doctrines of their belief system. Jesus himself is the ultimate example of service and humanitarian acts, and most Christians have a strong desire to emulate his life as closely as possible.

Christians are involved in a wide range of volunteer activities, such as short- and long-term missionary work that involves proselytizing, providing health care, educating and feeding the poor, constructing homes and other buildings, working with orphans and troubled youth, rebuilding after natural disasters and many other humanitarian efforts. They also travel to China, the Holy Land and other areas of the world to stand in solidarity with their co-religionists wherever they feel Christians are being oppressed, or where political statements need to be made in fulfillment of biblical prophecy or in accordance with the Word of God as revealed in the Bible. Many believers travel to volunteer at archaeological sites, which is an especially auspicious undertaking when it involves digs in settings associated with the Bible. Additionally, thousands of sacred sites, historic churches, shrines, hallowed gardens and Christian theme parks throughout the world rely heavily on the goodwill and unpaid altruistic efforts of people who are willing to sacrifice their time, talents and financial means to help support the causes of conservation, evangelization, interpretation and healing.

No two Christian denominations have exactly the same patterns of volunteer travel behavior, desires or outcomes. Yet, for everyone involved, volunteering in any of the capacities described throughout this chapter becomes a form of personal pilgrimage that has temporal and spiritual implications for this life and for the eternal life to come (Engberg, 2017).

6 Christian Themed Environments

Introduction

Theming is an important part of tourism promotion efforts today. It reflects the efforts of destinations or individual establishments to differentiate themselves from their competitors. It also illustrates changing tastes among consumers. The theming of space entails the development of theme parks, themed environments and themed landscapes (Shaw & Williams, 2004). For Christians, it entails the development of faux landscapes that depict scenes from the Holy Land, biblical themes or scaled models of events and places. Thus, the visitor experience is intended to be more important than the veracity of the physical sites themselves, although some themed Christian places have attempted to claim a degree of scientific legitimacy of their stories, replica artifacts, ceremonies and staged ways of life, as a way of lending a degree of 'authenticity' to their establishments (Rowan, 2004).

Theming is no less important in the Christian religious market than it is in general tourism markets. Theming of the sacred is an important approach in religious destinations and among service providers. There is even a significant degree of differentiation between Catholic and Protestant groups. Several globally known religious theme parks and theme sites have been developed in the United States, Western Europe, East Asia and Israel by various Protestant non-governmental organizations (NGOs) and other faith-based organizations. Roman Catholic organizations have also been active in developing spiritual theme parks in Argentina, Poland and other places. Most theming is carried out by various evangelical Protestant groups and Roman Catholic organizations and NGOs, which also determines their visitor markets.

This chapter examines the concept of Christian and biblical theming of various environments, spaces and localities. It highlights the development of themed sites in the United States, Israel and elsewhere in relation to authenticity and addresses many of the controversies associated with these various locales and the visitors' needs they are trying to fulfill.

The Theming of Tourism

The term 'themed environment' has been defined and widely examined. According to Gottdiener (2001),

> When I refer to a *themed environment*, I explicitly mean the material product of two social processes. First, I am talking about socially constructed, built environments – about large material forms that are designed to serve as containers for commodified human interaction (for example, malls). Second, I have in mind themed material forms that are products of a cultural process aimed at investing constructed spaces with symbolic meaning and at *conveying* that meaning to inhabitants and users through symbolic motifs. (Gottdiener, 2001: 5)

Themed environments or spaces can include many types of cultural landscapes. The best known types are amusement parks and theme parks, restaurants and hotels, shopping centers and malls, heritage centers and religious-themed attractions (Beeton, 2005; Hannigan, 1998; Josiam *et al.*, 2004; Paradis, 2004; Urry, 2002; West, 2006).

The historical beginnings of themed environments are not fully clear. Knott's Berry Farm (established in 1954) was among the first officially recognized theme parks, but American amusement parks (e.g. Luna Park on Coney Island) have been developed since the beginning of the 20th century with their predecessors having been established in the 1700s. Likewise, world expositions were quite popular in 19th-century Europe and America (Mitchell, 1988; Urry, 2002). Some observers include zoos and pleasure gardens as types of themed environments as well, which means the beginnings of themed spaces are older than generally supposed by several hundred years.

Walt Disney's original theme park was not the first (opened to the public on 17 July 1955) (Wharton, 2006), but surely it was the foundation of contemporary tourist theming. According to Shani and Logan (2010: 155), 'The perceptions around the design and operation of amusement parks changed forever, as a result of Disney's ideas and actions. So revolutionary and innovative were his thoughts that their influence went far beyond merely shaping the nature of modern amusement attractions'. The innovative concepts that Disney introduced have also been successfully applied in other tourism, hospitality and service contexts, such as restaurants, hotels, shopping centers and airports. Social and cultural critics have even claimed that Disney's theme park principles have spread to wider sectors of society, in what has been termed by Bryman (1999) as 'the Disneyization of society', meaning that the characteristics of modern society are beginning to resemble the characteristics of Disney's theme parks – theming, de-differentiation of consumption, emotional labor and merchandising.

The study of themed environments, or themed spaces, has expanded significantly over the past several years (Edensor, 2001; MacLeod, 2017). The theming craze today is a direct result of capital accumulation and the increased materialism that is pervading Western societies (Gottdiener, 2001; Shaw & Williams, 2004). Theming aims to provide increasingly titillating experiences and entertainment for an increasingly disinterested and materialistic population, whose attention span has shortened and who have grown bored of other tourist offerings. Shaw and Williams (2004: 255) outline three types of themed spaces: theme parks, themed environments and themed landscapes – all part of today's postmodern tourism spaces that are characterized by the intertwining of the real and the fake (Figure 6.1).

Shaw and Williams' (2004) theme park category includes various types of specific attractions, including cultural parks, heritage centers, nature parks and specialized theme parks, together with Disney-type amusement parks. All of these are united by their use of theme park technology and their amalgam of elements of staged authenticity, fakery, representations of reality and reality. Themed malls, festivals, restaurants, museums and galleries characterize their 'themed environments'. Old-fashioned specialty shops, thematic cafes and specialized markets are examples of spaces of everyday life and tourist attractions that define Shaw and Williams' themed environments. Their final category, themed landscapes, is comprised of intentional marketing efforts and the deliberate creation of spaces for tourist consumption. These include, but are not limited to, literary landscapes, film and television landscapes, fictional places and tourism trails. The Christian-themed environments described below include elements of these three types of contrived spaces, but they illustrate best the characteristics of theme parks and themed landscapes.

At the core of this discussion is the notion of authenticity within the tourist experience. Many standard tourists care little about whether or not they are visiting 'authentic places' or consuming 'authentic

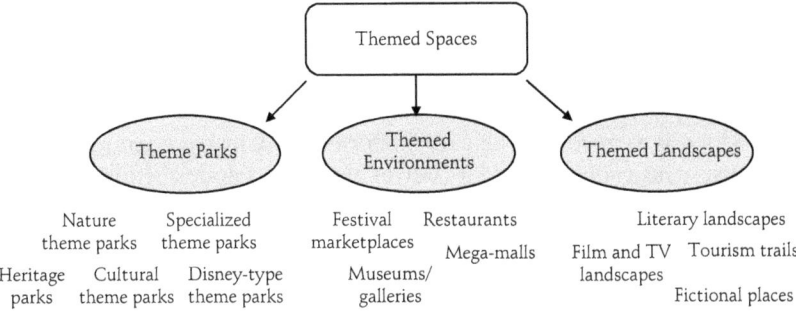

Figure 6.1 A typology of themed tourism spaces (Source: Redrawn from Shaw & Williams, [2004])

experiences'; instead, they desire to focus on fun and pleasure. Hard-core heritage tourists and religious travelers, however, generally tend to feel otherwise (Timothy & Boyd, 2003).

There has been a long and robust debate about authenticity in the realm of tourism (Chhabra, 2007, 2008; Cohen, 1988; Hughes, 1995; Kim & Jamal, 2007; MacCannell, 1973; Urry, 1995). Many scholars have argued that in plenty of cases and in many ways, authenticity might be an objective notion that can be measured and verified, and is manifested in the inherent characteristics of an object, event or place (Chhabra, 2012; Timothy, 2011). However, the majority of observers today conclude that authenticity is more likely a subjective concept that is influenced by an individual's own lived experiences or personal attachments to a place, object, event or person (Chhabra, 2007; Chhabra *et al.*, 2003; Wang, 1999).

Authenticity is often defined with descriptors such as 'original', 'traditional' or 'genuine', but scholars have now moved away from such a narrow interpretation of the authentic to understand it more holistically as being more experiential and existential – subject to one's own interpretation (Breathnach, 2006; Timothy, 2011). What is authentic to one person might not be authentic to another. Nowhere is this more evident than in the context of religious tourism (Cohen, 2006; Collins-Kreiner, 2010a; Eade & Garbin, 2007; Gil & de Esteban Curiel, 2008; Olsen & Timothy, 2006; Shapiro, 2008). No two travel experiences are the same, and different people experience religious encounters with the sacred differently. Their experiences might be negotiable, fluid and dynamic, depending on their own understandings and circumstances (Olsen, 2010). According to Coleman and Elsner (2004: 274), 'Pilgrimage ritual... often appears to be most "authentic" to such practitioners when it gives them the most freedom to create their own modes of participation'. Thus, pilgrimage becomes a vehicle that people might use to construct their own authentic spiritual experiences (Coleman, 2004).

Some people may regard themed environments as the epitome of inauthentic spaces. They are artificial geographies that bear little resemblance to reality (Timothy, 2011). They may be scale models of sacred spaces, exaggerated places or invented locations that never existed, such as in the case of make-believe localities from famous movies. Many tourists seek representative sites and experiences over the objectively real, which is very much the case with themed Christian environments. For those who cannot afford a tour of the Holy Land, visiting the Holy Land Experience (HLE) in Florida (see below) might satisfy their desire until they are able to visit the holy city of Jerusalem in person. Urry (1995) insists that travelers are keenly able to distinguish between the authentic and the inauthentic but that they choose to ignore the fakery of Disneyized landscapes because their main objective is to enjoy their journey. The same could be said of pilgrims and other Christian travelers who seek representations of biblical reality rather than reality itself.

Themed Environments and Religious Tourism

The link between contemporary themed environments and religion should not be taken for granted, as theming, especially in the context of modern tourism, is commonly associated with secularism, amusement, fun, pleasure and fantasy (Shaw & Williams, 2004). In the context of religion and pilgrimage, and especially in Christianity, the word 'pleasure' would be somewhat incongruent in many cases, and to a degree perhaps inappropriate depending on the situation. A visitor might say that he or she was pleased to visit a site, but the word pleasure has a hedonistic connotation of fun and delight, whereas seeing representations of the crucifixion would generally not be considered fun or delightful.

Religious-themed environments are known by many different names, including spiritual or religious theme parks (Bielo, 2018b; Gupta, 1986; Kaelber, 2006; Mitrašinović, 2006), religious theme sites (Rivera *et al.*, 2009; Ron & Feldman, 2009; Shani *et al.*, 2007), biblical theme parks (Branham, 2008; Pinsky, 2007; Taylor, 1999), Bible parks or inspiration parks (Beal, 2005), biblical gardens (Bielo, 2018b) and mythological theme parks (Brereton, 2006). Christian-oriented themed environments are frequently known as Christian theme sites or Christian theme parks (Mitrašinović, 2006; Ron, 2009; Ron & Feldman, 2009).

Few religious-themed environments can be considered multifaith in nature. One exception to this is Museumpark Orientalis in the Netherlands (Kloek, 2009), but even there the multifaith element is limited to monotheistic religions. The scarcity of multifaith-themed environments is similar in essence to the scarcity of multifaith museums of religion, which have been explored by Carnegie (2009):

> One reason [for their scarcity] might well be the difficulty of making 'religion exhibitable'… In attempting to define the rituals of religious expression there is the danger of exposing seemingly bizarre customs and actions which cannot be readily understood by adherents of other faiths. Such 'normalised' acts as… animal sacrifice, ancestor worship or the use of body parts can have the opposite effect than the intended attempt to encourage mutual respect and understanding between people of all faiths and cultures. Equally, as religion is often cited as a cause of, or contributing to, war, genocide, persecution and oppression, it can be difficult to reconcile the tenets and expressions of a faith with such acts which might be done in the name of religion. (Carnegie, 2009: 158)

One example of a mono-faith religious environment is Gangadham, a planned Hindu theme park in Hardiwar, India. The aim of this attraction is 'to recreate great moments in Hindu mythology through hi-tech rides, an animated mythological museum, a "temple city", food courts and a sound and light show' (McCaul, 2005: np). Although there are a number of themed environments in Muslim countries (Anton-Clavé, 2007), with the exception of Taman Tamadun Islam in Malaysia (Moal-Ulvoas, 2016), we are unaware of any other Muslim-themed environments or theme parks.

Christian-Themed Spaces

One must distinguish between contemporary and historical Christian-themed environments. Places like the HLE in Orlando did not exist before Walt Disney, but the idea of a Christian-themed environment is not new. For example, sacred mountains in northern Italy, known as *Sacri Monti*, are considered to have been a medieval spiritual theme park that was established 'to bring the foreign spiritual experience closer to home' (Kaelber, 2006: 50; see also Morris, 2005; Wharton, 2006).

Bielo (2016b: 3) identified five different types of Bible-based themed environments, including re-creations, creation museums, Bible history museums, biblical gardens and art collections. To this list should be added three additional types of artificial spaces: outdoor Holy Land models, fairs/exhibitions and contrived theme parks and sites.

Re-creations depict replicas of Bible stories, characters or scenes. Creation museums aim to discredit evolutionary science by supporting the creationist view. Bible history museums exhibit ancient Holy Writ, biblical artifacts and replicas, and other material objects that testify of the Bible's divine origins. In biblical gardens, plants, trees, flowers and other vegetation mentioned in the Bible are cultivated (Figure 6.2). Art collections highlight various art forms that represent biblical stories, scenes and characters. An example of an outdoor Holy Land model is Palestine Park at Chautauqua, New York – 'a half-acre tract of land outfitted in 1874 with a scaled Jordan River, Galilee, and Jerusalem, [which] allowed late nineteenth century visitors to stroll symbolically through the land of the Bible – many decked out in "oriental" costume' (Rogers, 2003: 60; see also Long, 2003; Ron & Feldman, 2009; Ward, 2008).

Today, there are more than 200 such attractions throughout the world (Bielo, 2016b). Many of these Christian-themed spaces materialize from ecumenical desires, although many have evolved out of specific sectoral traditions, the most common being Roman Catholic and fundamentalist Protestants. Regardless of their origins, they all strive to animate the Bible and ministry of Jesus by 'transforming written scriptural words into a material, experiential environment. And, they seek to integrate religious faith with pleasure and religious education' (Bielo, 2016b: 3).

The Christian interest in simulated Holy Lands also found its expression in fairs and exhibitions. In the 1904 St Louis World's Fair,

Figure 6.2 The Bible Garden in the Vatican Gardens, Vatican City (Photo: D. Timothy)

a large-scale model of Jerusalem was built (Rubin, 2000), and 'inside the city's walls, as well as riding camels and having their fortunes told, visitors could take a tour through familiar landscapes of Christian piety' (Long, 2003: 51). A more recent example took place at the Canadian Expo in 1967, where the Christian Pavilion presented Christianity in a more modern light.

Christian theme parks and sites

Christian theme parks and themed sites are becoming more prevalent in large segments of contemporary Christianity (Figure 6.3). Shackley (2003) refers to these as religiously themed environments without any authentically or inherently sacred elements. In many Western societies, images and the desire for multisensory experiences have found their way from mass secular culture into the heart of Protestant worship (Luhrmann, 2004), as may be attested to by the proliferation of video screens and staged performances in churches, as well as the taking of communion in cinemas after a screening of Mel Gibson's *The Passion of the Christ* (Pinto, 2004). One result has been an increase in the theming of the Bible in several tourism destinations (Beal, 2005; Feldman & Ron, 2011; Rivera *et al.*, 2009; Ron, 2010b; Ron & Feldman, 2009; Rowan, 2004; Shani *et al.*, 2007; Shoval, 2000; Ward, 2008), which is both a catalyst of those changes and a response to them. Some countries and destinations are more themed than others. Currently, Christian theme parks and

110 Contemporary Christian Travel

Figure 6.3 The Life of Christ Museum in Fatima, Portugal, is an example of a themed Christian space (Photo: D. Timothy)

sites exist at least in Argentina, Germany, Israel, Poland, Brazil, China and the United States.

Christian-themed environments in the United States

The United States has the highest number of Christian-themed environments in the world (Corbett, 1997; Mitrašinović, 2006; Ron & Feldman, 2009; Rivera et al., 2009; Shackley, 2001; Shani et al., 2007). Many of them still function (see Table 6.1), while others have been abandoned for a variety of reasons, and remain in a state of dereliction in the landscape (Beal, 2005).

The HLE is one of the most researched Christian-themed environments in the United States (Beal, 2005; Branham, 2008, 2009; Rowan, 2004; Ward, 2008; Wharton, 2006). It is a 15-acre biblical theme park that

> brings together the sights and sounds of the world of the Bible in a unique and interactive way… It is a living, biblical museum that takes you 7000 miles away and 2000 years back in time to the land of the Bible. Its combination of sights, sounds, and tastes will stimulate your senses and blend together to create a spectacular new experience. (Holy Land Experience, 2017: np)

Several researchers have compared the HLE to various other biblical parks, and even to amusement parks such as Disneyland and Universal

Table 6.1 A sample of Christian-themed environments and theme parks in the United States

Themed environment	Location	Date opened
Ark Encounter	Williamstown, Kentucky	2016
Ave Maria Grotto	Cullman, Alabama	1961
Biblical Mini-golf	Lexington, Kentucky	1987
Biblical History Center	Lagrange, Georgia	2006
Christ in the Smokies Museum & Gardens	Gatlinburg, Tennessee	2010
Creation Museum	Petersburg, Kentucky	2007
Don Brown Rosary Collection	Skamania County, Washington	1973
Holy Land Experience	Orlando, Florida	2001
Museum of the Bible	Washington, DC	2017
Precious Moments Inspiration Park	Carthage, Missouri	1989

Studios, as well as to living museums (e.g. Colonial Williamsburg) and movies (Beal, 2005; Branham, 2009; Rowan, 2004; Wharton, 2006). Many of these observers have levied heavy criticism of the place and its commodification of the Bible and the life of Christ, suggesting that it is more an amusement park than a sacred place:

> I've observed people, sort of not knowing what to do: are they supposed to be enjoying the show?... are they supposed to enjoy the ice cream that they're eating, at the same time as they're watching Jesus get nailed to the cross? Or are they supposed to be crying? And it's true that I have seen people cry. So it's a very strange place to be as to how you react. (Branham, 2008: np)

Much of the criticism expressed relates to the question of authenticity; although all are critical of the HLE and what it stands for, some are more critical than others on issues of authenticity. In Rowan's (2004: 263) opinion, 'visitors wishing to become closer to the biblical narrative are only one additional step removed from authenticity, that of proximity, than those who actually walk in one of the various putative Garden Tombs in Jerusalem or along the Via Dolorosa'. At the other end of the authenticity spectrum is Beal's (2005) assertion that what repelled him most about

> the Holy Land Experience was its lack of authenticity... it was inauthentic in that the actual physical place lacked personality and soul. It was a production rather than a creation. There was no sense of creative process or personal investment in its various displays. No finger prints, no paint strokes, no mistakes, no signatures, no whimsy. The perfectly landscaped gardens around the Empty Tomb, the perfectly plumb walls

of the Temple, and the expertly made costumes of the performers left me longing for the bumpy roads of Journey Trail, the blue barrels of the Dome of the Ark, and the hand-painted cutouts of biblical characters at Holy Land USA. (Beal, 2005: 68)

Beal also views the Jewish–Christian relations presented at the HLE as being quite disingenuous. Its Baptist founder, a converted Jew named Marvin Rosenthal, did not conceal his missionary evangelical Judeophilic agenda in developing the theme park. For Beal (2005: 68), this fact intensifies the attraction's inauthenticity 'in that it is not forthright about its larger agendas, especially its mission to proselytize Jews into its own peculiar form of Christianity, preferring... to present itself as an educational mission'.

Controversy has also followed the opening of the Museum of the Bible in November 2017 in Washington, DC, in two different ways. The first was a recent controversy (2010–2017) over the company's purchase of biblical artifacts from war-torn Iraq, which were believed by the US government to have been looted from museums and archaeological sites. The US Department of Justice forced the museum's parent company, Hobby Lobby, to return the Mesopotamian artifacts to Iraq and pay a US$3 million fine. The company maintains that its officials were unaware of the illicit nature of the objects, which were not planned to be displayed at the museum. The second controversy surrounds the establishment's intended goals. Management claims that the purpose of the Museum of the Bible is to share the historical importance of the Bible in a non-sectarian manner and to allow visitors to draw their own conclusions regarding the veracity of the book. Critics, however, contend that its covert aim is to sell an extremely conservative version of evangelical Christianity, and its location in Washington, DC, only a few blocks from the Capitol building reveals an effort to exert influence in the capital (Ortiz, 2017). Regardless of the extant cynicism, the museum has seen reasonable success, and hundreds of Christian groups have booked tours of the institution for the duration of 2018.

The 2016 opening of the Ark Encounter in Kentucky was celebrated widely in evangelical Christian circles (Lovan, 2016). The 155-meter long Noah's ark replica cost nearly US$100 million to construct to the specifications described in the Book of Genesis. It depicts life before the flood, aims to advocate a creationist perspective and is emblematic of the crossover between religion, entertainment, tourism, publicity and creativity (Bielo, 2018a) with an apocalyptic twist (Bloomfield, 2017). The site is said to have received more than 1 million visitors during its first year of operation, and that number is expected to grow in 2018 and 2019, with many community members anticipating the attraction's economic promise.

Christian-themed environments in Israel

In Israel, the two best-known Christian-themed environments are the Biblical Resources Museum (BRM) in Jerusalem and Nazareth Village (NV) in Nazareth. Both of these are important religious attractions in the Holy Land that feature prominently on Christian itineraries (Bielo, 2018b).

The BRM was founded over a quarter century ago. The location of the museum has changed several times. Between 1998 and 2006, it was located in the neighborhood of Ein Kerem (the traditional birthplace of John the Baptist) in Jerusalem. The site was recently relocated to LaGrange, Georgia, USA (now the Biblical History Center). The Ein Kerem site is now called the Bible Times Center, and is operated by a different group. The BRM was founded by J.W. Fleming, a biblical scholar and educator. Visitors there encountered several staged biblical elements, including a threshing floor, a quarry, a goat's hair tent, a sheepfold, a watchtower, a water well, olive and wine presses and a crucifixion site with Roman-style crosses. The two highlights of the site were a replica of the tomb of Jesus and a Last Supper event offered as an optional meal for tour groups (Ron & Timothy, 2013).

Even while still in Israel, the site was operated by non-Israeli Christian volunteers, who presented themselves to visitors as devout Christians. While using volunteers is not necessarily cheaper than employing local salaried workers (Pinto, 2004), it has invisible advantages, insofar as it suggests a comparison with well-established holy places in Israel (e.g. the Garden Tomb), and endows the BRM with the aura of a spiritual site of sacred worship, rather than of a commercial enterprise.

Nazareth, located in the north of Israel, was the site of the Annunciation to Mary and the childhood home of Jesus. In recent years, Nazareth has become the largest Arab town in Israel, and represents an extremely important destination in most Christian travel itineraries to the Holy Land. Up to the end of the 20th century, however, despite its being the hometown of Jesus, Nazareth had very little to offer the Protestant visitor, as most of its churches and Christian Arab population belong to various Catholic or Orthodox churches (Emmett, 1995). According to one promotional tome, 'this idyllic town has been transformed into a teeming city of 70,000… Horns blare from the cars and buses that jam the streets from dawn to dusk…' (Kauffmann & Hostetler, 2005: 70).

A typical Protestant tour of Nazareth lasts less than two hours and includes a visit to the Church of the Annunciation and a short walk through a small Arab bazaar. Like the native Arab population, the religious sites in Nazareth are mainly Catholic and Orthodox. In fact, the overbuilt and oftentimes garish church settings around these sites repulse many Protestant visitors who seek to spend their time in more natural and biblical-looking environments (Shoval, 2000). Consequently, most Protestant tour itineraries regard Nazareth as a 'drive-through town' on their way to other Christian destinations, such as the Sea of Galilee or Jerusalem.

At the turn of the millennium, in the late 1990s, the Israeli Ministry of Tourism made serious attempts to renew the appearance of Nazareth, especially in areas frequented by tourists. The plan, *Nazareth 2000*, included the construction of new promenades and hotels, repaving the streets of the old bazaar and improving the infrastructure generally (Cohen-Hattab & Shoval, 2007; Gelbman & Laven, 2016). The main drive for the project was the anticipation of millions more Christian believers visiting the Holy Land and the city of Jesus for the new millennium, a hope that, in the end, was only partly fulfilled (Kliot & Collins-Kreiner, 2003). These great expectations also stimulated private tourist development initiatives, the most prominent of which was NV.

Established in 2000 by a local Protestant Arab, N. Beshara, and supported by the Mennonite Mission Network, NV was designed to breathe life into a Galilean village and farm, recreating Nazareth as it might have been 2000 years ago. It aims to open a window into the life of Jesus Christ, Nazareth's most famous citizen. According to the site's founding director, the concept of NV was inspired by three well-known heritage sites: Colonial Williamsburg (USA), Plimoth Plantation (USA) and Ecomusée d'Alsace (France). All three sites are themed to certain periods and geographies, frozen in time (Timothy, 2011). At NV, visitors encounter costumed actors, staged buildings and streets, and artifacts, which site managers proudly suggest are designed after scientific and archaeological evidence.

The site itself includes a traditional rural area with representative 'biblical' artifacts, such as a threshing floor and water well, newly built 'traditional' homes, streets and a synagogue. When tourists come to the village, they encounter local men, women and children, as well as volunteer actors and missionaries, dressed in traditional attire, performing traditional jobs, such as plowing, picking and crushing olives, manufacturing and repairing tools, weaving, winnowing and more. The visitors also have the option of ordering a biblical meal. At NV's opening, Shoval (2000: 258) predicted that North American Christians would be very enthusiastic about the idea, whereas Europeans, in general, would fear that NV would be an '"American production", that is, a site that would sacrifice authenticity on the altar of technological sophistication'. Almost two decades later, NV receives visitors from many different countries. Nearly 10 years into its operations, some 30% of the attraction's visitors came from Europe, while about 65% came from the United States (Roth, 2008). These statistics, along with the presence of Christian theme parks in Poland, Hong Kong and Argentina and plans for more in Asia, seem to indicate that the appeal of religious-themed environments reaches much further than the North American Protestant market.

Both the BRM and NV are located in important biblical towns central to Jesus' mission. Both depict themselves as biblical, natural, agricultural, ancient and Christian. Both claim to be based upon archaeological truths and claim the scientific veracity of their reconstructions. Both establishments exhibit contemporary rustic remains without identifying them as recent, and perform daily Bible-period practices, such as weaving and herding sheep, without framing them as staged. By refraining from inauthenticating themselves, NV and the BRM make themselves appealing to the Protestant gaze and satisfy certain Protestant expectations of 'authentic' New Testament villages. The operation of the attractions by non-profit, charitable Christian organizations and their partial staffing by devout volunteers serve to increase the sites' religious and historical authority. Yet, in Bryman's (1999: 39) view, both locales should be regarded as Disneyfied environments, because they demonstrate characteristics of intentional theming, de-differentiation of consumption, merchandising and emotional labor. Shoval (2000: 262) laments that these sorts of places may 'seriously undercut the significance of the authentic historical locations' in Israel.

While both locales may demonstrate many characteristics of a Disneyized commercial landscape, the relationship between the two sites and their host communities, as well as their representations of the past, differ significantly. The BRM is detached from the local community and is staffed by Christians from abroad. There, guides are primarily instructors, and scientific cross sections of models and scholarly language dominate interpretation and historical depictions. NV, on the other hand, was founded by members of the local community, and portrays itself as reflecting the values of, and contributing to, the Christian community of Nazareth, which has endured over two millennia. The majority of NV's staff are local Christian Arabs, supplemented by some short-term missionaries, who dress in costumes and use primitive tools to play the roles of weavers, carpenters and shepherds. As it is more oriented toward the local community, NV demonstrates a few characteristics of an eco-museum that, according to Davis (2005: 370), emphasizes the relationship with the local population, and represents them and their heritage. The BRM, on the other hand, appears to be more committed to the theme and less to local community embeddedness, which is reflected by the fact that its location has changed several times – its first three in the Jerusalem area and its current location in the United States.

Both representations accommodate the same orientalizing tendencies of the Protestant gaze. Whereas at the BRM, the global Western volunteer is perceived by visitors as 'one of us' and presents a (pseudo-)scientific discourse; the physical features and accents of the NV narrators mark them as being from elsewhere. The NV website, for example, portrays contemporary urban Christians as biblical shepherd girls. Thus, they may convincingly play characters of the past in ways that would be perceived as alienating make-believe, had they been performed by the Westerners of the BRM. Given the power of the Protestant orientalizing gaze, the best way for Arab Christians to find a place in conservative Protestant itineraries may be by portraying themselves as 'Living Stones' (Palestinian Christians) in a heritage site.

Both sites are very successful in terms of visitor satisfaction (Hostetler, 2005; Pinto, 2004; Roth, 2008), which may reflect the presence of three dominant elements: theming, nature and science (Figure 6.4). Theming the sacredscapes of Nazareth in a theme park-like environment shapes the architecture, landscape, actors, performances, foods and souvenirs. By doing so, sites might fulfill the need for religious visualization, thus acting as more spiritual alternatives to the traditional holy sites, which are sometimes perceived by Protestants as alienating, cold and overly ornate.

Significant resources are currently being invested in scientific research to get a more accurate picture of biblical-period living. The fact that some scientists have given the two attractions their seal of approval contributes to their reputation and increases their scientific validity among Protestant visitors and tour operators. In addition, this scientific 'authentication' adds to the distinction made by visitors between an ordinary 'Disney-ized' theme park and a more authentic experience. Nature is emphasized in two parallel narratives: the visual and the audio. The first narrative consists of natural elements that dominate the sites: trees, flowers, water and animals, all of which educe biblical associations. The latter narrative is more evasive and depends greatly on the circumstances. In accordance with this narrative, local guides are trained to emphasize nature by referring to relevant biblical events through stories and parables.

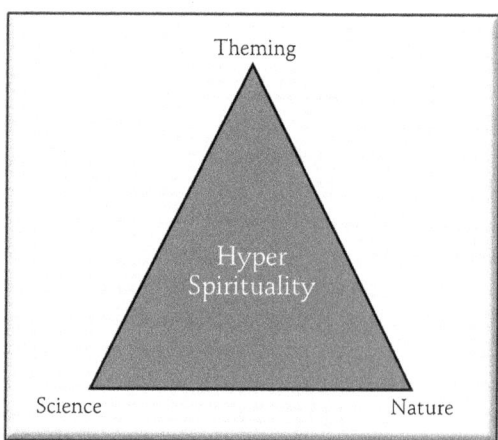

Figure 6.4 Common features of a Protestant theme site in Israel

An analysis of the two sites and their above-mentioned elements suggests that we are dealing with a contemporary phenomenon, which will be called here 'hyper-spirituality', to borrow from Eco's (1986) concept of hyperreality. The combination of spiritual context and meaning, on the one hand, and active visitor participation, on the other, leads to a unique and enhanced experience that can be viewed as making a significant contribution to the spectrum of the religious spiritual tourist experience.

Christian-themed environments elsewhere

Although Israel and the United States still possess the highest number of Christian-themed environments per capita of any other country, there are dozens of other artificial sites throughout the world, and there are many ongoing plans to develop future attractions in other countries (see Table 6.2) (Bielo, 2016a). One of the more unusual Christian-themed environments is Golgotha in Licheń Stary, Poland. It is unusual because it is in fact a part of the Religious Complex of Licheń, which includes the Sanctuary of Our Lady of Licheń, the Sorrow Queen of Poland (Haładewicz-Grzelak & Lubos-Kozieł, 2014; Sekerdej, 2005; Sekerdej *et al.*, 2007). Licheń, a village about 10 km from the city of Konin, has been a pilgrimage destination for decades. During the 1990s, the parish priest decided to build a huge basilica, meant to be a 'votive of the Polish nation for the year 2000'. The basilica is considered to be the largest in Poland and the seventh largest in Europe. The Religious Complex in many ways resembles an amusement park, part of which is Golgotha, a hill topped by a large cross and containing a sepulcher, pathways, monuments and fountains. In the words of Sekerdej (2005: 5–6), the place is over-commercialized and lacks 'visible borderlines between the sacred and the profane... [creating] an impression that there is no qualitative difference between the... market of religious objects and the [Religious Complex] itself'. Local nuns conduct tours of the complex, and the place is a popular attraction for Poles. While some people criticize the attraction for its overly touristic features and commercialization, it appears to overlap the boundaries between the sacred and the profane, wherein

Table 6.2 A sample of Christian-themed environments and theme parks outside Israel and the United States

Themed environment	Location	Date opened
Xingsha Ecological Park	Changsha, China	2017
Holy Land Subic	Subic Bay, Philippines	2010
Golgotha	Licheń Stary, Poland	1976
Tierra Santa	Buenos Aires, Argentina	2000
Temple of Solomon	São Paolo, Brazil	2014
Noah's Ark Park	Hong Kong	2009

Licheń 'offers the grandeur and splendor of a huge church, on the other it does not demand detaching oneself from popular religiosity. Although it is monumental, by alluding to commonly familiar symbols, it is also understandable' (Sekerdej, 2005: 9).

A completely different example of a Christian-themed environment in a Roman Catholic setting is Tierra Santa in Buenos Aires, Argentina. This New Testament theme park is one of the earliest of its kind. It is 7 hectares in size and attracts hundreds of thousands of visitors every year (Alegro, 2008). The attraction, which is endorsed by the Roman Catholic Church, tells stories from the life of Jesus and is populated with plastic animals and mechanical characters, including an 18-meter Christ, which resurrects every 30 minutes (Ward, 2008). Beyond telling the stories of Jesus and emphasizing his ministry, Tierra Santa is also widely recognized as an entertainment complex – replete with entertainers and performers, puppet shows and musical performances (Alegro, 2008).

While the park's main audience is overwhelmingly Roman Catholic, its managers have made an effort to cater to a wider range of other Christians and even non-Christians. In addition to the chapel of Jesus of Nazareth and various themes of Mother Teresa, the park also houses a mosque and a synagogue (Alegro, 2008), and the entertainment brought in is seen to appeal to everyone regardless of their religious background.

Visitors' reactions to Tierra Santa are mixed. Some are cynical about the attraction's apparent commercialization of Jesus Christ, the Disneyfication of the savior, while others convey a sense of reverence about the place and what its purpose is supposed to be. As an example, Davies (2007: 48) writes that 'We saw Jesus rise from the dead, and then 30 minutes later it happened again. The crowd stood transfixed as a vast, hydraulic Messiah emerged from the fiberglass mountain and Handel's "Hallelujah Chorus" boomed from loudspeakers'. There are at least 37 depicted scenes from the Bible, but the main focus is the birth, ministry, crucifixion and resurrection of Jesus. Staged scenes, fake topography, fiberglass electronic characters and faux streets of Jerusalem create a Disneyesque landscape that does not escape the observations of critics. In the words of Clarke (2015),

> Perhaps more open to historical debate is Tierra Santa's interpretation of the resurrection: every half an hour a… statue of The Good Shepard himself gloriously rises out of the Holy Mount, towering above the park to the rapturous delight of the audience… within the artificial confines of the Holy Mount lies an economic miracle'. (Clarke, 2015: 10)

Likewise, Sandberg (2009) sums up her visit in a tone of ambivalence:

> Overall, Tierra Santa in Buenos Aires, Argentina was a bizarre experience. There were elderly people and families there who were obviously

having religious experiences. Then there were teenagers giggling as they posed with a statue of Jesus enduring a crown of thorns. I'm still not quite sure what to make of this supposed 'holy land', but it was worth the trip for me. Where else can you pose with a life-size statue of a prostitute, dine on falafel, watch a dance show, and see a gigantic Jesus rise out of a mountain to the soundtrack of Handel's Hallelujah Chorus? (Sandberg, 2009: np)

Opened in 2009, Noah's Ark Park in Hong Kong is an evangelical Christian theme park that aims to encourage a creationist narrative (Bielo, 2016b; Chi-Keung, 2017) by 'harvesting interest in nature and the environment to create a Christian learning experience' (Goh, 2014: 208). The park's main attraction is the full-sized replica of Noah's Ark, which is supplemented by various children's activities, a hotel, an ark garden, a nature garden, a solar tower and dining services. In congested Hong Kong, this park is a prized piece of uncrowded green space, a popular getaway for the city's Christian population to enjoy open space and learn about the gospel simultaneously.

Conclusion

Christian-themed environments are on the rise. Until relatively recently there where none to speak of. Nowadays, however, there are more than 200 of them in various parts of the world, and several more are being planned. One of the reasons for this increase in interest is no doubt part and parcel of the growing popularity and pervasiveness of themed environments and contrived spaces in general (Åstrøm, 2017; Erb & Ong, 2017; Urry, 2002). A concomitant reason may be the growing desire to seek spiritual experiences in spaces beyond traditional holy sites (Hall, 2006b), which for many people might be less accessible financially, politically or in other ways. This growing desire correlates well to the pervasive Protestant concept that God is everywhere; consequently, all places have just as much right to be sacred as those officially sanctioned by the church (Ron & Feldman, 2009: 203), but it is noteworthy that Christian theming is not exclusively in the Protestant domain.

The themed environments described in this chapter vary greatly in several aspects of form and content. One of the ways to distinguish between them is by seeing their relationship to traditional sacred sites. Most of the themed environments discussed here are physically detached from the sacred spaces that they are imitating, representing and replicating. Some (e.g. BRM and NV) are located in sacred cities, near traditional sacred sites, but only one (Golgotha in Poland) is in fact a themed environment that is part of a traditional pilgrimage shrine.

Despite our increased knowledge and understanding about Christian-themed environments, there are still many islands of ignorance in the sea of knowledge. To name a few, why do Christian-themed environments exist only in certain denominational contexts? To what extent do these themed environments replace the 'real world' of traditional sacred sites? To what extent are these sites a positive, negative or neutral contribution to their surrounding communities? How is authenticity sought, ignored or perceived in Christian-themed spaces? These questions and others remain unanswered. However, one should remember that this form of contemporary Christian edutainment feeds and maintains the faith and spirituality of many.

7 Heritage Trails and Cultural Routes

Introduction

Since the commencement of the Anthropocene, humankind has forged trails and routes of various sorts. Earliest among these were hunting paths, trade routes and migratory trails. These were often designated ways of getting from point to point and eventually evolved into many of the current transportation corridors in the modern world, and some are utilized as salient recreation and tourism trails today.

Trails are an important part of the spatial manifestation of traditional Christian pilgrimages. Medieval pilgrimages tended to follow earlier trade routes but also began to forge their own distinct paths (Stopford, 1994). Throughout the centuries, Christian pilgrim paths were blazed, standardized and marked for large-scale traffic. With their near abandonment between the 16th and 20th centuries, the use of official trails by many Christian pilgrims, particularly by Protestants, waned considerably, so that the trails were abandoned and fell into disuse. In recent years, however, many of these disused pilgrim paths have been researched, reinstated and repopularized as trails for religious and non-religious tourists (Pack, 2010). In many communities and regions, these contemporary routes comprise the single most important part of their tourism economies.

This chapter examines the role of trails, routes and other linear attractions as resources for pilgrimages and other forms of tourism in a Christian context. The chapter describes some of the most important Christian heritage trails in the world, organized around the dual concepts of organic and purposive trails, as well as the issues surrounding them as an important part of the supply of Christian travel.

Routes, Trails and Linear Resources

Several different sorts of tourism and recreation trails and routes have been identified. Ramsay and Truscott (2003) suggested three types: evolved, designed and associative trails. 'Evolved' routes began anciently as lines of human mobility for indigenous peoples and later became the foundations for modern-day vehicle roads and highways. Ramsay and

Truscott's 'designed' tracks are purpose-built corridors that were constructed for the socio-economic development of places. These include railroads, fire management trails, roads and timber industry access trails. 'Associative' tracks, according to Ramsay and Truscott, are historic ways that are still valued by the people whose ancestors created them and also by contemporary recreationists.

Timothy and Boyd (2015) incorporated this three-part typology and suggested that tourism and recreation trails can be viewed broadly from two perspectives: organically developed and purposefully constructed routes. Organic trails best resemble Ramsay and Truscott's (2003) evolved tracks but also include some of the features of their designed and associative tracks as well. Organic trails are those that developed spontaneously as explorer or migration routes, trade routes or religious pilgrimage trails. However, these also include constructed linear corridors such as political borders, canals, roads or railways. Some of the most famous organic trails include the Great Wall of China and Hadrian's Wall, the Silk Road, the Oregon Trail and the way to Santiago de Compostela. All of these can be used as modern-day tourist trails but were not developed specifically to be such.

Original pilgrim trails were arduous and harsh, and their purpose was to humble the repentant traveler, so that he or she would be better prepared to be in the presence of the holy, to demonstrate contrition and seek forgiveness (Kong, 2001; Potter, 1982; Timothy & Olsen, 2018). However, through the centuries and with the restoration of many former pilgrim routes in the past quarter century for recreational purposes, the austerity of the way itself has yielded to the idea of the final destination, or end point, being the main goal of the modern-day pilgrim. Today, relatively few Christian pilgrims follow the toilsome trails of yesteryear. Instead, most people travel directly to the memorial site, shrine or attraction where divine interventions occurred. In the process of secularization or desanctification of pilgrim routes, they have simultaneously become commoditized into all-purpose tourism venues that are now revered by general tourists as well as by pilgrim tourists (Kušen, 2010; Liutikas, 2014; Metreveli & Timothy, 2010; Timothy, 2011).

Based upon their assessment of the Way of St James, Murray and Graham (1997: 522–523) outlined a five-phase evolutionary model that depicts the transformation of pilgrim roads into general tourism trails as part of their organic life cycle (Figure 7.1). The initial medieval pilgrimage circuit was characterized by a wide-ranging and imprecise zone of human mobility without a set course or support infrastructure. However, in the beginnings of phase two, the way became formalized as people began to use common, well-trodden and generally accepted pathways. During this stage, support infrastructure begins to develop, including bridges, pilgrim rest houses, wells, shelters and intermediate churches and shrines. During stage three, the trail becomes multinodal, suggesting

Heritage Trails and Cultural Routes 123

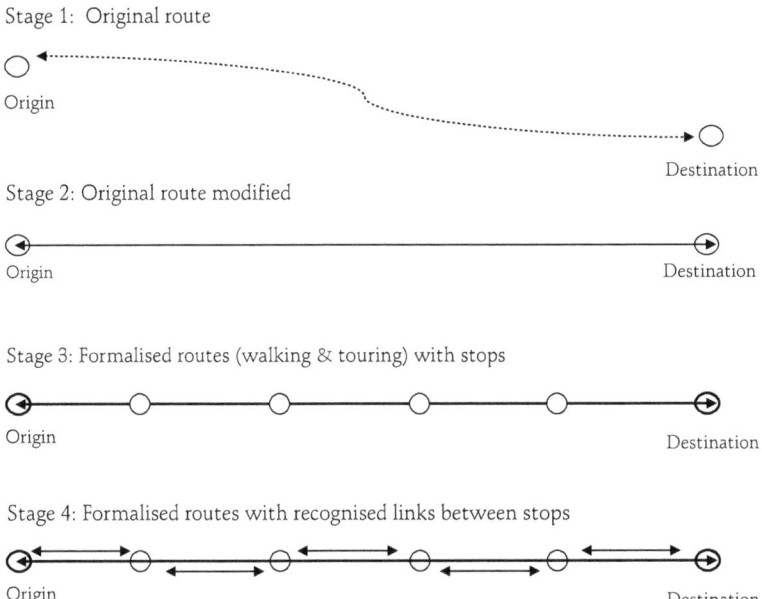

Stage 1: Original route

Stage 2: Original route modified

Stage 3: Formalised routes (walking & touring) with stops

Stage 4: Formalised routes with recognised links between stops

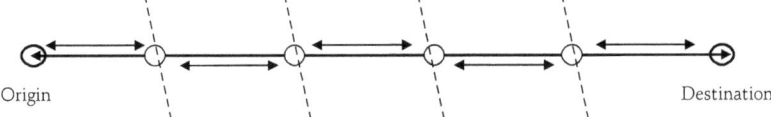

Stage 5: Mini routes within formalised routes developed and promoted

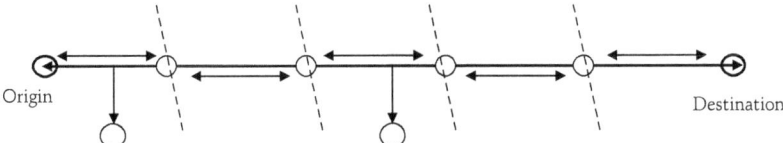

Stage 6: Developments take place beyond the recognised route

Figure 7.1 Evolution of original tracks to developed routes and trails (Source: adapted from Murray & Graham, 1997)

that historic cities along the way become a more important part of the journey and provide multiple opportunities for pilgrims to join the route at various geographical locations, thereby allowing different participants to experience certain segments or bypass the most challenging ones. These attraction nodes also come to deliver many services to sojourners, including lodgings, food services, souvenir shops and transportation hubs. This facilitates the adoption of multimodal transportation – foot, bicycle, horse or motorized vehicle – and travelers can then bypass the less interesting or more strenuous sections of the pathway. At this juncture, the initial emphasis on origin and destination becomes ancillary to the encounters and experiences of the route itself.

The fourth stage is defined by the path itself becoming the main attraction for tourists, more so than the original destination, and in fact the original shrine at the end of the trail may in some cases be forgotten almost entirely as distractions along the track vie for tourist attention. By this time, there are multiple access points, and motorway-based transportation will be closely linked and integrated in some cases with the original pedestrian circuit. Tensions between pilgrims and non-pilgrim tourists will be evident, and much of the tourism economy of the villages and towns along the trail will be based on religious and other tourist expenditures. Finally, in stage five, many trailside communities will depend on modern tourism for their economic well-being, and efforts will be made in relevant regions to diversify the product and spread the benefits of route-based tourism to less-affluent communities. In some instances, the trail will become more widely used and socio-economically dependent on non-pilgrim tourists than on pilgrims.

Purposive trails are different from the organic trails previously described by Murray and Graham (1997) in that they are created, specifically where no original trail necessarily existed, to be recreation and tourism routes and resources by linking together common attractions around a central theme and where the network itself possesses 'a set of values whose whole is greater than the sum of the parts' (Logan, 2002: 23). Food and wine routes, literary heritage trails, industrial trails, architectural corridors and urban heritage walks are examples of purposive trails (Timothy & Boyd, 2015: 18). Many religiously themed routes are being developed as purposive trails for Christian travelers in various parts of the world, some of which will be highlighted later in the chapter.

Religious routes are becoming a more prominent subject of academic inquiry (Olsen & Trono, 2018; Timothy, 2014; Timothy & Boyd, 2006). They provide an unparalleled mix of sensory experiences in natural and cultural settings. Many studies show the spiritual value of being in nature (Heintzman, 2009; Langelo, 2006; Sharpley & Jepson, 2011; Snell & Simmonds, 2012). Many outdoor enthusiasts, even those who would not describe themselves as 'religious', often report having 'spiritual' experiences in wilderness settings (Fredrickson & Anderson, 1999; Heintzman, 2003; Stringer & McAvoy, 1992). Something about being immersed in nature, alone with one's thoughts and undistracted from the harried lifestyles of modern society, allows individuals to develop connections with an otherworldy force beyond themselves. Many people describe their trail-based encounters with nature to be uplifting, energizing or spiritual. For others, it may be an outright manifestation of their faith in a divine creator (Timothy, 2013). For many people, pilgrim trails provide such experiences. Religious trail users can draw closer to deity, while secular tourists may also appreciate the beauty of the natural landscapes through which the route passes (Amaro *et al.*, 2018; Timothy & Boyd, 2015) and have a desire to utilize mobile phone pilgrimage apps to help them interpret their experiences (Antunes & Amaro, 2016).

By the same token, pilgrimage paths are in every way an important part of a region's cultural heritage, and in many instances a sojourner's own personal heritage (Badone, 2014; Timothy, 1997). Heritage is what we inherit from the past and value and utilize in the present day (Graham *et al.*, 2000). This includes both tangible and intangible elements of the past (Timothy, 2014). Religious routes demonstrate heritage characteristics in many ways. First, the pathways themselves are an important heritage element. They were developed by early pilgrims as a way of accessing places of spiritual importance (Turner, 1973). Second, the faith that drives people to undertake a pilgrimage is an important element of the intangible heritage. This includes the rituals, rites and ceremonies that might take place along the route or in the final destination. Third, the shrines, churches, groves and grottos along the way or in the destination are an important tangible manifestation of past and present religious beliefs and practices. Finally, the events, people and places encountered on the journey become a collage of memories that pilgrims will look back on with memories of their experience.

Several geographical concepts are crucial in understanding Christian routes and trails. The first is scale. This refers to the length, spread and impact of a particular path or route. Wall (1997) outlined a spatial typology of attraction types that is useful not only in understanding how particular attractions appear on the ground but also how they can be better managed. Wall's first attraction type, points, refers to single attractions (e.g. a museum, gold mine, shopping center or castle). These are relatively easy to manage and plan, and the physical impacts of tourism are limited to the point attraction and its immediate surrounds. Areas are the second type of attraction. They are larger in scale than points and may include several point attractions within a bounded area. Small towns, villages and national parks would be indicative of area attractions. In areas, visitors can undertake a variety of activities, and their impacts will likely be more widespread than at point attractions. Wall's (1997) final category is linear attractions, which possess physically linear properties and which direct travelers along specific physical corridors. These can be natural (e.g. rivers, lakeshores or mountain ranges) or human created (e.g. railways, roads, trails or paths) and typically link individual nodes, or points, along a common rectilinear space. Use and visitation is usually more dispersed than at point attractions, yet many scenic routes and heritage trails have seen considerable economic success in being able to attract significant tourist attention and link individual points together for a higher economy of scale.

In terms of size and catchment, scale is a salient concept that has conservation, economic impact and management repercussions.

Timothy and Boyd (2015) suggest that route scale can be considered from two primary perspectives. The first is the size or linear extent of a given path or corridor. Large-scale trails may include several countries and cover vast distances. These may be multi-nucleic and encompass many feeder trails from other regions. An example of this is the Way of St James, which extends through several countries of Europe. The shortest trails might include walkways and paths only several meters long between shrines or historic structures in a sacred destination.

The second perspective on scale is understanding a route's symbolic or market reach beyond its geographical location. Timothy (1997) examined this perspective from the perspective of heritage attractions, but it can also easily be applied to the situation of Christian trails. Some religious trails, such as the Way of St James noted above, are of a truly global scale in that they are world famous, they are known to most Christians, at least of certain denominations, and some have been branded UNESCO World Heritage Sites or received other global commendations that increase their visibility to an international audience. National religious trails stay within national borders but tend to have countrywide appeal in their value and use. Local trails are important for a more limited audience and rarely exude national or international appeal. Nonetheless, they are very important for resident worshippers, who with their co-congregants may undertake same-day pilgrimages to local shrines along locally prescribed paths and routes (Bradley, 2009; Bremborg, 2013; Eade & Katić, 2014; Rodrigues & McIntosh, 2014).

Christian Routes and Trails

Religious routes, or pilgrimage trails, are among the most popular and widespread tourism corridors today. Traditional Christian pilgrimages were walking pilgrimages, and while many modern-day pilgrims prefer to travel by motorized vehicle, many still opt to walk long or short distances (Hall *et al.*, 2018). Christian routes in Europe and North America serve a dual purpose: pilgrim trails for travelers who are religiously or spiritually motivated and resources for other tourists who are motivated by a desire to experience nature, improve their health or immerse themselves in a cultural experience (Cerutti & Dioli, 2013; Digance, 2006; Horák *et al.*, 2015; Olsen & Timothy, 2006; Singh, 2006; Timothy & Iverson, 2006; Timothy & Olsen, 2018). Pilgrimage routes are among the most important linear resources today in many tourist destinations (Garín-Muñoz, 2009; Rizzello & Trono, 2013; Ruthven, 2012; Sánchez y Sánchez & Hesp, 2015) and can be seen as either organic or purposive.

Organic Christian trails

There are many examples of Christian routes that developed as religious trails centuries or millennia ago and continue today to be important religious, recreational and tourism byways. Many of them were abandoned during the Reformation and have in recent decades been resurveyed and resuscitated, based upon archaeological evidence (Stopford, 1994), to become important tourism trails and tools for regional economic development. This section describes some of the most prominent organic Christian trails in the world today.

Camino de Santiago

Perhaps the best-known Christian trail is the Way of St James, or Camino de Santiago, which is comprised of a few major routes and several smaller courses stretching from as far as the United Kingdom, Belgium, Switzerland, Italy and Portugal and ending in Santiago de Compostela, Spain. In 819 AD, the remains of St James were ostensibly discovered in northwestern Spain. A church was immediately built over the site to protect it and to venerate it as sacred space. By the end of the 9th century, the route to Santiago had become an extremely popular journey (Costen, 1993; Council of Europe, 2014; Mullins, 1974; Rudolf, 2004; Slavin, 2003; Thomas-Penette, 2010; Wright, 2014), and according to some estimates, by the 11th century, pilgrim numbers varied from half a million to 2 million arrivals per year. Stopford (1994: 59) estimated that anciently some 1400–5500 pilgrims might have arrived at the shrine each day, after which they faced the arduous return journey home.

Gradually, the tomb became more popular among Christians to the point that during the Middle Ages, it became the third most visited Christian destination, after Jerusalem and Rome (Timothy & Boyd, 2015). Traversing the Way of St James enabled pilgrims to seek forgiveness for their sins and pay a penance for wrongdoings. The arduous journey was seen as a way to cleanse the pilgrim, build faith, humble oneself and build a community spirit (*communitas*) with other believers (Schmidt, 2012; Thomas-Penette, 2010). Roads and trails to Santiago developed significantly in the years after 819 AD as the site grew in importance. The pilgrimage to Santiago entailed people blazing their own trails from home until they met with an established trail, which then connected them to one of the main routes. By the 12th century, the main way (*Camino Francés*), which started in France, and a number of secondary branches were established throughout much of Western Europe, and the location became more accessible to the masses (Graham & Murray, 1997; Murray & Graham, 1997).

Despite the trail's popularity from the 9th century on, several factors played a role in decreasing its use and importance in religious worship in later centuries. First, the Protestant Reformation beginning in the early 1500s discouraged, and even forbad, the outward manifestation of faith through pilgrimage (Bremborg, 2013; Dyas, 2014; King, 1920; Przybylska & Sołjan, 2010). This discounted the notion that blessings or forgiveness could be garnered by traveling any of the sacred routes of the Christian world. Second, the political instability of 16th- and 17th-century Europe made traveling more difficult and dangerous (Hess, 1978; Kagan, 1990), which put additional stress on potential pilgrims, who might not have acceded with the Reformation. Third, for Catholics and others who still desired to undertake pilgrimages, alternative destinations became more popular, such as Jerusalem. With transportation innovations and easier access to the Holy Land, some of the attention on European religious routes was diverted to the lands where Jesus walked (Przybylska & Sołjan, 2010). Finally, Black Death, or the Plague, starting in the 14th century and recurred several times between the 15th and 17th centuries, killing millions of Europeans. There was a profound and widespread fear that it could easily be transmitted during pilgrimages to Rome and Santiago (Byrne, 2012; Parker, 2001). As a result of these factors and others, the Camino lost its appeal, and trail-based pilgrimage to Santiago declined considerably for a few hundred years.

While small numbers of Roman Catholics continued to visit Santiago in the 1960s and 1970s, by the 1970s the Way of St James had almost become just a memory in the history books. After the fall of Spain's Franco dictatorship (1939–1975), the tides began to turn and the number of pilgrims from abroad began to grow, although during the 1980s, the use of the Way of St James remained at a mere trickle (Aviva, 2001).

Four main events prompted the resurrection of pilgrimage and other touristic uses of the route after the 1980s. First, in 1987, the Council of Europe established its Cultural Routes Program to raise awareness of Europe's cultural identity, to promote intercultural dialogue, to protect the continent's heritage, to promote quality of life and socio-economic development and to encourage sustainable development (Berti, 2010; Grabow, 2010; Timothy & Saarinen, 2013). At the time the program was established, the Camino de Santiago was selected to be the council's first cultural route, being officially designated in Belgium, France, Germany, Italy, Luxembourg, Portugal, Spain and Switzerland (Mariñas Otero, 1990). 'By providing people of varied backgrounds, believers and nonbelievers, Christians and non-Christians, with an opportunity to gather together, the Santiago Routes serve both as a symbol, reflecting over one thousand years of European history, and as a model of cultural cooperation for Europe as a whole' (Council of Europe, 2014: np).

The second major event was the holding of World Youth Day in 1989 in Santiago de Compostela. World Youth Day was initiated by Pope John Paul II in 1985 to unite Catholic youth and help them develop their spiritual selves in a cross-cultural setting. In 1989, this celebration in Santiago was attended by approximately 400,000 Roman Catholic youth from around the world, bringing additional attention to the shrine of St James and the Pilgrim's Way leading to it (Przybylska & Sołjan, 2010).

Third, 1993 was a jubilee year (Holy Year) for Roman Catholics and celebrated in Santiago to commemorate St James Day. That year's jubilee was considered by the Galician regional government to be an ideal time to promote the trail for its potential economic impacts through tourism (Ambrósio, 2011; Calaf, 2003; Garín-Muñoz, 2009). More people utilized the route that year than in recorded history, with a spike to nearly 100,000 users; additional lodgings, food services and cultural events were established, and old city centers along the way were gentrified (Gonzáles & Medina, 2003). Finally, that same year (1993), the Way of St James was inscribed on UNESCO's World Heritage List, thereby increasing its global visibility even further.

Since these occurrences, worldwide media, including travel shows and guidebooks, as well as promotional efforts by Spain and France, have resulted in tremendous growth in the use of the Camino as a unique travel experience. Today, the Camino is one of the most popular heritage trails in Europe and attracts contrite pilgrims, as well as other tourists who follow the way for the scenic villages, natural environments and rural landscapes it traverses (Cazaux, 2011; Doi, 2011; Downie, 2013; Frey, 1998; Gonzáles, 2006; Santos, 2002; Thomas-Penette, 2010, 2011; Trono & Oliva, 2017), as well as health improvement, personal reflection and self-confidence building, much the same way pilgrimages in other Christian contexts are seen to provide restorative therapy sometimes more than spiritual upliftment (Bond *et al.*, 2015; Lopez *et al.*, 2017; Scandolara, 2008).

Today, the trail is well marked and signed (Figure 7.2), and provides adequate lodgings and dining facilities, some of which have been around since medieval times (Scandolara, 2008). Pilgrim hostels provide inexpensive overnight lodgings for pilgrims with official credentials, although some pilgrims camp along the way. Most of the communities through which the main routes pass have developed a well-oiled hospitality sector to service the needs of tourists. Each year, between 5 and 6 million tourists visit Santiago de Compostela, but not all of them arrive via the Camino. In 2017, approximately 301,036 people completed a sufficient length of the Camino to qualify as 'official' pilgrims, according to authorities in Santiago. Slightly more than half (50.9%) were male, while 49.1% were female. A large majority completed the route by foot (92.51%), followed by bicycle (7.29%), horseback (0.14%) and wheelchair (0.01%). Pilgrims from nearly 150 countries negotiated the trail, with the majority from Spain (44.01%) (see Table 7.1); 60.04% of official pilgrims sojourned to Santiago on the Camino Francés, the main route leading from France. Interestingly, even though being officially distinguished and certified a 'pilgrim', religious or spiritual purposes were not always the main motive for arriving by trail. Only 43.46% of 2017's pilgrims claimed to be motivated to undertake the journey for religious reasons. Nearly half (47.39%) of 2017's pilgrims were prompted to travel the way by both

Figure 7.2 The Way of Saint James crosses the French–Spanish border at the location shown – note the border stone in the middle of the picture (Photo: D. Timothy)

religious and other motives, and 9.15% claimed to have embarked on the trek for non-religious, cultural reasons (Oficina del Peregrino, 2018). These numbers do not reflect the thousands of additional trekkers who use the trail but do not qualify as official pilgrims.

To be a certified pilgrim, travelers must acquire a credential or 'pilgrim passport', which is awarded to anyone who completes 100 km or more of the route by foot or 200 km or more by bicycle. This credential is marked at strategic locales along the way to prove one has traveled the

Table 7.1 Top origin countries of Santiago de Compostela pilgrims in 2017

Country of origin	Number of pilgrims	Percent of total
Spain	132,478	44.01
Italy	27,073	16.06
Germany	23,227	13.78
United States	17,522	10.40
Portugal	12,940	7.68
France	8,835	5.24
Ireland	6,643	3.94
United Kingdom	5,768	3.42
Brazil	5,113	3.03

Source: Compiled from Oficina del Peregrino (2018).

required distance and on the approved pathway. After arriving at Santiago, the pilgrims can then exchange these credentials for a *compostela*, or certificate of completion, thereby satisfying all requirements for their designation as a pilgrim (Gonzáles & Medina, 2003; Murray & Graham, 1997; Timothy & Boyd, 2015).

As already noted, the French Way (Camino Francés) is the most popular and widely used long-distance portion of the Way of St James. It is several hundred kilometers long and can require one to three months to complete (Timothy & Boyd, 2015). It crosses the Spanish border in the Pyrenees and passes through several important historic cities, some of which have been regenerated through the Galician region's route-based tourism initiatives. In addition to the French route, several ancillary pathways through France, Spain and Portugal can also be used to access the shrine at Santiago (Fernandes, 2012; Fernandes *et al.*, 2012) (see Figure 7.3).

Although this discussion about the Camino de Santiago reflects the idea of an organically developed route, it is also worth mentioning that new routes, or purposive routes, are also being developed to reach Santiago. Archaeological records (e.g. icons and souvenirs) indicate that some wealthy and powerful Polish nobility had in fact undertaken the pilgrimage to Santiago during the Middle Ages (Przybylska & Sołjan, 2010). Since 2005 there has been a growing interest in creating new pilgrimage trails to Santiago. As of the end of 2009, the composite length of the Polish Ways of St James was 2016 km, comprised of 13 sections of trails (Przybylska & Sołjan, 2010: 211).

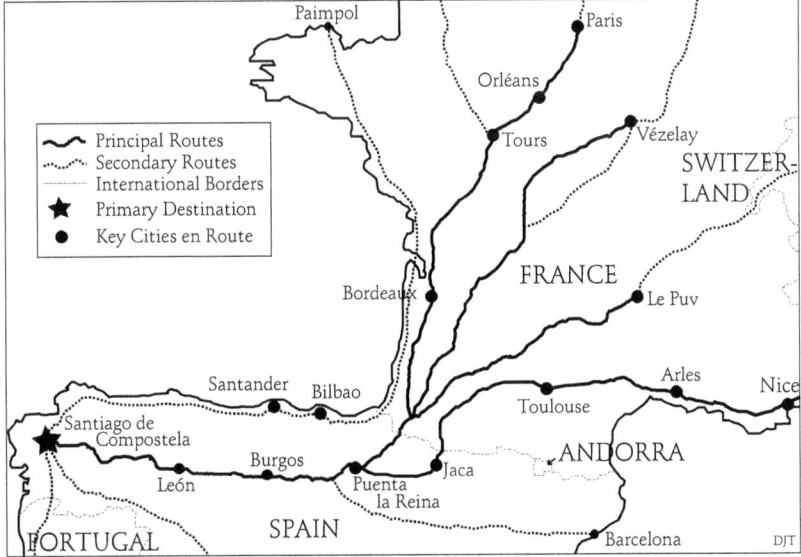

Figure 7.3 The Way of Saint James and its various routes

Via Francigena

By the 7th century AD, Rome had become an important destination for religious travelers and was designated a 'major pilgrimage' destination by the Church in the 13th century, affording it special status in the company of Santiago de Compostela and Jerusalem (Stopford, 1994). Rome was best known as the center of the Christian faith, as well as the burial location of the apostles Peter and Paul.

The original routes to Rome were a series of connected ways whose courses varied in length and location over time. The trail that eventually became the most used pilgrim and trade route ran from Canterbury, England, to Rome through France and Switzerland. This way became known as the *Via Francigena* (the road from France) or *Via Romea*. Today, the Via Francigena is an increasingly popular resource for both religious pilgrims and other tourists, although its reputation is not as widespread globally as that of the Camino de Santiago, and it is used more by day hikers and overnight tourists than by devout pilgrims like the Camino is.

The Via Francigena is sometimes said to be the oldest long-distance cultural route in Europe, originating more than two millennia ago as a transportation and trade corridor. Much of it follows original ancient Roman roads and medieval footpaths (Tencer, 2011) and was the main travel corridor of European kings and English archbishops to Rome from the 6th to the 13th centuries (Stopford, 1994). In 990 AD, Sigeric, the Archbishop of Canterbury, traveled to Rome on the Via Francigena to receive his vestment from Pope John XV. The archbishop kept a concise record of the trail, which has allowed historians and modern trail enthusiasts to retrace, map and demarcate it (Cerutti & Dioli, 2013; Council of Europe, 2014). In 1985, the original route was surveyed and charted based upon Sigeric's description, and in 1994 the trail was added to the list of European Cultural Routes, increasing its visibility further for general recreational use (Cofraternity of Pilgrims to Rome, 2014).

In April 2001, the European Association of Via Francigena was established to help mark, maintain, promote and 'rediscover' the 1800 km route from the North Sea to Rome (Council of Europe, 2014). Much of the way follows country lanes, rural footpaths and sleepy backroads. It is fast becoming an increasingly popular pilgrim circuit and cultural tourism experience (Cropera, 2006; Ruini, 2007). In the view of Via enthusiasts, the trail passes through some of Europe's most beautiful and unspoiled regions and includes ancient cobble-stoned Roman roads and medieval footpaths, and bypasses ancient ruins and hilltop villages (Cofraternity of Pilgrims to Rome, 2014; Tencer, 2011). While the Via Francigena is not as well developed for pilgrimage and other forms of tourism, the way the Camino de Santiago is in terms of services and infrastructure, the situation is changing. There are increasing numbers of accommodation and meal services along or nearby the route (Giotta, 2007), and increasing numbers of health spas are being developed along the way, including thermal baths, owing to the emerging theme of the Via Francigena as a wellness and health experience (Cropera, 2007).

The Via is sometimes noted as Europe's 'second pilgrimage trail'. After the renaissance of the Way of St James as a popular tourist route in the 1980s and 1990s, the public began focusing on the Via Francigena. The route to Rome is often traveled by pilgrims and other hikers, cyclists or horseback riders as the next long-distance route after they have completed the Camino (Mooney, 2010), and is often seen as a scenic and quieter alternative to the Way of St James (Cofraternity of Pilgrims to Rome, 2014).

While the Via is not as well known as the Camino and fewer people utilize the route for religious or other cultural heritage purposes, it is emerging as an important long-distance walkway for people of different backgrounds and interests. In the words of Tencer (2011: 35), '...the Via Francigena provides an exceptional opportunity to experience the contemporary culture, intricate cuisine, and rich history of Italy, one footstep at a time. Moreover, it is one of the world's important religious and spiritual modern-day Christian pilgrimages'. Since 2005, the Italian government and local governments have devoted a great deal of attention to developing the route as a tourism product. Projects are currently underway to develop the Via Francigena as a religious and cultural tourism route, including mapping exercises, resource inventories, marketing initiatives, developing mobile phone apps and other global positioning system (GPS) devices and promoting tour packages (Cerutti & Dioli, 2013).

Much like on the Camino de Santiago, people who complete the journey to Rome on the Via can be certified 'bonafide pilgrims' by having their pilgrim documents stamped at each point along their journey, walking or riding horseback for the last 130 km or cycling the last 400 km, and declaring a religious or spiritual motivation to qualify for the *testimonium*, or pilgrimage certificate (Cofraternity of Pilgrims to Rome, 2014).

Via Dolorosa, Jerusalem

Via Dolorosa (the Way of Sorrows or the Way of the Cross) is the traditional route Jesus walked through Jerusalem while carrying his cross to the place of the crucifixion (Dakkak, 1981; Shachar & Shoval, 1999). While archaeological evidence is still unclear about the original course of the route within Roman Jerusalem at the time of Christ, the current trail begins near the Lion's Gate and ends at the Church of the Holy Sepulcher. Along the way are nine Stations of the Cross with five more located within the Church of the Holy Sepulcher. Each of the stations represents the location where a certain event occurred during the final hours of Jesus' life beginning with his condemnation and ending with his entombment (Bowman, 2000; Peterson, 1998). Many Christians follow Via Dolorosa as part of their visit to Jerusalem, but it is especially popular among Roman Catholics and Orthodox Christians. The Stations of the Cross are used as points of information, pondering and prayer. Other denominations use other routes they believe to be more accurate, but what they all have in common is their desire to follow the footsteps of Christ during the final day of his life (Sacred Destinations, 2014).

Each Friday, pilgrim processions are led by priests from Station 1 to Station 14. For many Christians, this is a major highlight of their journey to the Holy Land (Sacred Destinations, 2014). Via Dolorosa, like many important sites in Jerusalem, is especially crowded during Easter and Christmas when pilgrims and other tourists from around the world descend on the Holy City to celebrate the life of Christ and commemorate his crucifixion and resurrection (Timothy & Boyd, 2015). Re-enactments are common along the way, some with costumed actors (e.g. Roman soldiers, Jesus and stalwart disciples), while small church groups from across the world frequently stage their own 're-enactments' throughout the year (Figure 7.4).

St Olav's Way

The primary route of St Olav's Way, also known as the Old King's Road and the Pilgrim's Way, is a 640 km trail that begins in Oslo, Norway,

Figure 7.4 Christian pilgrims symbolically 're-enacting' the burden of the cross in Jerusalem (Photo: D. Timothy)

heads north through scenic landscapes of lakes, valleys, mountains, rural farmland and villages until it reaches Nidaros Cathedral in Trondheim, Norway, the final resting place of St Olaf. Like most of the other original pilgrimage routes throughout Europe, St Olav's Ways encompass a main trail, the pilgrim's route and several ancillary trails from various locations in Norway, Sweden and Denmark, all leading to Nidaros Cathedral and all having been directly linked to journeys that St Olaf undertook during his lifetime or the original pilgrim routes that followed his death (Bradley, 2009; Gamlem, 2009; Pilegrimsleden, 2014; Thue, 2008). There are approximately 5000 km of St Olav's Ways throughout Scandinavia, with 2000 km in Norway; the rest are in Sweden and Denmark (Lånke, 2012).

In ancient times, the King's Road was an important transportation corridor, not only for pilgrims but also for traders, hunters and migrants. Historical records indicate that King Olaf traveled between Oslo and Trondheim on a few occasions between 1021 and 1024 AD, as many ancient kings of Norway did at other times. King Olaf was born in southern Norway in 995 and was martyred in the Battle of Stiklestad in 1030. During his life he was said to have converted to Christianity in modern-day France and labored diligently the rest of his life to Christianize Norway. A year after his death, his coffin was opened, revealing that his body ostensibly had not deteriorated, and his hair and nails had grown since his death. Owing to this miracle and his earlier efforts to Christianize Scandinavia, he was canonized a saint by Bishop Grimkell a year following his demise. Pilgrimages to his burial place in Trondheim began immediately (Lånke, 2012).

Pilgrims visited St Olaf's grave for more than 500 years. The tomb became the fourth most visited Christian pilgrimage site after Rome, Jerusalem and Santiago and received thousands of visitors each year from as far away as Russia, Greenland, Germany and the United Kingdom (Good Walking, 2014). With the Reformation in the Nordic region (1536–1537), however, pilgrimages in Lutheran countries were forbidden (Gunner, 2017; Lånke, 2012). The general use of the King's Road and other ways as a means of travel declined even further with the construction of railway lines and paved roads throughout Norway and Sweden in the 19th and early 20th centuries. In common with other popular routes in Europe, in recent years it has once again found favor among hiking aficionados, Protestant and Catholic pilgrims and holidaymakers.

Work on revitalizing the Pilgrim's Way began in 1994, with the first route, the King's Road, opening in 1997. Since then, several secondary pilgrim routes of St Olaf have been established in the Nordic states with trails being researched and demarcated with blazes and signs, interpreted, groomed and maintained (Lånke, 2012). In 2006, the Pilgrim's Way was selected to be a pilot project of Norway's Directorate for Cultural Heritage as a way of helping educate the public, preserve the past and stimulate economic growth through tourism (Kuiper & Bryn, 2013).

The pilgrim offices in Oslo and the Pilgrim Center in Trondheim provide information for visitors, and the office in Trondheim provides certificates of successful completion of the pilgrimage after one's arrival at the cathedral. Several pilgrim centers were founded along the main route in 2010 to provide information and assist sojourners, although pilgrim-type lodgings remain sparse along the way. Youth hostels and camping are the primary forms of accommodation (Good Walking, 2014).

The Mormon Trail

A discussion about organic Christian trails would not be complete without mentioning the Mormon Trail. In 1846, after years of maltreatment by many of their non-Mormon neighbors in the US Midwest, large numbers of members of the Church of Jesus Christ of Latter-day Saints began a westward migration from Illinois to the Great Salt Lake Valley, where they felt they could practice their religion without persecution. The first company of pioneers arrived in 1847 after many hardships on the open plains through Iowa, Nebraska and Wyoming. Harsh weather conditions, ill health and death, as well as many miraculous events were fodder for promoting faith, solidarity and pioneer folklore for many generations to follow (Hill, 1996). Some 70,000 pioneers eventually made it to the Great Salt Lake Valley and Utah Territory by the time the transcontinental railway connected the eastern and western portions of the United States. The 2092 km trail and its associated experiences are a very important part of the cultural heritage of the Mormons (Hill, 1996; Wahlquist, 2014) (Figure 7.5).

Although members of the church do not practice pilgrimage in the traditional sense, they are ardent travelers for religious and faith-promoting purposes (Hudman & Jackson, 1992; Olsen, 2006b). In common with many other Christian denominations, LDS tourists consider Jerusalem, Bethlehem and other sites in the Holy Land high on their list of desired destinations, to walk where Jesus walked and to witness the sites associated with his life and ministry. In addition to the Holy Land, pilgrimage-like travel to church history sites in various countries, particularly the United States, is very desirable for many Latter-day Saints (Ioannides & Timothy, 2010). Part of this trend involves people traveling by car along the Mormon Pioneer National Historic Trail to visit sites associated with the 19th-century westward movement of the early pioneers (Davis, 2014; Olsen, 2006b). Several guidebooks have been published throughout the years to help would-be route tourists follow the trail as closely as possible and understand the historic locations along the way (e.g. Chatterley, 2000; Kimball, 1988).

Since the mid-1990s, many pioneer trek re-enactments have been staged along the trail. In a major 1997 depiction of the pioneer journey,

Figure 7.5 The terminus of the Mormon Trail near Salt Lake City (Photo: D. Timothy)

approximately 10,000 trekkers in period clothing pushed handcarts or rode in covered wagons all or most of the 1640 km way from Omaha, Nebraska, to the Salt Lake Valley in Utah (Hill & Landon, 2000; Jones, 2006). This spurred additional re-enactments, which continue to take place in various lengths and forms. For many people, pioneer trail re-enactments help build faith and appreciation for the sacrifices of their forebears (Hill, 1998).

Purposive Christian trails

As noted earlier, the other major form of tourist route, the purposive trail, is comprised of trails and routes that did not necessary function as an original route for trade, commerce, migration or pilgrimage as the formerly discussed trails have done but which have been intentionally developed to become a linear tourism or recreation resource (Galbraith, 2000; Timothy & Boyd, 2015). In nearly all cases, they are developed to link together nodes or specific attractions and locations that have some sort of common history. In the case of Christianity, there are in existence many trails and routes, and a number of additional ones currently being developed, that commemorate the lives of celebrated religious figures (e.g. Jesus Christ, the apostles, saints and church leaders), Christian buildings and architecture styles, denomination-specific heritage, legendary events and sacred places associated with miracles or other divine manifestations. Several of these sorts of trails are described in the following sections.

Trails of Saints

The Saint Martin of Tours Route was established in 2005 and incorporated into the European Cultural Routes program the same year. Saint Martin was born in 316 in what is today Hungary. He eventually converted to Christianity, established monasteries, churches and abbeys, and traveled extensively throughout Europe spreading the gospel and administering to many nations. He is known to have performed many good deeds and miracles and is venerated throughout Europe by Roman Catholics, Eastern Orthodox, Anglicans and Lutherans. He died in 397 and was buried in Tours, France.

The route encompasses an impressive range of European countries (i.e. Albania, Andorra, Austria, Belgium, Bosnia and Herzegovina, Bulgaria, Croatia, Cyprus, the Czech Republic, Denmark, Estonia, Finland, France, Germany, Greece, Hungary, Iceland, Ireland, Italy, Latvia, Liechtenstein, Lithuania, Luxembourg, Malta, Moldova, Monaco, Montenegro, the Netherlands, Norway, Poland, Portugal, Romania, Serbia, Slovakia, Slovenia, Spain, Sweden, Switzerland, Macedonia, Ukraine and the United Kingdom) in true multinational collaborative fashion. The trail connects places associated with his birth, youth and death, as well as some of the places where Saint Martin traveled during his ministry (371–397 AD). Veneration of Saint Martin grew in popularity during the Middle Ages, and his influence had spread to nearly all parts of Europe by the 19th century (Fava, 2007). The Saint Martin of Tours trail links countries and communities where his influence is highly regarded by the general population and where shrines, churches and monuments are dedicated to his memory (Council of Europe, 2014). Saint Martin is regarded as one of the most truly pan-European religious heroes of the classical period in Europe.

Figure 7.6 A Station of the Cross along St Patrick's Trail in Northern Ireland (Photo: D. Timothy)

Similarly, St Patrick's Trail is a long-distance route in Northern Ireland that unites various locations related to the life of St Patrick, the patron saint of Ireland (Simone-Charteris & Boyd, 2010). The route stretches some 148 km from Bangor to Armagh and links 15 Christian sites, including a contemporary visitor center near the burial site of the saint in Downpatrick (Figure 7.6). The trail is one of Northern Ireland's most important heritage tourism resources and has been effective in spreading the economic benefits of Catholic pilgrims and other tourists along the route (Timothy & Boyd, 2015). The trail's development entailed cooperation between public bodies, community groups and private tourism organizations and was designed to be a touring route that can be completed by car or bus with three cluster nodes: Armagh, Downpatrick and Bangor. The trail is meant to reflect a literal and symbolic network of journeys through cultural landscapes that usher visitors in the footsteps of Patrick's own voyage from ordinary man to saint (Boyd, 2013).

Christ-centered trails in the Holy Land

Several trails have been established at various times recently in Israel and Palestine to attract and meet the needs of Christian travelers (Rosenblum, 2008). In 2000, as part of the celebrations associated with Pope John Paul II's visit to the Holy Land, the Nativity Trail was inaugurated by the Palestinians to connect Nazareth and Bethlehem and to bring tourists and their spending to certain parts of the West Bank (Troen & Rabineau, 2014).

Currently, there are two trails in the northern part of Israel that commemorate the life of Jesus and direct hikers to various locations associated with his life and ministry. In the early 2000s, the Israeli Ministry of Tourism began talks to establish a Christian pilgrim trail in Galilee, but it did not come to fruition until 2011. In the meantime, the Jesus Trail, a 65-km walking and hiking path in Galilee that links together specific places mentioned in the biblical accounts of Jesus, was established by a non-profit organization in 2007 (Burge, 2009; Dershowitz, 2014; Dintaman & Landis, 2013; Klangwisan, 2012). The primary aim of the Jesus Trail organization is to provide educational, authentic and salient trekking opportunities that will help users of all religions and nationalities better understand and appreciate the life of Jesus (Timothy & Boyd, 2015). The route begins in Nazareth and includes numerous places of importance to Christians, such as Cana (the location of Jesus turning water into wine), Capernaum, the Jordan River and Mount Tabor (Ynetnews, 2008) (Figure 7.7).

The second major northern path, the Gospel Trail (63 km), was founded in 2011 by the Israeli Ministry of Tourism (Figure 7.8). It also aims to highlight the sojourns of Jesus, although it focuses more on the natural environment than the Jesus Trail does. Both routes parallel one another at various points, and they even converge at a few locations. However, they start at different locations in Nazareth, go through different settlements and tell slightly different stories (Timothy & Boyd, 2015; Tourism Review, 2011).

In a part of the world where almost everything is political, the pilgrimage trails in Israel and Palestine are inherently political as well, just as they are religious in nature. For example, the Nativity Trail noted above was ostensibly developed for the benefit of Christian pilgrims to visit places of importance in the life of Christ. However, from the Palestinians' perspective the trail was initiated largely as a tool for building solidarity between visiting Christians and their Palestinian brothers and sisters (the 'Living Stones'), to show the deep connections between the Palestinian people and their land, and to stress some of the mistreatment inflicted on them by Israel (Troen & Rabineau, 2014: 180).

Likewise, the Israeli government has received considerable criticism for its efforts to develop the Gospel Trail when the Jesus Trail was already in operation by a non-profit organization (Lewon, 2012; Mansfeld, 2012). The Gospel Trail was seen by observers as a competitor to the Jesus Trail – the government was viewed by some as a pariah that had attempted to usurp the market from the Jesus Trail organization. Many of the sites along the Jesus Trail are located in Arab towns and villages.

Figure 7.7 Jesus Trail guides and souvenirs in Israel (Photo: D. Timothy)

Figure 7.8 The head of the Gospel Trail on the outskirts of Nazareth (Photo: D. Timothy)

The Gospel Trail, however, bypasses many of these important Christian locations, ostensibly for security reasons, instead focusing on the natural landscapes and forests of northern Israel. Fewer Christian tourists utilize the Gospel Trail than they do the Jesus Trail, largely because the latter sidesteps too many holy sites until the end of the route, when it overlaps with the Jesus Trail (Troen & Rabineau, 2014: 180).

Architectural routes

Several long-distance trails have been established to memorialize and underscore the importance of the Christian architectural landscape of Europe. At least three of them have been developed and inscribed on the European Cultural Routes list in recent years: the European Route of Cistercian Abbeys, the Cluniac Sites in Europe and Transromanica: The Romanesque Routes of European Heritage.

The European Route of Cistercian Abbeys became a European Cultural Route in 2010 and includes segments in Belgium, the Czech Republic, Denmark, France, Germany, Italy, Poland, Portugal, Spain, Sweden and Switzerland (Council of Europe, 2014). The Roman Catholic Cistercian Order, which began in approximately 1098 AD, eventually spread throughout Europe to include 750 abbeys, 1000 monasteries and many churches. The order's dictates are to 'pray far from the world and live by the work of one's hands'. The Cistercian Order played an important role in the development of European states, the Roman Catholic Church and the Christian architectural heritage of Europe (Berman, 2000). The notion of manual labor and simplicity spurred the development of a unique architectural style that is considered one of the most striking medieval religious building forms in Europe, characterized by simplicity, utilitarianism and a dearth of inessential extravagance (Kinder, 2002). The trail aims to emphasize the architectural style, the simple life of the 'white monks' of the Cistercian Order and the advanced agricultural technique they developed (Council of Europe, 2014).

The Cluniac Sites in Europe route was added to the European Cultural Routes in 2005, and is currently designated in Austria, Belgium, the Czech Republic, France, Germany, Hungary, Israel, Italy, Portugal, Spain, Switzerland and the United Kingdom. Circa 910 AD, William the Pious founded a Benedictine abbey in Cluny, France, which became a center for monastic reform in Europe in response to corruption in the church. Some 1400 other Cluniac sites were built in Western Europe with similar architectural styles, distinctive musical forms, paintings and sculptures (Klingelhofer, 2003), but the most salient common feature of the sites was their role in the Cluniac Reforms, which restored traditional monastic life, such as the development of art forms and caring for the poor. The artworks and largely Romanesque architectural style provide much of the foundations for this cultural route, which is continuing to add countries and kilometers to its network each year (Council of Europe, 2014; Graf & Popesku, 2016).

Initiated and listed as a European Cultural Route in 2007, Transromanica: The Romanesque Routes of European Heritage celebrates the built environment of Romanesque heritage. While it is not solely a religious-oriented route, many of its linked sites and buildings have Christian origins. Transromanica includes castles, monasteries and cathedrals built between the 10th and 12th centuries in eight different countries: Austria, France, Germany, Italy, Portugal, Romania, Serbia and Spain. The aim of the trail is to preserve Romanesque buildings that are distinguished by the use of rounded arches, thick walls and symmetrical layouts, make them accessible to the general public and develop tourism in communities from the Baltic Sea to the Mediterranean (Council of Europe, 2014).

Trails in the development stage

Besides numerous trails that have existed for many years, purposive trails are being developed all the time. Multitudes of other Christian trails are currently under construction at various stages from delineation and planning to actual marking on the ground.

In Croatia, there are ongoing efforts to revive abandoned pilgrimage trails, increase the use of paths to Marian shrines, such as Marija Bistrica, and develop new ones to memorialize locally important priests (Kušen, 2010). Other emerging trails in the Republic of Georgia and in Lithuania have significant potential appeal for domestic and foreign religious tourists (Liutikas, 2014; Metreveli & Timothy, 2010). A trail in Portugal based on sites associated with the life of the 15th-century Portuguese military hero-turned-friar, St Nuno, was recently proposed to attract tourists to locations associated with the saint (Braga *et al.*, 2013). St Nuno is revered in Roman Catholicism, especially in Portugal, because of his support of the Portuguese dynasty, his efforts to keep Portugal independent from Spain and his integrity and spirit of holiness. Plans are underway to develop brochures, maps and historical data to support the way of St Nuno. It will encompass religious and non-religious sites and 'facilitate the development of cultural tourism in less developed touristic areas, attracting visitors with different motivations' (Braga *et al.*, 2013: 81), much the same way the Via Francigena and Camino de Santiago have done in recent years.

Conclusion

The use of pilgrimage routes remains strong and in many cases is growing steadily. Additionally, many original pilgrimage routes are being developed and promoted as general tourist trails, increasing their popularity even further. This gives rise to potential problems on the trail, such as conflict between curious tourists and religious pilgrims whose spaces coincide simultaneously (Lois González & Santos, 2015; Lois González *et al.*, 2016). This is especially the case when religious tourists perceive the routes to be overcrowded or desanctified by non-spiritual sojourners. In most cases, however, both groups get along. Another emerging concern among planners, tourism officials and government agencies is the increase in pilgrim numbers, which can have significant negative impacts on the natural landscapes through which a Christian trail passes (Kuiper & Bryn, 2013), owing to souvenir hunting, fires and camping, garbage build-up and off-trail activities. Likewise, dissonance has been noted where parallel or competing Christian purposive routes have been developed. This is a common problem in natural and cultural contexts whenever tourism is involved, and the situation of Christian travel is no different.

Physical, observable trails are not the only Christian pilgrimage routes. There are also more abstract notions, such as 'In the Footsteps of Paul' cruises noted in Chapter 3 and locally important trail walks for individual congregations. Bremborg (2013: 550) noted that because the Swedish Lutheran Church has no official policy or practice regarding pilgrimage, 'any trail could be a pilgrim route' because the destination is the least important element of a pilgrimage. In fact, there may be no destination or designated trail at all. Rather, the quietude, the walking, peacefulness, immersion in nature and opportunities to meditate are the most important part of modern pilgrimage in the Swedish context. Among Nordic Lutheran congregants, pilgrimage routes are planned according to the needs of the congregation and should be beautiful and interesting. As well, walking old pilgrim trails between historical places and visiting abbeys, springs or other traditional sacred spots are salient elements of modern pilgrimage, but the walking is emphasized more commonly over the arrival (Bremborg, 2013: 551).

Christian travel routes are an important tourism product in many parts of the world. Purposive and organic linear corridors bring economic benefits to adjacent and terminal communities, help build *communitas* among co-religionists, serve to prepare pilgrims for their encounters with the holy and help preserve cultural and natural assets. The bigger the scale of the pilgrimage route, the more impactful it is in these ways.

8 Christian Events and Gatherings

Introduction

Events and other gatherings are among the most visible motives and manifestations of Christian travel and tourism. Events may be held at various scales, including very local, regional, national or international mega-events (Dowson, 2017; Rubio Gil & de Esteban Curiel, 2008), with each one serving a different purpose. Obviously, national and international events are the most likely to attract Christian tourists in the conventional sense, although regional and local events may also attract day-trippers or overnight visitors from around the region. The Zion Christian Church in South Africa, for example, holds an annual Easter weekend celebration that attracts over 1 million participants from throughout the country and in just strictly numerical terms is said to be one of the largest pilgrimages in the world (Saayman *et al.*, 2014). Religious events on any scale may serve a variety of purposes and aims, including hearing the word of God, fellowshipping, evangelizing, celebrating milestones or important church events, celebrating holidays or fundraising. In the majority of cases, religious events encompass a mix of some or all of these.

It is not possible within the frame of this book to examine all the different types of Christian events that could potentially be discussed. These may include parades, picnics, camps, revivals, crusades and reunions. Instead, this chapter examines several key events and mega-events that are most common and most pertinent for our discussion on travel and tourism. First, the chapter examines the travels of church leaders as a form of pilgrimage and also as a significant pilgrimage attraction for devotees. The popes of the Roman Catholic Church are used as a prime example. Secondly, the chapter looks at national conventions, mission symposia and international conferences where people gather to hear from church leaders, conduct business and make future plans. The role of youth motivational meetings is examined as an important event in the lives of Christian young people in an ever-changing world. Finally, the chapter describes the importance of certain liturgical dramas as attractions for spreading the word and commemorating historical occurrences.

Religious Events

In ancient times, public events were common reasons for traveling from nearby communities and the countryside to towns and villages. Hunting competitions and harvest festivals were among the earliest planned events. Sporting contests appeared thousands of years ago in many locations, but the ancient Greeks are often attributed with developing the world's earliest large-scale mega-events, particularly the Olympics. This ancient celebration was revived by Greece in 1896 to the delight of the global athletic community (Bowdin *et al.*, 2011). Throughout history, festivals and events have had an important role to play in community life. They often commemorated battlefield victories, harvest and hunting successes, marriages, births, deaths and other important life events. Many such celebrations grew organically through time into major tourist spectacles, particularly as they offered something that visitors could not witness in their own spheres of daily life. As a result, many such events became commoditized as tourism products, which has often led to their embellishment and reorientation from their original purpose. Special events have also been planned and carried out deliberately as a means of bringing tourists and other visitors into a place for economic development and social purposes (Curtis, 2016, 2018; Fernandes *et al.*, 2016). Many destinations have elected to develop festivals and events as a way of creating an image or tourism brand, commemorating important events or people from that community and stimulating economic growth.

Religious occasions have become one of the most salient forms of events throughout the world. The hajj Muslim pilgrimage happens each year, attracting approximately 2.5 million people to Mecca, Saudi Arabia, at one time in a relatively small space. The Hindu pilgrimage Kumbh Mela is the largest gathering of people in any one place on earth at any given time (in the tens of millions) and occurs at individual holy cities in India every 12 years (Singh, 2006).

Christianity also has a wide range of planned events that draw pilgrims and other visitors from near and far to participate. These take many forms including, but not limited to, church leader visits, church conferences and conventions, youth motivational meetings and liturgical drama. These are all an important part of the broader meetings, incentives, conferences and exhibitions (MICE) tourism system, and each one is described in more detail next.

Church leader visits

Esteemed religious leaders often draw large crowds whenever they visit places. One of the best illustrations of this is the Dalai Lama. Whenever he travels, he draws large crowds of Buddhist believers and non-Buddhist admirers. Perhaps the best example from a Christian perspective, however, is the Pope. Papal visits are overwhelmingly viewed positively by destination residents and usually entail presiding at liturgical events and meetings, attending to official church business, offering blessings at sites of disaster, attending to humanitarian crises or undertaking a pilgrimage himself. While it is likely that the travel patterns and behaviors of many church leaders draw substantial attention, this section focuses on the role of the Pope as a world traveler.

A distinction should be made between the Vatican as a pilgrimage destination and the Vatican as a source of pilgrimage – in other words, the Pope as attraction and the Pope as a pilgrim. Although the Vatican City is a major Catholic pilgrimage destination, with approximately 7 million annual visitors (Orcutt, 2012), hardly any academic work has been done on the touristic aspects of the Vatican City state (Kim & Kim, in press). Nonetheless, several scholars have mentioned the touristic importance of this miniature microstate (Digance, 2006; Olsen, 2006a; Shackley, 2001; Timothy, 2001; Timothy & Olsen, 2006; Vukonić, 1996, 2006), which includes far more than just devout Catholic pilgrims. The Vatican City itself is a foremost tourist destination owing to its unique heritage of art, architecture and faith, and it is the only example in the world where an entire country is listed by UNESCO as a World Heritage Site. Aside from its global heritage appeal, many Catholics are motivated to visit the Vatican City in the hopes of seeing the Pope during his weekly address at St Peter's Square (Figure 8.1), while for others, audiences with the Holy Father may be arranged ahead of time (Ptaszycka-Jackowska, 2000).

As for papal pilgrimages to destinations outside and apart from the Vatican City, recent popes have been very avid travelers. Today, the job of the Holy Father includes frequent travels to nearby and distant destinations. On the one hand, the popes visit as pilgrims, while on the other hand, multitudes of believers follow them. In that sense, the Pope functions also as a mobile and temporary tourist attraction. For example, it is estimated that during Pope Francis' visit to the Philippines in 2015, 6 million devotees attended his outdoor mass (BBC News, 2015).

According to Table 8.1, the last three popes undertook 298 apostolic voyages between 1979 and 2017. Some journeys were short, lasting only a few hours, but some were long, covering several nations on more than one continent over a period of several days. Some popes have traveled more than others, possibly owing to reasons of health, age, media hype and technology. The last four popes visited 155 countries over many hundreds of journeys and were accompanied or visited by millions of followers. For the destinations involved, these papal visits constitute an extremely significant economic impact in numbers of tourists and revenues generated from their expenditures (TotusTuus, 2017).

During his long ministry, Pope John Paul II travelled extensively, and there are many indications and references to his highly developed mobility. Because he hailed from Poland, John Paul II's travels were followed

Figure 8.1 Tourists clamber to photograph jumbotron images of Pope Francis in the Vatican City (Photo: D. Timothy)

extensively by the Polish media and researched extensively by Polish religious scholars (e.g. Felak, 2014; Górecki, 2009; Jabłoński, 2009; Jackowski *et al.*, 2009; Mach, 2009; Ołdakowski, 2002). Many other academics took great interest in his worldwide travels, discussing his mobility patterns and the social and spiritual outcomes of his visits (Bajc, 2011; Felak, 2014; Katz, 2003; O'Mahony, 2005).

Pope Francis is also known for his frequent apostolic journeys. Many of his trips are to non-Catholic destinations, such as South Korea, Albania, Turkey, Azerbaijan, Greece and Bangladesh. Part of Pope Francis' credo has been to reach out to Eastern Orthodox communities and to non-Christian organizations and countries as a means of building bridges and reaching out to people of other faiths that some previous popes have avoided. Since his papacy began in 2013, his frequent travels have taken him across the globe to Latin America, Africa, the Caribbean, the Middle East, Southeast Asia and North America (FitzGerald, 2014; Lanuza, 2015; Levine, 2016; Lundgren, 2017). He has visited the Holy Land to stand with the Israelis and the Palestinians, Africa and Latin America to stand with the poor, and North America to represent his social justice causes. Pope Francis' efforts toward ecumenical outreach and social justice has changed the way in which popes have traditionally been viewed and broadened his appeal as a potential 'tourist attraction' wherever he travels.

Table 8.1 Apostolic voyages of the last three popes (1979–2017)

Pope	Year	Journeys in Italy	Journeys outside Italy
Francis	2017	5	4
	2016	2	6
	2015	3	5
	2014	4	5
	2013	3	1
Benedict XVI	2012	4	2
	2011	5	4
	2010	4	5
	2009	5	3
	2008	4	4
	2007	5	2
	2006	1	4
	2005	1	1
John Paul II	2004	1	2
	2003	1	4
	2002	1	3
	2001	0	3
	2000	0	3
	1999	2	5
	1998	2	4
	1997	1	6
	1996	2	6
	1995	3	7
	1994	2	2
	1993	7	6
	1992	3	4
	1991	5	4
	1990	7	5
	1989	4	4
	1988	7	4
	1987	3	4
	1986	5	4
	1985	6	5
	1984	6	4
	1983	4	4
	1982	9	6
	1981	3	1
	1980	10	4
	1979	3	5
Total	38	143	155

Source: Holy See (2018).

While popes have always drawn large crowds during papal visits (Di Giovine, 2016; Dowson, 2017), John Paul II and Francis stand out as being especially popular in their liturgical and ecumenical appeal, as well as their eschatological approach to comfort the masses during times of terrorism and natural disasters. In the modern world, the notion of a pope being an attraction is more tangible than ever before. He has the power to draw millions of people from near and far to admire, participate and feel the spirit. Research by Marine-Roig (2016) found that Pope Benedict's visit to Barcelona to consecrate the world-famous church La Sagrada Familia lent an extraordinary boost to tourists visiting the church. Even though La Sagrada Familia is already one of Barcelona's most popular tourist attractions, Pope Benedict's visit sparked an immediate tourism response and a six-fold increase in online travel reviews during the year following the event. As noted elsewhere in this book, papal visits to shrines and sacred sites also infuse an additional layer of spiritual value, which often results in these places being deemed more sacrosanct and therefore more worthy of a visit. In this sense then, a papal visit is not only an attraction itself; it also 'brands' certain localities with an extra measure of valorization that makes it more appealing to potential Catholic visitors.

Conferences, Conventions and Business Meetings

Conferences and conventions are an important part of the event sector of the travel industry. In the tourism industry, MICE refers to meetings, incentives, conferences and exhibitions and includes essentially all sorts of business travel. Christianity, like many other organizations and enterprises, sponsors a wide array of business meetings that spur MICE tourism. Many Christian denominations have annual or semi-annual churchwide conferences that aim to provide doctrinal statements, policy changes, Bible study, musical entertainment, elections and other business (Chibaya, 2017). For example, each year, the Southern Baptist Convention has its annual meeting wherein the organization reviews its ministry efforts and discusses future directions. It provides a nationwide (USA) 'old-fashion revival meeting with an open-microphone business meeting' (Southern Baptist Convention, 2018: np). The annual meetings typically last two days and have become an extremely important tourism event for the cities that host them. The 2018 meeting will be hosted in Dallas, Texas, with future meetings scheduled many years in advance in Alabama, Florida, Tennessee, California, North Carolina and Indiana at high-capacity conference centers.

The LDS Church holds general conferences every six months at its Conference Center in Salt Lake City. Church members gather from all over the world for two days to confirm their support for church leadership, listen to sermons and participate in other churchwide business.

Tickets are required but are free and can be obtained from local congregation leaders from anywhere in the world. These conferences are also seen as major tourism attractions for Salt Lake City. With somewhere between 125,000 and 175,000 attendees, with many coming from out of town, many of the city's hotels are fully booked for the weekend of General Conference. The conference is also attended virtually online or by satellite television throughout the world.

Youth Motivational Meetings

Many Christian churches hold periodic motivational meetings at local, national or international level, that bring people together to share faith, participate in music and prayer, fellowship with one another, study the Bible in a multinational context, meet other co-religionists, listen to guest speakers and participate in various leisure pursuits (Caton *et al.*, 2013; Cleary, 2011; Pastoor *et al.*, 2018). Many such meetings are oriented toward youth (and also frequently women [see Dowson, 2016]) by evangelizing and helping to build and maintain faith among youth in an increasingly secular world (Hanson, 2016; Norman & Johnson, 2011) in an intentional campaign that Berger (1999) dubs the 'desecularization' of the world.

Hanson (2016: 11) writes about four major youth ministries that aim to bring millennials together 'to provoke a young generation to passionately pursue Jesus Christ and to take his life-giving message to the ends of the earth'. Rendezvous, Acquire the Fire, the Passion Conference and Winterfest are just some examples of large-scale youth meetings that aim to counter the effects of an increasingly secular world and declining Christian adherence among millennials. According to Hanson (2016), branding and effective marketing are key to attracting the millennial market back to Christ, which many motivational conferences are doing in their efforts to desecularize.

One of the best-researched examples of youth motivational meetings is the Roman Catholic World Youth Day (Hepp & Krönert, 2010; McIntosh & Zahra, 2013). World Youth Day (WYD) is a staged media mega-event that is designed for Catholic youth from around the globe (Hepp & Krönert, 2010). The idea was initiated, developed and promoted by Pope John Paul II in 1984. It was based on the UN International Youth Year in 1985 'as a way to interior renewal, to a deepening of faith, a strengthening of the sense of communion and solidarity' for the purpose of discovering their personal vocation (Cleary, 2011: 19; see also Jackowski *et al.*, 2017; van der Plancke, 1992). WYD is becoming increasingly important for the Roman Catholic Church owing to increased competition for followers between Christian denominations and also the pervasive shift toward secularism noted above. The event cements the church's position as a 'powerful opponent of the trend toward secularization' (Halter, 2013: 261). Norman and Johnson (2011: 372) argue that WYD is also ever more important for the church as a new way of evangelizing to an increasingly modern, media-dependent and materialistic world.

This event is one of the largest, or some say the very largest, organized event for youth in the world (Hutton *et al.*, 2010: 273). It takes place every two or three years in different locations around the globe, always in the presence of the Pope. Since its founding, 15 WYD events have been held, and attendance has grown from 300,000 in 1984 to approximately 3 million in 2016 (United States Conference of Catholic Bishops, 2018).

Most WYDs have been held in Europe and the Americas. The activity has yet to take place in continental Asia or Africa (Table 8.2), and this is likely owing to the easier access of Europe and the Americas for large numbers of Catholic youth. The event is usually held in countries with large Catholic populations. Also noteworthy is the fact that in most cases these events occur in cities that are not considered sacred by the church. This affirms Norman and Johnson's (2011) distinction between pilgrimage sites and pilgrimage events. According to their view, WYD is a pilgrimage event.

> Despite lacking the historical authority of longer established pilgrimages and despite not taking place at a noted sacred site, the use of the term

Table 8.2 Chronology and geography of WYD celebrations

	Year	Date	City	Country	Estimated attendance
1	1984	14–15 April	Vatican City[a]	Vatican City	300,000
2	1985	30–31 March	Rome[a]	Italy	300,000
3	1987	1–12 April	Buenos Aires	Argentina	1,000,000
4	1989	19–20 August	Santiago de Compostela[a]	Spain	600,000
5	1991	10–15 August	Częstochowa[a]	Poland	1,600,000
6	1993	10–15 August	Denver	USA	700,000
7	1995	10–15 January	Manila	Philippines	5,000,000
8	1997	19–24 August	Paris	France	1,200,000
9	2000	15–20 August	Rome[a]	Italy	2,000,000
10	2002	23–28 July	Toronto	Canada	800,000
11	2005	16–21 August	Cologne	Germany	1,200,000
12	2008	15–20 July	Sydney	Australia	400,000
13	2011	16–21 August	Madrid	Spain	1,400,000–2,000,000
14	2013	23–28 July	Rio de Janeiro	Brazil	3,700,000
15	2016	26–31 July	Kraków	Poland	3,000,000
16	2019	22–27 January	Panama City	Panama	n/a

[a]Considered sacrosanct by the Catholic Church.
Source: Based on Jackowski *et al.* (2017) and United States Conference of Catholic Bishops (2018).

'pilgrimage' in reference to the event should be of particular note to scholars of religion, as traditional uses of the term connect it with one or both of these features. (Norman & Johnson, 2011: 371)

The variable attendance rates, including the high of 5 million in the Philippines in 1995 and 3.7 million in 2014 in Brazil, likely has something to do with the critical mass of Catholics in those countries and the intensity of believers compared to non-believers in the population. It might also relate to the popularity of the pope in power at the time.

Like WYD, Christian music festivals are becoming an increasingly popular medium for devotion, worship and fellowship (Johnston, 2011). In these, youth (and others) learn the gospel through the language of music but also through the spoken word. These events become 'spaces of ideological consumption' and

> …always felt like an incredible adrenaline rush… the high-pitched fervour of the emotional spiritual experiences to be had under the swirling lights, as Christian rock and pop musicians worked the stage, their messages of testimony pouring out of the loudspeakers… It was hard not to be swept away into this environment – to ground oneself in the weight of the promises on offer. Following Jesus and living in accord with his plan would bring peace and happiness (not to mention eternal life!) – a welcome prospect in the world of stress, loneliness and uncertainty that often characterizes teenage existence. (Pastoor *et al.*, 2014: 47)

Dozens of Christian youth music festivals are held each year throughout the world. Lifest, held each year in Oshkosh, Wisconsin, is one of the most popular in the United States and draws 15,000–20,000 participants each year and a star-studded lineup of Christian rock musicians. Lifest's purpose is to help Christian youth affirm their faith and to convert non-Christians to conservative Christianity. It also provides 'a space in which Christian youth can experience elements akin to mainstream popular culture that they will find attractive… but in a protective setting' (Pastoor *et al.*, 2014: 50; see also Pastoor *et al.*, 2018).

Liturgical Drama

Pageants and other theatrical performances are the best examples of Christian liturgical drama. Plays and pageants are a unique way in which Christian churches commemorate historical events, evangelize and provide public worship. Perhaps the most famous Christian theatrical performance in the world takes place in the German village of Oberammergau. Since 1634, this passion play has been performed on outdoor stages, depicting the final part of Jesus' life from the time he arrived in Jerusalem until his crucifixion and resurrection three days later. The performance occurs every 10 years and lasts 5 months during that year (Stevenson,

2015). At the time of writing, the last scheduled presentation took place from May to October 2010, so the next play iteration will be performed in 2020. In 2010, approximately half a million people were privileged to have seen the performance (Stevenson, 2011). The play involves more than 2000 cast members, technical assistants and musicians selected from the village's population. Owing to its fame and infrequency, there is very high demand for the decadal performance. The passion play is a hot commodity, and package tours of Europe during years that end in zero frequently include participation in the event. Many tour operators buy the best seats in the open-air 4700-person capacity Passion Play Theater for resale to their traveling customers, and the village streets are overrun by commercial establishments selling passion play-related souvenirs (Stevenson, 2011). The theater has been expanded and renovated several times to accommodate the growing popularity of the play, and the community is heavily dependent upon the performance for its economic well-being.

Over the past 350 years, this Bavarian Alpine play has become an essential part of Oberammergau's identity. Only people born in the village or who have lived there for at least 20 years are eligible to perform. Only then are they reckoned to be vested enough in the community's theater-based heritage identity. Any changes to the play must be approved by the community by popular consent, which enables community members to be more empowered in producing this event and more identifiable with this liturgical theater performance (Montgomery, 2011).

Despite its tremendous popularity, since the Second World War, Oberammergau's Passion Play has been dogged by controversy. One issue has been the Catholic monopoly over the play. The Protestant faithful from the area of Oberammergau have argued for the right to be involved in its production; they won the right to participate in 1990 (Montgomery, 2011).

The most serious debate surrounding the performance has been its anti-Semitic bent and accusations that it was sympathetic to the Nazi cause during the 1930s (Friedman, 1984). Until relatively recently, it tended to over-blame the Jews for the execution of Christ. Even Adolf Hitler was said to have approved of the production's anti-Semitic undertones (Shapiro, 2000). During the 1970s, and even into the 1990s, with input from Jewish organization representatives, the pageant's contents were revised to reflect a more Jewish-friendly and more authentic New Testament version of the Easter story. A few Jewish characters have been eliminated, Jesus is portrayed more as a Jew, Jesus and his disciples pray in Hebrew, Romans are emphasized more as the 'bad guys' rather than the Jews and certain scriptural references have been removed (Shapiro, 2000).

There are many other Easter dramas throughout the Christian world that are important manifestations of community Christian theater.

Outside the famous passion play of Oberammergau, many different Christian denominations put on Easter pageants, although the most common are Catholic productions in Europe (Baraniecka-Olszewska, 2014a, 2014b; Cerutti & Piva, 2015). Nonetheless, in North America, many are held by various Lutheran, Latter-day Saint, Baptist, Anglican, Cornerstone Full Gospel, Methodist and Church of Christ denominations. There are several in North America also that are produced in ecumenical fashion by interfaith groups and community theater organizations.

Baraniecka-Olszewska (2014b: 41) suggests that these passion theater productions in Poland are a new way of involving modern Catholics in the liturgical aspects of the church due to crucial changes in Polish Catholicism. Observing these plays and participating in them can help meet the evolving spiritual needs and requirements of the contemporary faithful in ways that invest their emotions and engage them personally.

The LDS Church has established several liturgical dramatic events around several themes, including the Easter story (passion of Christ), the establishment of the church and the events leading up to it, occurrences depicted in the Book of Mormon and later events in the history of the church. Six major pageants are held in the United States and one in the United Kingdom with hundreds of thousands of Mormon and non-Mormon spectators attending each year (LoMonaco, 2009; Todras-Whitehall, 2007). The most famous of these is the Hill Cumorah Pageant in Palmyra, New York, where the church's founder ostensibly received ancient plates from which he translated the Book of Mormon in the 19th century (Gurgel, 1975). These events, together with accounts from the Book of Mormon, are the focus of this liturgical drama (Armstrong & Argetsinger, 1989; LoMonaco, 2009; McHale, 1985). With the exception of the Easter Pageant in Mesa, Arizona, which is based strictly on the New Testament account of the passion of Christ, most of the LDS Church's sanctioned pageants are distinctive in that they demonstrate a unique simultaneity of witnessing of Christ and retelling church history – the church's hallmark inseparability of doctrine and heritage.

Conclusion

Business meetings, conferences, conventions and revivals have long been an important part of the missionary efforts of Christian churches and a means of conducting official business. Related to these are the increasingly popular youth festivals or youth revivals that are aimed at evangelizing among younger generations who are more technology dependent and who face many forces in the world that run counter to Christian teachings. The programming and execution of such mega-events demonstrate efforts to desecularize the lives of participants in a world that is becoming progressively secular and which is increasingly choosing to distance itself from biblical teachings. Most Christian churches put on events geared toward the youth in an effort to offset the worldly influences they face each day. Desecularization is undertaken in many ways, including through music, motivational speakers, sharing testimonies, instructional media, social media, mobile phone apps, fellowship with hundreds or thousands of other Christians and field trips to shrines and sacred sites.

Liturgical theater has been an important messenger of the biblical gospel for hundreds of years. Small-scale events are portrayed locally each Christmas with the Nativity being re-enacted countless times all over the world. Several Easter pageants, or passion plays, are very well known and attract the gaze of hundreds of thousands of believers and non-believers each year, with the hope that the non-believers will be touched by what they see and hear. This type of community theater provides spiritual nourishment for attendees and cast members. Many such activities are uni-denominational, while it is becoming more common for inter-denominational efforts to share the Christian message. Some of these are one-off events, while others are long-standing occurrences that are performed regularly, having become significant tourist attractions – anchor attractions of iconic value in some cases (e.g. Oberammergau).

The journeys of religious leaders influence their followers to travel and attend religious gatherings of various sorts by setting a personal example (e.g. Pope John II, a very frequent traveler) or by recommending travel to followers. The appearance of church heads, such as during papal visits, often increases tourist visitations to certain places and can even render them quasi-sacred spaces on a temporary basis.

Christian events are manifold and diverse, and they occur throughout the world. While most traditional pilgrimage in Christianity has focused on physical spaces, either a religious shrine or the pathway to get there, the rapid growth of celebrations and events and how participants view their experiences while attending them show that pilgrimage now reaches more broadly. Thus, even events taking place in traditionally non-sacred spaces are deemed sacrosanct, and attendance becomes just as much a pilgrimage as traditional physical mobilities ever were. Through this process, ephemeral spaces and times can become sanctified by the messages they share and the spirit they educe.

9 Conclusion

Religious travel is a multidimensional phenomenon that encompasses spiritual growth, fulfilling obligations, communion with deity and expressions of devotion (Barber, 1993; Eade & Albera, 2017; Tomasi, 2002). However, it also involves commercialization and commoditization, economic development, community resources and public relations, conflict and conflict resolution, health and wellness, as well as geopolitics and propaganda. In the modern era, the boundaries between pilgrimage and tourism no longer exist. They are in many ways a reflection of one another. This book aims to address many of these issues. It describes, assesses and illuminates many of the patterns and trends associated with modern-day Christian travel and tourism.

Moufakkir *et al.* (in press) have clarified with regard to Muslim travelers that not all journeys undertaken by Muslims qualify as 'Islamic tourism' or 'halal tourism'. Many Muslims, including non-practicing Muslims, in fact seek leisure experiences that have nothing to do with their religion. Likewise, just as Moufakkir *et al.* suggest regarding Muslims, our focus in this book has been travel for religious or spiritual purposes, but we recognize that not all Christians undertaking trips or holiday vacations qualify as being part of 'Christian travel'. Christians are prolific travelers for a wide range of purposes; not all of their motives are faith oriented and not all have been a part of this discussion, nor should they be. Here, we have focused attention on the manifestations and outcomes of Christians' faith-based travel.

While the Catholic and Orthodox churches have maintained the importance of pilgrimage as an outward demonstration of faith shortly after the death of Christ to the present, the Protestant Reformation and its anti-pilgrimage stance ended the widespread practice among many reformist Christian organizations. Although mainstream Protestantism forbade pilgrimage after the 16th century, today Protestants of many denominations are enthusiastic travelers who visit sites in the Holy Land, throughout the Mediterranean and places in Europe associated with the Reformation (Breger *et al.*, 2012). Because newer Protestant and Restorationist denominations were not involved in the 1517–1648 Christian schism, they are generally not restricted from undertaking pilgrimages, although many do not have official doctrines or practices regarding this devotional form of travel. However, this does not prevent them from carrying out pilgrimage-like journeys to places associated with the life of Christ and his apostles or to church history sites. In fact, in many younger Christian denominations, such journeys are encouraged as a way of connecting with God, building faith, strengthening testimony and evangelizing.

These basic tenets, which vary widely throughout Christianity, have resulted in various patterns of travel, some of which are unique to certain denominations while others are standard across the realm of Christianity. Denominational differences in sites and activities derive from diverse churches' histories, their views of deity, their heroification of particular characters, their contrasting scriptural interpretations and how they view their apostolic and proselytizing responsibilities. These diverging perspectives have resulted in inimitable Christian geographies, particularly in the Holy Land and the Mediterranean where certain places are venerated above others or neglected altogether.

By virtue of following Christ's example, most Christians are service oriented. They serve others frequently and in many ways. This is an underlying tenet of Christianity that derives from the Bible and the teachings of Jesus. This is typically observable in people rendering humanitarian aid during times of crisis, visiting the widowed and needy, volunteering in public service agencies (e.g. foodbanks and homeless shelters), donating money to worthwhile causes (e.g. animal shelters, Christian charities, environmental foundations), serving missions and working with troubled youth, to name but a few opportunities. These altruistic endeavors manifest in travel in what is commonly referred to as volunteer tourism. Christian volunteer tourists play many different roles, including short-term missionaries, longer-term missionaries, amateur archaeologists, solidarity supporters and workers at shrines, sacred sites and church history locations. These efforts are an act of personal pilgrimage, a way of giving of oneself for the greater good of society.

Demand for Christian travel has also resulted in the development of themed spaces, especially during the past 20 years. There are more than 200 Christian-themed places throughout the world, but the majority of them that function as salient tourist attractions are located in the United States and Israel, although increasing numbers are being built in South America, Asia and Europe (Bielo, 2016b). For some people who might not have the time or means to visit the Holy Land in person, many Bible theme parks, museums, gardens and Jesus-centered monuments become 'intervening opportunities', or affordable substitutes that can pacify their desire to visit the lands where Jesus walked (Goh, 2017). For many consumers, the lack of authenticity and the hyper-reality of these Disneyized landscapes have little bearing on their experience, for their Holy Land encounter is subjective; it lies within them and is determined by how they choose to experience it rather than being literally in Israel and Palestine.

Historically, Christian pilgrimage was as much about the route taken as it was about the destination, or even more so. Through the centuries after the crucifixion of Jesus, as devotees began journeying to sacred shrines in the Holy Land and to sites of Marian apparitions, clear and distinct pathways or trails were developed in an organic manner. Through the Reformation, when pilgrimage was frowned upon, many pilgrim ways fell into dereliction and were overgrown with vegetation and construction. Even Catholics, diverging from centuries of tradition, became more fixated on the pilgrimage center rather than the pathway leading to it. However, in recent decades, many of the old-time pilgrim trails have been revived, renovated and re-marked, and they have once again become distinguished pathways on which pilgrims can commune with deity, humble themselves, seek forgiveness through physical exertion and prepare themselves psycho-spiritually to arrive at their sacred terminus. Simultaneously, these organic trails have become consumable products for non-pilgrims, or pilgrims of a different sort. Non-Christians now frequently utilize these footpaths (e.g. Camino de Santiago and Via Francigena) as sightseeing trails and for cathartic reasons they might not acknowledge being true pilgrimages in the Christian sense of the word. Instead, they represent secular pilgrimages for appreciating nature and culture, undertaken out of a desire to find their own place in the universe (Digance, 2006; Liutikas, 2014).

The growing socio-economic importance of these organic pilgrim trails since the 1980s has prompted the deliberate development of new forms of religious routes whose aim is economic development, heritage awareness and conservation. These purposive trails are found throughout the world, but organizations such as the European Institute of Cultural Routes have encouraged their establishment for these very purposes (Berti, 2010; Timothy & Saarinen, 2013), making them extremely popular throughout Europe. Many of these intentional trails and routes have Christian themes, particularly those associated with saints, church and monastery architectural styles, and certain churchly political movements. Regardless of whether or not a trail is purposive or organic, it plays a salient part in the lives of communities of pilgrims and communities along them in developing solidarity and a sense of *communitas* and pride in place.

All Christian sects organize and carry out events. These may be for business, missionary, fundraising, cultural celebrations, religious holidays or many other purposes. Visits by ecclesiastical leaders can be a major event that draws thousands or millions of people from a local area and abroad. Papal visits, for example, are large-scale mega-events, which from the community's perspective, is a major tourism occurrence. The same is true of church conferences and revival meetings. In Catholicism, papal visits to a shrine or holy place can render it holier and more desirable as a visitor attraction. This can be used as a 'brand' or an image enhancer for both spiritual and commercial purposes. Many denominations and multifaith ecumenical groups organize one-off or annual women's conferences and youth motivational congresses. The main aims of these are to provide continued Bible instruction, fellowship with like-minded believers and conversions and re-conversions, all in an effort to 'desecularize' an increasingly secular world in a safe and protected Christian environment. Liturgical theatrical performances have similar goals but are usually more open to multidenominational participation and traditional tour package-oriented tourism. Many churches and multi-church organizations hold plays, pageants and holiday celebrations that meet the needs of community members and tourists.

Finally, despite many faith societies' desire to remain altruistic, service oriented and spiritual in their quest to satisfy the needs of pilgrims and other religious travelers, the commoditization of the sacred has become inevitable. Signs of the commercialization of Christianity can be found in the writings of early pilgrims to the Holy Land, Rome and Santiago de Compostela. Today, for the most part, destination communities view religious travel as an economic development tool that should be promoted among pilgrims and other tourists. Branding exercises, quality customer care, massive marketing, developing biblical and Jesus theme parks, selling tour packages and cruises, organizing mega-events and catering souvenirs and symbolisms to the wants and needs of tourists have resulted in the commercialization of the Christian sacred, probably more so than in relation to any other religion, Hinduism, Buddhism, Judaism, Sikhism and Islam included.

What Lies Ahead?

As this book has clearly indicated throughout, we know much about Christianity and Christian beliefs as stimuli for travel, but many questions remain unanswered. As Christianity is the largest religion in the world and its travel and tourism components manifest in so many unique ways, there is considerable scope for additional work.

Many studies have examined people's motivations for undertaking pilgrimages, although most of the work has been done outside the realm of Christianity. Pilgrims and other Christian devotional travelers are assumed to be motivated overwhelmingly by the desire to seek communion with God, to walk in the footsteps of Jesus, to seek clemency for wrongdoing, to build faith and to fellowship with co-religionists. These customary incentives, however, may no longer even comprise the primary motives in the dynamic travel marketplace of the new millennium, yet many researchers continue to operate instinctively based on these assumptions, whether tested or not. Little is known about other motivations for utilizing sacred spaces. For instance, increasing numbers of monasteries are becoming involved in non-religious tourism, especially that of a holistic and restorative nature, capitalizing on their role as 'spiritual centers' to help people re-balance their lives, get back to nature and seek guidance for healthful living (Bond *et al.*, 2015; Ouellette *et al.*, 2005; Ryan & McKenzie, 2003). The same is true regarding pilgrimage trails. Frequently, recreational and touristic use of traditional pilgrim routes exceeds their use by puritan wayfarers. These trends reflect a current paradigmatic shift from pilgrimage and religious tourism to spiritual tourism and well-being, which is much broader and encompasses deeper experiences and more diverse parameters. This is even more poignant when one considers that spirituality and religiosity are not synonymous; non-believers can have spiritual experiences, and some believers may not seek transcendent growth.

One of the most vexing questions is how the Christian travel experience affects a person's life following the journey. Like the work on motivations, or the assumptions related thereto, many conjectures are made about the short- and long-term outcomes of Christian tourism encounters. Most research on this topic has been done in the context of volunteer tourism, especially as regards mission service, but it is also important for us to know how other religious volunteer experiences and other Christian travel events affect people's lives. This is particularly needful for the subfields of events, volunteer work, themed environments and use of pilgrim trails (Frey, 2004). What outcomes beyond deeper faith, tighter testimonies and enriched socialization can be expected from these sorts of experiences? Understanding the socio-spiritual, cultural and inner journeyings that result from the wide range of faith opportunities and encounters described herein is crucial to being able to manage sites, experiences and products more effectively.

Sacred spaces, holy shrines, fabricated themed environments and Christian events necessarily have unique management requirements that are different from other heritage localities and consumer milieus (Hughes *et al.*, 2013; Olsen, 2006a; Olsen & Ron, 2013; Trono, 2017; Wiltshier & Griffiths, 2016). Because so many people visit with preconceived ideas and expectations about what they will encounter, policies, practices and management frameworks must be adaptable and take into account the unique needs of the spiritually driven, as well as the secularly minded who share overlapping spaces and consumer corresponding experiences.

In addition, management approaches should consider the new age of technology in how the Christian travel message is disseminated. Changes in demand among younger generations for alternative enterprises and occurrences, as illustrated by the growing number of Christian rock festivals and other outreach programs that appeal to more youthful church cohorts, are a necessity in the current religious climate. The degree to which pilgrimage organizations, religious site managers, Christian tourism service providers and destination communities adopt modern technology may determine whether or not they remain competitive as visitor destinations in the decades to come. How places, organizations and services can use social media to their advantage in a religious travel context compared to other forms of tourism has not been well addressed (Gelbman & Laven, 2016; Goh, 2017). Likewise, with only a few minor exceptions, recent work on smart tourism and smart destinations (Narbona & Arasa, 2016) all but ignores religious tourism. These and progressively more important technology tools, such as mobile phone apps and augmented reality (Antunes & Amaro, 2016; Ramos *et al.*, 2016), may have particularly beneficial uses in religious tourism contexts, yet they are understudied. Perhaps these new technologies run counter to the long-held pilgrimage associations of simplicity, plainness and austerity, but without additional research, this remains unknown.

Despite all that is currently known about religion and tourism, there remains a sizable dearth of knowledge about Christianity-driven travel. Within Christianity, there are multitudes of different denominations, all of which sponsor or encourage some types and scales of mobility, whether local or global. While all of Christianity shares a common belief in the divinity of Jesus Christ, each denomination has unique beliefs, doctrines and practices that translate into human mobility for touristic purposes or otherwise. It would behoove researchers to move beyond the mainstream denominations to investigate nuanced differences between sects to understand how differing doctrines and practices play out in travel-seeking. The extant literature focuses overwhelmingly on several main denominations, including Eastern Orthodoxy, Roman Catholicism, Protestantism in general and Latter-day Saints. This is obvious from the examples provided in this book. The heavy reliance on these churches for empirical fodder is not a reflection of these being more highly prioritized by the authors but rather a result of the high volume of published knowledge in the academic literature. We need to know about a broader range of denominations and sub-denominations. What are their differences and commonalities? What are their unique church sacredscapes? And how do these differences or similarities manifest in travel?

While the focus of this book has been the physical movement of people from their home environments to hallowed localities throughout the world, perhaps the most important Christian voyage is the journey within. The inner journey from selfishness to service, from secularity to spirituality, from self to solidarity and from skeptic to Savior is what most Christians desire. Dowson (2016: 12) concedes that although Christians make physical and geographical journeys of spiritual importance, 'they also make a spiritual journey of inner transformation', for there is no requirement for physical mobility to gain salvation. We hope this book reflects this transformation in people and place, has set the tone for additional research in this needful area of scholarship and has raised more questions than it has answered.

References

Abu Dayyeh, H.E. (2005) Rethinking Holy Land and the Lands of the Bible: Marketing a Strategy for the Future. Unpublished manuscript in possession of Amos Ron.

Adair, J. (2016) Mesa Easter pageant: 'Jesus the Christ'. *Deseret News*, 17 March. See https://www.deseretnews.com/article/865650276/Mesa-Easter-Pageant-Jesus-the-Christ.html (accessed 10 November 2017).

Adie, B.A., Hall, C.M. and Prayag, G. (2018) World Heritage as a placebo brand: A comparative analysis of three sites and marketing implications. *Journal of Sustainable Tourism* 26, 399–415.

Afferni, R., Ferrario, C. and Mangano, S. (2011) A place of emotions: The sacred mount of Varallo. *Tourism* 59 (3), 369–386.

Agnew, M. (2014) *Where heaven touched earth: Encountering place and person at Lourdes*. Doctoral dissertation, McMaster University.

Agnew, M. (2015) 'Spiritually, I'm always in Lourdes': Perceptions of home and away among serial pilgrims. *Studies in Religion/Sciences Religieuses* 44 (4), 516–535.

Aguilar Ros, A. (2017) Transcending symbols: The religious landscape of pilgrimage studies in Mexico. In D. Albera and J. Eade (eds) *New Pathways in Pilgrimage Studies: Global Perspectives* (pp. 142–161). London: Routledge.

Ahmed, Z.U. (1992) Islamic pilgrimage (Hajj) to Ka'aba in Makkah (Saudi Arabia): An important international tourism activity. *Journal of Tourism Studies* 3 (1), 35–43.

Ahn, Y.K. (2007) Adaptive reuse of abandoned historic churches: Building type and public perception. Unpublished PhD dissertation, Texas A&M University.

Albala, K. (2011) Historical background to food and Christianity. In K. Albala and T. Eden (eds) *Food and Faith in Christian Culture* (pp. 7–19). New York: Columbia University Press.

Alegre, J. and Garau, J. (2010) Tourist satisfaction and dissatisfaction. *Annals of Tourism Research* 37 (1), 52–73.

Alegro, C. (2008) Aquí la gente siente paz y vuelve con más fe. *La Milonga Argentina* 3 (30), 26–27.

Alexopoulos, G. (2013) Management of living religious heritage: Who sets the agenda? The case of the monastic community of Mount Athos. *Conservation and Management of Archaeological Sites* 15 (1), 59–75.

Allison, R.S. (1997) Great tradition/little tradition. In T.A. Green (ed.) *Folklore: An Encyclopedia of Beliefs, Customs, Tales, Music, and Art* (Vol. 1; pp. 426–428). Santa Barbara, CA: ABC-CLIO.

Al-Rimmawi, H. and Butcher, S. (2015) Trends of tourism in Bethlehem, Palestine: 1994–2015. *Tourism* 63 (3), 317–335.

al-Saadi, Y. (2014) Mecca's changing face: Rejuvenation or destruction? *Al-Akhbar*, 5 March. See http://english.al-akhbar.com/content/meccas-changing-face-rejuvenation-or-destruction?utm_source=feedburner&utm_medium=feed&utm_campaign=Feed%3A+AlAkhbarEnglish+(Al+Akhbar+English) (accessed 15 July 2016).

Amaro, S., Antunes, A. and Henriques, C. (2018) A closer look at Santiago de Compostela's pilgrims through the lens of motivations. *Tourism Management* 64, 271–280.

Ambaw, Z.G. (2015) Potentials and challenges of Entoto Saint Mary Church to heritage tourism development. *Journal of Hospitality Management and Tourism* 6 (5), 47–59.

Ambrósio, V. (2011) Religious tourism and the Lent pilgrimages in Sao Miguel, Azores. *International Journal of Business and Globalisation* 7 (1), 14–28.

Ambrósio, V. and Pereira, M. (2007) Christian/Catholic pilgrimage: Studies and analyses. In R. Raj and N.D. Morpeth (eds) *Religious Tourism and Pilgrimage Festivals Management: An International Perspective* (pp. 140–152). Wallingford: CABI.

Ambrósio, V. and Santos, C. (2012) Understanding parish pilgrimages in Portugal. In K. Griffith and R. Raj (eds) *Reflecting on Religious Tourism and Pilgrimage* (pp. 14–28). Arnhem: ATLAS.

Anderson, P.L. (1980) Heroic nostalgia: Enshrining the Mormon past. *Sunstone* 22, 47–55.

Andriotis, K. (2009) Sacred site experience: A phenomenological study. *Annals of Tourism Research* 36 (1), 64–84.

Answers in Genesis (2016) Prepare to believe. See http://creationmuseum.org/ (accessed 30 July 2016).

Anton-Clavé, S. (2007) *The Global Theme Park Industry*. Wallingford: CABI.

Antunes, A. and Amaro, S. (2016) Pilgrims' acceptance of a mobile app for the Camino de Santiago. In A. Inversini and R. Schegg (eds) *Information and Communication Technologies in Tourism* (pp. 509–521). Cham: Springer.

Apostolopoulos, Y., Sönmez, S. and Timothy, D.J. (eds) (2001) *Women as Producers and Consumers of Tourism in Developing Regions*. Westport, CT: Praeger.

Archaeological Seminars Institute (2006) Dig for a day. See http://www.archesem.com/dig.asp (accessed 30 January 2018).

Ariel, Y. (2006) An unexpected alliance: Christian Zionism and its historical significance. *Modern Judaism* 26 (1), 74–100.

Armstrong, R.N. and Argetsinger, G.S. (1989) The Hill Cumorah Pageant: Religious pageantry as suasive form. *Text and Performance Quarterly* 9 (2), 153–164.

Arya, A.N. and Nouvet, E. (2018) Host experience: A brief survey of the literature. In A.N. Arya and J. Evert (eds) *Global Health Experiential Education: From Theory to Practice* (pp. 163–179). London: Routledge.

Aslan, D. and Andriotis, K. (2009) Clustering Visitors to a Religious Island: The Case of Tinos. Paper presented at the International Conference on Tourism Development and Management (ICTDM): Tourism in a Changing World: Prospects and Challenges, 11–15 September, Kos Island, Greece.

Associates for Biblical Research (2018) The Shiloh Excavations 2018. See https://www.biblearchaeology.org/page/Volunteer-to-Dig-at-Shiloh.aspx (accessed 14 February 2018).

Åstrøm, J.K. (2017) Theme factors that drive the tourist customer experience. *International Journal of Culture, Tourism and Hospitality Research* 11 (2), 125–141.

Aulet, S. and Hakobyan, K. (2011) Turismo religioso y espacios sagrados: Una propuesta para los santuarios de Catalunya. *Revista Iberoamericana de Turismo* 1 (1), 63–82.

Aulet, S., Mundet, L. and Vidal, D. (2017) Monasteries and tourism: Interpreting sacred landscape through gastronomy. *Revista Brasileira de Pesquisa em Turismo* 11 (1), 175–196.

Aviva, E. (2001) *Following the Milky Way: A Pilgrimage on the Camino de Santiago*. Boulder, CO: Pilgrim's Process.

Avraham, E. and Ketter, E. (2008) *Media Strategies for Marketing Places in Crisis: Improving the Image of Cities, Countries and Tourist Destinations*. Oxford: Butterworth-Heinemann.

Badone, E. (2014) New pilgrims on a medieval route: Mobility and community on the Tro Breiz. *Culture and Religion* 15 (4), 452–473.

Badone, E. and Roseman, S.R. (2004a) Approaches to the anthropology of pilgrimage and tourism. In E. Badone and S.R. Roseman (eds) *Intersecting Journeys: The Anthropology of Pilgrimage and Tourism* (pp. 1–23). Chicago, IL: University of Illinois Press.
Badone, E. and Roseman, S.R. (2004b) *Intersecting Journeys: The Anthropology of Pilgrimage and Tourism*. Chicago, IL: University of Illinois Press.
Bajc, V. (2006) Christian pilgrimage groups in Jerusalem: Framing the experience through linear meta-narrative. *Journeys* 7 (2), 101–128.
Bajc, V. (2007) Creating ritual through narrative, place and performance in evangelical Protestant pilgrimage to the Holy Land. *Mobilities* 2 (3), 395–412.
Bajc, V. (2011) Security meta-framing of collective activity in public spaces: The Pope John Paul II in the Holy City. In V. Bajc and W. de Lint (eds) *Security and Everyday Life* (pp. 49–76). London: Routledge.
Bajc, V., Coleman, S. and Eade, J. (2007) Introduction: Mobility and centering in pilgrimage. *Mobilities* 2 (3), 321–329.
Bakalova, E. (2002) La vénération des icônes miraculeuses en Bulgarie: Aspects historiques et contemporains d'un pèlerinage. *Ethnologie Française* 37, 261–274.
Ballantyne, R., Hughes, K. and Bond, N. (2016) Using a Delphi approach to identify managers' preferences for visitor interpretation at Canterbury Cathedral World Heritage Site. *Tourism Management* 54, 72–80.
Bandyopadhyay, R. (2018) Volunteer tourism and religion: The cult of Mother Teresa. *Annals of Tourism Research* 70, 133–136.
Bandyopadhyay, R. and Patil, V. (2017) 'The white woman's burden': The racialized, gendered politics of volunteer tourism. *Tourism Geographies* 19 (4), 644–657.
Banica, M. (2016) Coach pilgrimage: Religion, pilgrimage, and tourism in contemporary Romania. *Tourist Studies* 16 (1), 74–87.
Bar, D. and Cohen-Hattab, C. (2003) A new kind of pilgrimage: The modern tourist pilgrim of nineteenth century and early twentieth century Palestine. *Middle Eastern Studies*, 39 (2), 131–148.
Baraniecka-Olszewska, K. (2014a) Golgotha on city peripheries: The passion play in Bygdoszcz Fordon. *Folklore* 56, 67–92.
Baraniecka-Olszewska, K. (2014b) The role of the religious crowd in the mass Catholic events: The passion play and nativity play in Warsaw. *Anthropological Notebooks* 20 (2), 27–43.
Barber, R. (1993) *Pilgrimages*. London: The Boydell Press.
Bartholomew, C. and Llewelyn, R. (2004) Introduction. In C. Bartholomew and F. Hughes (eds) *Explorations in a Christian Theology of Pilgrimage* (pp. xii–xvi). Aldershot: Ashgate.
Battour, M.M., Ismail, M.N. and Battor, M. (2010) Toward a halal tourism market. *Tourism Analysis* 15 (4), 461–470.
Battour, M.M., Ismail, M.N. and Battor, M. (2011) The impact of destination attributes on Muslim tourists' choice. *International Journal of Tourism Research* 13 (6), 527–540.
BBC News (2015) Pope Francis in Manila: Six million attend outdoor Mass. 18 January. See http://www.bbc.com/news/world-asia-30869019 (accessed 30 January 2018).
Beal, T.K. (2005) *Roadside Religion: In Search of the Sacred, the Strange, and the Substance of Faith*. Boston, MA: Beacon Press.
Bebbington, D.W. (2008) *Evangelicals in Modern Britain: A History from the 1730s to the 1980s*. London: Unwin.
Beck, J.A. (2017) *The Holy Land for Christian Travelers: An Illustrated Guide to Israel*. Grand Rapids, MI: Baker Books.
Beeton, S. (2005) *Film-Induced Tourism*. Clevedon: Channel View Publications.
Belhassen, Y. (2007) Evangelical tours to the Holy Land: A study on the theopolitics of Christian pilgrimages. Unpublished doctoral dissertation, University of Illinois.

Belhassen, Y. (2009) Fundamentalist Christian pilgrimages as a political and cultural force. *Journal of Heritage Tourism* 4 (2), 131–144.

Belhassen, Y. and Ebel, J. (2009) Tourism, faith and politics in the Holy Land: An ideological analysis of evangelical pilgrimage. *Current Issues in Tourism* 12 (4), 359–378.

Belhassen, Y. and Santos, C.A. (2006) An American evangelical pilgrimage to Israel: A case study on politics and triangulation. *Journal of Travel Research* 44 (4), 431–441.

Belhassen, Y., Caton, K. and Stewart, W.P. (2008) The search for authenticity in the pilgrim experience. *Annals of Tourism Research* 35 (3), 668–689.

Belhassen, Y., Uriely, N. and Assor, O. (2014) The touristification of a conflict zone: The case of Bil'in. *Annals of Tourism Research* 49, 174–189.

Benson, A. (ed.) (2008) *Volunteer Tourism: Theoretical Frameworks and Practical Applications*. London: Routledge.

Ben-Yehuda, N. (1995) *The Masada Myth: Collective Memory and Mythmaking in Israel*. Madison, WI: The University of Wisconsin Press.

Berger, P.L. (1999) The desecularization of the world: A global overview. In P.L. Berger (ed.) *The Desecularization of the World: Resurgent Religion and World Politics* (pp. 1–18). Grand Rapids, MI: Ethics and Public Policy Center.

Berman, C.H. (2000) *The Cistercian Evolution: The Invention of a Religious Order in Twelfth-Century Europe*. Philadelphia, PA: University of Pennsylvania Press.

Berti, E. (2010) European Institute of Cultural Routes: New strategies for high quality tourism in Europe. *Via Francigena* 16, 36.

Bethel Tour Vacations (2016) Scandinavia and Russia Cruise. See http://www.betheltourvacations.com/scandinavia-and-russian-cruise-2016/ (accessed 22 August 2016).

Bethlehem Christian Families Mission (2010) Olive wood history. See http://www.bcfmission.com/olive-wood-history.html (accessed 28 February 2010).

Beyerlein, K., Trinitapoli, J. and Adler, G. (2011) The effect of religious short-term mission trips on youth civic engagement. *Journal for the Scientific Study of Religion* 50 (4), 780–795.

Bhardwaj, S.M. (1973) *Hindu Places of Pilgrimage in India: A Study in Cultural Geography*. Berkeley, CA: University of California Press.

Biblical Archaeology Society (2018) Find a dig. See http://digs.bib-arch.org/ (accessed 13 February 2018).

Bideci, M. and Albayrak, T. (2016) Motivations of the Russian and German tourists visiting pilgrimage site of Saint Nicholas Church. *Tourism Management Perspectives* 18, 10–13.

Bielo, J.S. (2016a) Creationist history-making: Producing a heterodox past. In J.J. Card and D.S. Anderson (eds) *Lost City, Found Pyramid: Understanding Alternative Archaeologies and Pseudoscientific Practices* (pp. 81–101). Tuscaloosa, AL: University of Alabama Press.

Bielo, J.S. (2016b) Materializing the Bible: Ethnographic methods for the consumption process. *Practical Matters Journal* 9, 54–69.

Bielo, J.S. (2018a) *Ark Encounter: The Making of a Creationist Theme Park*. New York: New York University Press.

Bielo, J.S. (2018b) Biblical gardens and the sensuality of religious pedagogy. *Material Religion* 14 (1), 30–54.

Biema, D., Beyer, L., Klein, A., Burke, G. and Mitchell, E. (2000) Inside the pilgrimage. *Time* 155 (11), 55. See http://search.ebscohost.com/login.aspx?direct=true&db=aph&AN=2875510&site=ehost-live (accessed 27 November 2010).

Binns, J. (2002) *An Introduction to the Christian Orthodox Churches*. Cambridge: Cambridge University Press.

Blackwell, R. (2007) Motivations for religious tourism, pilgrimage, festivals and events. In R. Raj and N.D. Morpeth (eds) *Religious Tourism and Pilgrimage Management: An International Perspective* (pp. 35–47). Wallingford: CABI.

Blewett, J.E. (2004) A geography of Marian Shrines in the United States: A preliminary comparison with Western Europe. Unpublished PhD dissertation, University of Cincinnati.

Bloomfield, E.F. (2017) Ark Encounter as material apocalyptic rhetoric: Contemporary creationist strategies on board Noah's Ark. *Southern Communication Journal* 82 (5), 263–277.

Bobbitt, R.S. (2008) Applying movement success models to Marian apparition movements. Unpublished master's thesis, Central European University, Budapest.

Bond, N., Packer, J. and Ballantyne, R. (2015) Exploring visitor experiences, activities and benefits at three religious tourism sites. *International Journal of Tourism Research* 27 (5), 471–481.

Bowdin, G., Allen, J., O'Toole, W., Harris, R. and McDonnell, I. (2011) *Events Management* (3rd edn). London: Routledge.

Bowman, G. (1989) Fucking tourists: Sexual relations and tourism in Jerusalem's Old City. *Critique of Anthropology* 9 (2), 77–93.

Bowman, G. (1992) The politics of tour guiding: Israeli and Palestinian guides in Israel and the Occupied Territories. In D. Harrison (ed.) *Tourism in the Less Developed Countries* (pp. 121–134). London: Wiley.

Bowman, G. (2000) Christian ideology and the image of a Holy Land: The place of -Jerusalem pilgrimage in the various Christianities. In J. Eade and M.J. Sallnow (eds) *Contesting the Sacred: The Anthropology of Christian Pilgrimage* (pp. 98–121). Urbana, IL: University of Illinois Press.

Boyd, S.W. (2013) The Causeway Coastal Route and Saint Patrick's Trail: Heritage tourism route development in Northern Ireland. In B. Garrod and A. Fyall (eds) *Contemporary Cases in Heritage* (pp. 204–228). London: Goodfellow.

Bradley, I. (2009) *Pilgrimage: A Spiritual and Cultural Journey*. Oxford: Lion Books.

Braga, C., Soares, M. and Brito, M. (2013) A new pilgrimage in Portugal: Following the steps of Saint Nuno. *International Journal of Religious Tourism and Pilgrimage* 1 (1), 72–82.

Branham, J.R. (2008) The Crucifixion and Ice Cream: Inside Orlando's most Unusual Theme Park, the Holy Land Experience. *Newsweek*, 23 May. See http://www.newsweek.com/2008/05/22/the-crucifixion-and-ice-cream.html (accessed 14 July 2010).

Branham, J.R. (2009) The Temple that won't quit: Constructing sacred space in Orlando's Holy Land theme park. *CrossCurrents* 59 (3), 358–382.

Brayley, R.E. (2010) Managing sacred sites for tourism: A case study of visitor facilities in Palmyra, New York. *Tourism* 58 (3), 289–300.

Breathnach, T. (2006) Looking for the real me: Locating the self in heritage tourism. *Journal of Heritage Tourism* 1 (2), 100–120.

Breger, M.J., Reiter, Y. and Hammer, L. (eds) (2012) *Sacred Space in Israel and Palestine*. London: Routledge.

Bremborg, A.D. (2013) Creating sacred space by walking in silence: Pilgrimage in a late modern Lutheran context. *Social Compass* 60 (4), 544–560.

Bremer, T.S. (2000) Tourists and religion at Temple Square and Mission San Juan Capistrano. *Journal of American Folklore* 113, 422–435.

Brendon, P. (1991) *Thomas Cook: 150 Years of Popular Tourism*. London: Secker & Warburg.

Brent Plate, S. (2009) Introduction: The varieties of contemporary pilgrimage. *CrossCurrents* 59 (3), 260–267.

Brereton, B.G. (2006) Taiwan's mythological theme parks: Mnemonic guardians and uncanny imaginaries. *Acta Orientalia Vilnensia* 7 (1–2), 61–76.

Brice, J., Busby, G. and Brunt, P. (2003) English rural church tourism: A visitor typology. *Acta Turistica* 15 (2), 144–162.

Brin, E. (2006) Politically-oriented tourism in Jerusalem. *Tourist Studies* 6 (3), 215–243.

Brown, A. (2015) *Understanding Food Principles and Preparation*. Stamford, CT: Cengage.
Brown, S. (2005) Travelling with a purpose: Understanding the motives and benefits of volunteer vacationers. *Current Issues in Tourism* 8 (6), 479–496.
Brown, S. and Morrison, A.M. (2003) Expanding volunteer vacation participation: An exploratory study on the mini-mission concept. *Tourism Recreation Research* 28 (3), 73–82.
Bryman, A. (1999) The Disneyization of society. *The Sociological Review* 47 (1), 25–47.
Burge, G.M. (2009) *The Bible and the Land*. Grand Rapids, MI: Zondervan.
Burtea, I. (2009) Finding one's way into God's garden: Being a Romanian Orthodox nun. Unpublished master's thesis, Central European University, Budapest.
Busby, G. (2002) The Cornish church heritage as destination component. *Tourism* 50 (4), 371–381.
Bush, L. (2000) The long and short of mission terms: The director of AD2000 speaks of the virtues and vulnerabilities of long-term and short-term missions in Pakistan. *Mission Frontiers* 22 (1), 16–19.
Business Wire (2005) World's largest annual outdoor Easter Pageant draws crowds topping 150,000 during 10-day run. *Business Wire*, 9 March. See http://findarticles.com/p/articles/mi_m0EIN/is_2005_March_9/ai_n12416058/ (accessed 20 August 2011).
Butcher, J. and Smith, P. (2015) *Volunteer Tourism: The Lifestyle Politics of International Development*. London: Routledge.
Butler, R.W. (in press) Tourism and conflict in the Middle East. In D.J. Timothy (ed.) *Routledge Handbook on Tourism in the Middle East and North Africa*. London: Routledge.
Byrne, J.P. (2012) *Encyclopedia of the Black Death: Volume 1*. Santa Barbara, CA: ABC-CLIO.
Bywater, M. (1994) Religious travel in Europe. *Travel and Tourism Analyst* 2, 39–52.
Cahaner, L. and Mansfeld, Y. (2012) A voyage from religiousness to secularity and back: A glimpse into 'Haredi' tourists. *Journal of Heritage Tourism* 7 (4), 301–321.
Calaf, L.S. (2003) Turisme religiós: Montserrat, una destinació consolidada. *Estudis de Turisme de Catalunya* 6 (12), 18–23.
Campelo, A. (ed.) (2017) *Handbook on Place Branding and Marketing*. Cheltenham: Edward Elgar.
Campo, J.E. (1998) American pilgrimage landscapes. *Annals of the American Academy of Political and Social Sciences* 55, 40–56.
Carnegie, E. (2009) Catalysts for change? Museums of religion in a pluralist society. *Journal of Management, Spirituality & Religion* 6 (2), 157–169.
Carter, K.A. (2008) Volunteer tourism: An exploration of the perceptions and experiences of volunteer tourists and the role of authenticity in those experiences. Unpublished master's thesis, Lincoln University.
Caton, K., Pastoor, C., Belhassen, Y., Collins, B. and Wallin, M. (2013) Christian music festival tourism and positive peace. *Journal of Tourism and Peace Research* 3 (2), 21–42.
Cazaux, F. (2011) To be a pilgrim: A contested identity on Saint James' Way. *Tourism* 59 (3), 353–367.
Central Intelligence Agency (2018) *The World Factbook*. Washington, DC: Central Intelligence Agency. See https://www.cia.gov/library/publications/the-world-factbook/geos/xx.html (accessed 1 February 2018).
Černá, J. (2014) Religiousness and religious tourism in Slovakia case study. *European Journal of Science and Theology* 10 (1), 29–37.
Cerutti, S. and Dioli, I. (2013) Via Francigena mountain itineraries: The case of Piacenza Valleys. *International Journal of Religious Tourism and Pilgrimage* 1 (1), 83–92.
Cerutti, S. and Piva, E. (2015) Religious tourism and event management: An opportunity for local tourism development. *International Journal of Religious Tourism and Pilgrimage* 3 (1), 55–65.

Chadwick, J.R. (2003) Revisiting Golgotha and the Garden Tomb. *The Religious Educator* 4 (1), 13–48.
Chadwick, J.R. (2009) Khirbet Beit Lei and the Book of Mormon: An archaeologist's evaluation. *The Religious Educator* 10 (3), 17–48.
Chang, S. (2018) Experience economy in hospitality and tourism: Gain and loss values for service and experience. *Tourism Management* 64, 55–63.
Charters, S., Fountain, J. and Fish, N. (2009) 'You felt like lingering...': Experiencing 'Real' service at the winery tasting room. *Journal of Travel Research* 48 (1), 122–134.
Chatterley, L.M. (2000) *Wend Your Way: A Guide to Sites along the Iowa Mormon Trail.* Des Moines, IA: University of Iowa Press.
Chhabra, D. (2007) Exploring market influences on curator perceptions of authenticity. *Journal of Heritage Tourism* 2 (2), 110–119.
Chhabra, D. (2008) Positioning museums on an authenticity continuum. *Annals of Tourism Research* 35 (2), 427–447.
Chhabra, D. (2012) Authenticity of the objectively authentic. *Annals of Tourism Research* 39 (1), 499–502.
Chhabra, D., Healy, R. and Sills, E. (2003) Staged authenticity and heritage tourism. *Annals of Tourism Research* 30 (3), 702–719.
Chibaya, T. (2017) Pentecostalism as a drive for religious tourism development in new millennium Zimbabwe. In M. Mawere, T.R. Mubaya and J. Mukusha (eds) *The African Conundrum: Rethinking the Trajectories of Historical, Cultural, Philosophical and Developmental Experiences of Africa* (pp. 342–370). Bamenda: Langaa Research and Publishing.
Chi-Keung, Y. (2017) The curious case of discovering Noah's Ark in Hong Kong. In S. Travagnin (ed.) *Religion and Media in China: Insights and Case Studies from the Mainland, Taiwan and Hong Kong* (pp. 241–255). London: Routledge.
Chiş, A. and Ţîrca, A.M. (2009) Priors' perceptions of religious tourism and its spiritual, ethical, social and economical impacts: The case of Transylvania. Proceedings of the International Conference on Sustainable Tourism within High Risk Areas of Environmental Crisis, April 22–25, Messina, Italy.
Christensson, J. (2010) In search of learning and holiness: Scandinavians going abroad from the Middle Ages to the present. In R. Gothóni (ed.) *Pilgrims and Travellers in Search of the Holy* (pp. 53–68). Oxford: Peter Lang.
Clark, V. (2007) *Allies for Armageddon: The Rise of Christian Zionism.* New Haven, CT: Yale University Press.
Clarke, A. (2015) Paradise: The search for a better place. *Transylvanian Journal of Tourism and Territorial Development* 1 (1), 6–12.
Cleary, A. (2011) Young pilgrims: In search of treasure ancient and new. *Compass: A Review of Topical Theology* 45 (2), 19–24.
Cleary, E.L. (2009) *How Latin America Saved the Soul of the Catholic Church.* Mahwah, NJ: Paulist Press.
Cofraternity of Pilgrims to Rome (2014) All roads lead to Rome. See http://www.pilgrimstorome.org.uk/ (accessed 13 November 2017).
Coghlan, A. and Gooch, M. (2011) Applying a transformative learning framework to volunteer tourism. *Journal of Sustainable Tourism* 19 (6), 713–728.
Cohen, E. (1988) Authenticity and commoditization in tourism. *Annals of Tourism Research* 15 (3), 371–386.
Cohen, E. (1992) Pilgrimage and tourism: Convergence and divergence. In A. Morinis (ed.) *Sacred Journeys: The Anthropology of Pilgrimages* (pp. 47–61). New York: Greenwood Press.
Cohen, E. (2004) *Contemporary Tourism: Diversity and Change.* Amsterdam: Elsevier.
Cohen, E.H. (2006) Religious tourism as an educational experience. In D.J. Timothy and D.H. Olsen (eds) *Tourism, Religion and Spiritual Journeys* (pp. 78–93). London: Routledge.

Cohen, R. (2008) *Saving the Holy Sepulchre: How Rival Christians Came Together to Rescue their Holiest Shrine*. Oxford: Oxford University Press.

Cohen-Hattab, K. (2004) Zionism, tourism, and the battle for Palestine: Tourism as a political-propaganda tool. *Israel Studies* 9 (1), 61–85.

Cohen-Hattab, K. (2013) Public involvement and tourism planning in a historic city: The case of the old city of Jerusalem. *Journal of Heritage Tourism* 8 (4), 320–336.

Cohen-Hattab, K. and Shoval, N. (2007) Tourism development and cultural conflict: The case of 'Nazareth 2000'. *Social & Cultural Geography* 8 (5), 701–717.

Cohen-Hattab, K. and Shoval, N. (2015) *Tourism, Religion and Pilgrimage in Jerusalem*. London: Routledge.

Cohen Ioannides, M. and Ioannides, D. (2006) Global Jewish tourism: Pilgrimages and remembrances. In D.J. Timothy and D.H. Olsen (eds) *Tourism, Religion and Spiritual Journeys* (pp. 156–171). London: Routledge.

Coleman, S. (2004) Pilgrimage to 'England's Nazareth': Landcapes of myth and memory at Walsingham. In E. Badone and S.R. Roseman (eds) *Intersecting Journeys: the Anthropology of Pilgrimage and Tourism* (pp. 52–67). Chicago, IL: University of Illinois Press.

Coleman, S. and Elsner, J. (1995) *Pilgrimage: Past and Present in the World Religions*. Cambridge, MA: Harvard University Press.

Coleman, S. and Elsner, J. (2004) Tradition as play: Pilgrimage to 'England's Nazareth'. *History and Anthropology* 15 (3), 273–288.

Collins-Kreiner, N. (1997) Cartographic characteristics of current Christian pilgrimage maps of the Holy Land. *Cartographica* 34 (4), 45–54.

Collins-Kreiner, N. (2002) Is there a connection between pilgrimage and tourism? The Jewish religion. *International Journal of Tourism Sciences* 2 (2), 1–18.

Collins-Kreiner, N. (2010a) Researching pilgrimage: Continuity and transformations. *Annals of Tourism Research* 37 (2), 440–456.

Collins-Kreiner, N. (2010b) The geography of pilgrimage and tourism: Transformations and implications for applied geography. *Applied Geography* 30 (1), 153–164.

Collins-Kreiner, N. and Kliot, N. (2000) Pilgrimage tourism in the Holy Land: The behavioural characteristics of Christian pilgrims. *GeoJournal* 50 (1), 55–67.

Collins-Kreiner, N. and Zins, Y. (2011) Tourists and souvenirs: Changes through time, space and meaning. *Journal of Heritage Tourism* 6 (1), 17–27.

Collins-Kreiner, N., Kliot, N., Mansfeld, Y. and Sagi, K. (2006) *Christian Tourism to the Holy Land: Pilgrimage during Security Crisis*. Aldershot: Ashgate.

Conlin, M.V. and Jolliffe, L. (eds) (2011) *Mining Heritage and Tourism: A Global Synthesis*. London: Routledge.

Corbett, J.M. (1997) *Religion in America* (3rd edn). Upper Saddle River, NJ: Prentice Hall.

Corsale, A. (2017) Jewish heritage tourism in Bucharest: Reality and visions. *Geographical Journal* 183 (3), 261–271.

Costen, M. (1993) The pilgrimage to Santiago de Compostela in medieval Europe. In I. Reader and T. Walter (eds) *Pilgrimage in Popular Culture* (pp. 137–154). -London: Macmillan.

Council of Europe (2014) Cultural routes. See http://www.coe.int/t/dg4/cultureheritage/culture/routes (accessed 3 April 2016).

Cranston, R. (1958) A Protestant looks at Lourdes. See http://www.catholicpamphlets.net/pamphlets/A%20Protestant%20Looks%20at%20Lourdes.pdf (accessed 4 August 2010).

Cropera, C. (2006) On 'tour' along the Via Francigena. *Via Francigena* 24, 46–55.

Cropera, C. (2007) Spas, well-being and a break along the way. *Via Francigena* 26, 34–45.

Cunningham, L.S. and Egan, K.J. (1996) *Christian Spirituality: Themes from the Tradition*. Mahwah, NJ: Paulist Press.

Curran, J.R. (2002) *Pagan City and Christian Capital: Rome in the Fourth Century.* Oxford: Oxford University Press.

Curtis, S. (2016) English cathedrals: Events and spiritual capital. *International Journal of Religious Tourism and Pilgrimage* 4 (2), 1–11.

Curtis, S. (2018) Reaching out: Engagement through events and festivals – the cathedrals of England. In R. Butler and W. Suntikul (eds) *Tourism and Religion: Issues and Implications* (pp. 236–249). Bristol: Channel View Publications.

Dafuleya, G., Gyekye, A.B., Oseifuah, E.M., Nethengwe, T. and Sumbana, F. (2017) Religiously motivated travel and rural tourism in Vhembe District of South Africa. *Tourism Economics* 23 (4), 911–918.

Dahlberg, A. (2000) The body as a principle of holism: Three pilgrimages to Lourdes. In J. Eade and M.J. Sallnow (eds) *Contesting the Sacred: The Anthropology of Christian Pilgrimage* (pp. 30–50). Urbana, IL: University of Illinois Press.

Dakkak, I. (1981) Jerusalem's Via Dolorosa. *Journal of Palestine Studies* 11 (1), 136–149.

Daswani, G. (2013) The globalization of Pentecostalism and the limits of globalization. In J. Boddy and M. Lambek (eds) *A Companion to the Anthropology of Religion* (pp. 239–253). Oxford: Wiley.

Davidson, L.K. and Gitlitz, D.M. (2002) *Pilgrimage from the Ganges to Graceland: An Encyclopedia.* Santa Barbara, CA: ABC-Clio.

Davies, B. (2007) A divine experience. *New Statesman* 9 April, 48–49.

Davis, J.A. (2014) Historical sites. In B.S. Plewe, S.K. Brown, D.Q. Cannon and R.H. Jackson (eds) *Mapping Mormonism: An Atlas of Latter-day Saint History* (pp. 136–139). Provo, UT: BYU Press.

Davis, J.A. and Austin, K. (2002) Nauvoo, Illinois: A different kind of heritage tourism site. *Tourism Recreation Research* 27 (2), 35–40.

Davis, P. (2005) Places, 'cultural touchstones' and the ecomuseum. In G. Corsane (ed.) *Heritage, Museums and Galleries: An Introductory Reader* (pp. 365–376). London: Routledge.

de Pinho, M.R.I.B. and de Pinho, I.M.R.T. (2007) Fátima: The religious tourism altar. In R. Raj and N.D. Morpeth (eds) *Religious Tourism and Pilgrimage Festivals Management: An International Perspective* (pp. 211–221). Wallingford: CABI.

Della Dora, V. (2012) Setting and blurring boundaries: Pilgrims, tourists, and landscape in Mount Athos and Meteora. *Annals of Tourism Research* 39 (2), 951–974.

Della Dora, V., Maddrell, A. and Scafi, A. (2015) Sacred crossroads: Landscape and aesthetics in contemporary Christian pilgrimage. In S. Brunn (ed.) *The Changing World Religious Map: Sacred Places, Identities, Practices and Politics* (pp. 745–765). Dordrecht: Springer.

Dershowitz, L.K. (2014) A geographic examination of stakeholders' perceptions of ecotourism along the Israel National Trail and Jesus Trail in Israel. Unpublished master's thesis, Miami University, Ohio.

Di Giovine, M.A. (2011) Pilgrimage: Communitas and contestation, unity and difference – an introduction. *Tourism* 59 (3), 247–259.

Di Giovine, M.A. (2012) Padre Pio for sale: Souvenirs, relics, or identity markers? *International Journal of Tourism Anthropology* 2 (2), 108–127.

Di Giovine, M.A. (2016) Passionate movements: Emotional and social dynamics of Padre Pio pilgrims. In D. Picard and M. Robinson (eds) *Emotion in Motion: Tourism, Affect and Transformation* (pp. 117–138). London: Routledge.

Digance, J. (2006) Religious and secular pilgrimage: Journeys redolent with meaning. In D.J. Timothy and D.H. Olsen (eds) *Tourism, Religion and Spiritual Journeys* (pp. 36–48). London: Routledge.

Dinis, A. and Krakover, S. (2016) Niche tourism in small peripheral towns: The case of Jewish heritage in Belmonte, Portugal. *Tourism Planning & Development* 13 (3), 310–332.

Dintaman, A. and Landis, D. (2013) *Hiking the Jesus Trail and Other Biblical Walks in the Galilee* (2nd edn). Harleysville, PA: Village to Village Press.

Doi, K. (2011) Onto emerging ground: Anticlimactic movement on the Camino de Santiago de Compostela. *Tourism* 9 (3), 271–285.

Downie, D. (2013) *Paris to the Pyrenees: A Skeptic Pilgrim Walks the Way of Saint James*. New York: Open Road.

Dowson, R. (2016) Event as spiritual pilgrimage: A case study of the 'Cherish' Christian women's conference. *International Journal of Religious Tourism and Pilgrimage* 4 (2), 12–28.

Dowson, R. (2017) Towards a definition of Christian mega-events in the 21st century. *International Journal of Religious Tourism and Pilgrimage* 5 (3), 1–18.

du Plooy, S. (2017) South(ern) African journeys of reverance. In D. Albera and J. Eade (eds) *New Pathways in Pilgrimage Studies: Global Perspectives* (pp. 124–141). London: Routledge.

Dubisch, J. (1990) Pilgrimage and popular religion at a Greek holy shrine. In E. Badone (ed.) *Religious Orthodoxy & Popular Faith in European Society* (pp. 113–139). Princeton, NJ: Princeton University Press.

Dubisch, J. (1995) *In a Different Place: Pilgrimage, Gender and Politics of a Greek Island*. Princeton, NJ: Princeton University Press.

Dubisch, J. (2009) Toward a 'Poetics of Personhood': Beyond Honor and Shame. Lecture delivered at the 2009 Platsis Symposium, University of Michigan, 13 September.

Dugan, B. (1994) Religion and food service. *The Cornell Hotel and Restaurant Administration Quarterly* 35 (6), 80–85.

Duncan, K. (2009) *In the Footsteps of Paul: Experience the Journey that Changed the World*. Nashville, TN: Thomas Nelson.

Dunn, J.D.G. (2006) *The Theology of Paul the Apostle*. Grand Rapids, MI: Erdmans Publishing Co.

Dwyer, L., Forsyth, P. and Dwyer, W. (2010) *Tourism Economics and Policy*. Bristol: Channel View Publications.

Dyas, D. (2014) Pilgrims and Pilgrimage: The Reformation Onwards. See www.york.ac.uk/projects/pilgrimage/content/reform.html (accessed 25 September 2016).

Dyer, C.H. and Hatteberg, G.A. (2014) *The Christian Traveler's Guide to the Holy Land* (2nd edn). Chicago, IL: Moody.

Dziubiński, Z. (2009) Tourism through the eyes of the Holy See. *Physical Culture and Sport Studies and Research* 46, 254–250.

Eade, J. (1992) Pilgrimage and tourism at Lourdes, France. *Annals of Tourism Research* 19 (1), 18–32.

Eade, J. (2000) Order and power at Lourdes: Lay helpers and the organization of a pilgrimage shrine. In J. Eade and M.J. Sallnow (eds) *Contesting the Sacred: The Anthropology of Christian Pilgrimage* (pp. 51–76). Urbana, IL: University of Illinois Press.

Eade, J. (2012) Pilgrimage, the assumptionists and Catholic evangelisation in a changing Europe: Lourdes and Plovdiv. *Cargo* 10 (1–2), 27–46.

Eade, J. (2014) Pilgrimage and the development of Roman Catholic shrines in a changing Europe: Lourdes and Bulgaria. *Bulgarski Folklor* 40 (2), 105–127.

Eade, J. (2016) Parish and pilgrimage in a changing Europe. In D. Pasura and M. Bivand Erdal (eds) *Migration, Transnationalism and Catholicism: Global Perspectives* (pp. 75–92). London: Palgrave.

Eade, J. and Albera, D. (2017) Pilgrimage studies in global perspective. In D. Albera and J. Eade (eds) *New Pathways in Pilgrimage Studies: Global Perspectives* (pp. 1–17). London: Routledge.

Eade, J. and Garbin, D. (2007) Reinterpreting the relationship between centre and periphery: Pilgrimage and sacred spatialization among Polish and Congolese communities in Britain. *Mobilities* 2 (3), 413–424.

Eade, J. and Katić, M. (eds) (2014) *Pilgrimage, Politics and Place-Making in Eastern Europe: Crossing the Borders*. London: Routledge.

Eco, U. (1986) *Travels in Hyperreality: Essays*. Orlando, FL: Harvest.

Edensor, T. (2001) Performing tourism, staging tourism: (Re)producing tourist space and practice. *Tourist Studies* 1 (1), 59–81.

Egresi, I., Bayram, B. and Kara, F. (2012a) Tourism at religious sites: A case from Mardin, Turkey. *Journal of Geographica Timisiensis* 21 (1), 5–15.

Egresi, I., Bayram, B., Kara, F., and Kesik, O.A. (2012b) Unlocking the potential of religious tourism in Turkey. *GeoJournal of Tourism and Geosites* 5 (1), 63–80.

Egresi, I., Kara, F. and Bayram, B. (2014) Economic impact of religious tourism in Mardin, Turkey. *Journal of Economics and Business Research* 18 (2), 7–22.

Eid, R. (2012) Towards a high-quality religious tourism marketing: The case of hajj service in Saudi Arabia. *Tourism Analysis* 17 (4), 509–522.

Einstein, M. (2008) *Brands of Faith: Marketing Religion in a Commercial Age*. London: Routledge.

El-Gohary, H. (2016) Halal tourism: Is it really halal? *Tourism Management Perspectives* 19, 124–130.

Eliade, M. (1959) *The Sacred and the Profane: The Nature of Religion*. New York: Harcourt Brace.

Elsner, J. and Rutherford, I. (eds) (2005) *Pilgrimage in Graeco-Roman and Early Christian Antiquity: Seeing the Gods*. Oxford: Oxford University Press.

Emmett, C.F. (1995) *Beyond the Basilica: Christians and Muslims in Nazareth*. Chicago, IL: University of Chicago Press.

Engberg, A. (2017) Ambassadors for the kingdom: Evangelical volunteers in Israel as long-term pilgrims. In. M. Leppäkari and K. Griffin (eds) *Pilgrimage and Tourism to Holy Cities* (pp. 156–170). Wallingford: CABI.

Erb, M. and Ong, C.E. (2017) Theming Asia: Culture, nature and heritage in a transforming environment. *Tourism Geographies* 19 (2), 143–167.

Erekson, K.A. (2005) From missionary resort to memorial farm: Commemoration and capitalism at the birthplace of Joseph Smith, 1905–1925. *Mormon Historical Studies* 6 (2), 69–100.

Evans, G. (1998) Mementos to take home: The ancient trade in souvenirs. In J.M. Fladmark (ed.) *In Search of Heritage as Pilgrim or Tourist?* (pp. 105–126). Shaftesbury: Donhead.

Faith Journeys (2017) Faith Journeys: 'The most trusted provider of inspirational religious travel experiences'. See www.myfaithjourneys.com (accessed 30 December 2017).

Farra-Haddad, N. (2015) Pilgrimages toward south Lebanon: Holy places relocating Lebanon as a part of the Holy Land. In R. Raj and K. Griffin (eds) *Religious Tourism and Pilgrimage Management: An International Perspective* (2nd edn; pp. 279–296). Wallingford: CABI.

Fava, V. (2007) Saint Martin of Tours: A great European figure, a symbol of sharing. *Via Francigena* 26, 66–69.

Fedele, A. (2009) From Christian religion to feminist spirituality: Mary Magdalene pilgrimages to La Sainte-Baume, France. *Culture and Religion* 10 (3), 243–261.

Fedele, A. (2014) Energy and transformation in alternative pilgrimages to Catholic shrines: Deconstructing the tourist/pilgrim divide. *Journal of Tourism and Cultural Change* 12 (2), 150–165.

Feifer, M. (1985) *Going Places*. London: MacMillan.

Felak, J.R. (2014) Pope John Paul II, the saints, and communist Poland: The papal pilgrimages of 1979 and 1983. *The Catholic Historical Review* 100 (3), 555–574.

Feldman, J. (2007) Constructing a shared Bible Land: Jewish Israeli guiding performances for Protestant pilgrims. *American Ethnologist* 34 (2), 351–374.

Feldman, J. (2011) Abraham the settler, Jesus the refugee: Contemporary conflict and Christianity on the road to Bethlehem. *History & Memory* 23 (1), 62–95.

Feldman, J. (2014) Changing colors of money: Tips, commissions, and ritual in Christian pilgrimage to the Holy Land. *Religion and Society: Advances in Research* 5 (1), 143–156.

Feldman, J. (2016) *A Jewish Guide in the Holy Land: How Christian Pilgrims Made Me Israeli*. Bloomington, IN: Indiana University Press.

Feldman, J. and Ron, A.S. (2011) American Holy Land: Orientalism, Disneyization, and the evangelical gaze. In B. Schnepel, G. Brands and H. Schönig (eds) *Orient – Orientalistik – Orientalismus: Geschichte und Aktualität einer Debatte* (pp. 151–176). Bielefeld: Verlag.

Fernandes, C. (2011) Developing religious tourism in emerging destinations: Experiences from Mtskheta (Georgia). *International Journal of Business and Globalisation* 7 (1), 102–115.

Fernandes, C. (2012) Creating new forms of consumption along the Portuguese Camino de Santiago. *Revista Tourismo & Desenvolvimento* 17, 181–183.

Fernandes, C., Coelho, J. and Brázio, M. (2015) Revisiting religious tourism in northern Portugal. In R. Raj and K. Griffin (eds) *Religious Tourism and Pilgrimage Management: An International Perspective* (2nd edn; pp. 254–266). Wallingford: CABI.

Fernandes, C., Melo, C. and Cardoso, M. (2016) Monitoring the tourism impacts of a cultural and religious event: A case study in northern Portugal. *International Journal of Religious Tourism and Pilgrimage* 4 (2), 29–41.

Fernandes, C., Pimenta, E., Gonçalves, F. and Rachão, S. (2012) A new research approach for religious tourism: The case of the Portuguese route to Santiago. *International Journal of Tourism Policy* 4 (2), 83–94.

Finegan, J. (1981) *The Archeology of the New Testament: The Mediterranean World of the Early Christian Apostles*. Boulder, CO: Westview Press.

Finlayson, C. and Mesev, V. (2014) Emotional encounters in sacred spaces: The case of the Church of Jesus Christ of Latter-day Saints. *The Professional Geographer* 66 (3), 436–442.

Fish, J.M. and Fish, M. (1993) International tourism and pilgrimage: A discussion. *The Journal of East and West Studies* 22 (2), 83–90.

Fisher, D. (2004) The demonstration effect revisited. *Annals of Tourism Research* 31 (2), 428–446.

FitzGerald, T. (2014) Pilgrims for unity and witness. *Greek Orthodox Theological Review* 59 (1–4), 9–12.

Fleischer, A. (2000) The tourist behind the pilgrim in the Holy Land. *International Journal of Hospitality Management* 19 (3), 311–326.

Fleischer, A. and Nitzav, Y. (1995) *Christian Pilgrims: The Tourism Potential for Peripheral Regions in Israel*. Rehovot: Center for Development Studies.

Fletcher, R. (1997) *The Conversion of Europe: From Paganism to Christianity, 371–1386 AD*. London: Harper Collins.

Francis, L.J., Mansfield, S., Williams, E. and Village, A. (2010a) Applying psychological type theory to cathedral visitors: A case study of two cathedrals in England and Wales. *Visitor Studies* 13 (2), 175–186.

Francis, L.J., Mansfield, S., Williams, E. and Village, A. (2010b) The usefulness of visitor expectations type scales (VETS) for tourist segmentation: The case of cathedral visitors. *Tourism Analysis* 15 (5), 545–554.

Fredrickson, L.M. and Anderson, D.H. (1999) A qualitative exploration of the wilderness experience as a source of spiritual inspiration. *Journal of Environmental Psychology* 19 (1), 21–39.

Frenz, M. (2008) The Virgin and her 'relations': Reflections on processions at a Catholic Shrine in southern India. In K.A. Jacobsen (ed.) *South Asian Religions on Display: Religious Processions in South Asia and in the Diaspora* (pp. 92–103). London: Routledge.

Frey, N.L. (1998) *Pilgrim Stories: On and Off the Road to Santiago*. Berkeley, CA: University of California Press.

Frey, N.L. (2004) Stories of the return: Pilgrimage and its aftermaths. In E. Badone and S.R. Roseman (eds) *Intersecting Journeys: The Anthropology of Pilgrimage and Tourism* (pp. 89–109). Chicago, IL: University of Illinois Press.

Friedman, S.S. (1984) *The Oberammergau Passion Play: A Lance Against Civilization*. Carbondale, IL: Southern Illinois University Press.

Fuchs, G. and Reichel, A. (2011) An exploratory inquiry into destination risk perceptions and risk reduction strategies of first time vs. repeat visitors to a highly volatile destination. *Tourism Management* 32, 266–276.

Galbraith, M. (2000) On the road to Czestochowa: Rhetoric and experience on a Polish pilgrimage. *Anthropological Quarterly* 73 (2), 61–73.

Gamlem, T. (2009) *Step by Step from Oslo to Trondheim*. New York: Allaway Books.

Garay Tamajón, L. and Cànoves Valiente, G. (2017) Barcelona seen through the eyes of TripAdvisor: Actors, typologies and components of destination image in social media platforms. *Current Issues in Tourism* 20 (1), 33–37.

Garden Tomb Jerusalem (2017) Who we are. See http://www.gardentomb.com/about/ (accessed 22 December 2017).

Garín-Muñoz, T. (2009) Tourism in Galicia: Domestic and foreign demand. *Tourism Economics* 15 (4), 753–769.

Gayá, J. (2002) Pilgrimage in the Catholic Church: Pastoral care structures. *Peregrinus Cracoviensis* 13, 11–18.

Gelbman, A. and Collins-Kreiner, N. (2013) The host gaze on current Christian pilgrims in Israel: Tour guides gazing. In O. Moufakkir and Y. Reisinger (eds) *The Host Gaze in Global Tourism* (pp. 81–92). Wallingford: CABI.

Gelbman, A. and Laven, D. (2016) Re-envisioning community-based heritage tourism in the old city of Nazareth. *Journal of Heritage Tourism* 11 (2), 105–125.

Genesis Tours (2016) Footsteps of the Apostles: Mediterranean Cruise. See https://www.genesistoursusa.com/mediterranean-biblical-cruise/ (accessed 10 August 2016).

Gesler, W. (1996) Lourdes: Healing in a place of pilgrimage. *Health & Place* 2 (2), 95–105.

Getz, D. (1993) Planning for tourism business districts. *Annals of Tourism Research* 20 (3), 583–600.

Gil, A.R. and de Esteban Curiel, J. (2008) Religious events as special interest tourism: A Spanish experience. *PASOS: Revista de Turismo y Patrimonio Cultural* 6 (3), 419–433.

Gill, D.M. (2006) Called to serve: Mobilizing and training volunteers. *Enrichment Journal* (winter), 144.

Giotta, S. (2007) Accommodation facilities for pilgrims along the Via Francigena. *Via Francigena* 26, 17–25.

Goh, R.B. (2014) Noah's Ark: Evangelical Christianity and the creation of a value environment in Hong Kong. *Material Religion* 10 (2), 208–232.

Goh, R.B. (2017) The Jerusalem of Jesus: Space and Pentecostal-evangelical branding in Orland's Holy Land Experience and Eureka Spring's Holy Land Tour. *Culture and Religion* 18 (3), 296–323.

Goldingay, S., Dieppe, P. and Farias, M. (2014) 'And the pain just disappeared into insignificance': The healing response in Lourdes – Performance, psychology and caring. *International Review of Psychiatry* 26 (3), 315–323.

Gonzáles, R.C.L. (2006) The Way of St James: Religious and Cultural Tourism. Paper presented at the International Conference on Religious Tourism, 20 October, Nicosia, Cyprus.

Gonzáles, R.C.L. and Medina, J.S. (2003) Cultural tourism and urban management in northwestern Spain: The pilgrimage to Santiago de Compostela. *Tourism Geographies* 5 (4), 446–460.

Good Walking (2014) St Olaf's Way, Norway: The northern pilgrimage. See http://www.goodwalkingbooks.com/st_olafs_way.html (accessed 30 January 2018).

Goral, A. (2011) Research on cultural tourism development in sacral and spiritual sites from the UNESCO World Heritage List. *International Journal of Heritage & Sustainable Development* 1 (1), 49–59.

Gordon, B. (1986) The souvenir: Messenger of the extraordinary. *Journal of Popular Culture* 20, 135–146.

Górecki, J. (2009) John Paul II's pilgrimage to Our Lady of Piekary. *Peregrinus Cracoviensis* 20, 89–120.

Gothóni, R. (1993) *Paradise within Reach: Monasticism and Pilgrimage on Mt. Athos* Helsinki: University of Helsinki Press.

Gothóni, R. (1994) *Tales and Truth: Pilgrimage on Mount Athos: Past and Present*. Helsinki: University of Helsinki Press.

Gothóni, R. and Speake, G. (eds) (2008) *The Monastic Magnet: Roads to and from Mount Athos*. Oxford-Bern: Peter Lang.

Gottdiener, M. (ed.) (2000) *New Forms of Consumption: Consumers, Culture and Commodification*. Boulder, CO: Rowman and Littlefield.

Gottdiener, M. (2001) *The Theming of America: American Dreams, Media Fantasies, and Themed Environments* (2nd edn). Boulder, CO: Westview Press.

Govender, M. and Rogerson, C.M. (2010) Volunteer tourism: An emerging element of youth travel in Africa. *Commonwealth Youth and Development* 8 (1), 3–19.

Grabow, S. (2010) The Santiago de Compostela pilgrim routes: The development of European cultural heritage policy and practice from a critical perspective. *European Journal of Archaeology* 13 (1), 89–116.

Grabowski, S. (2013) Volunteer tourists: Why do they do it? In S. Wearing and N.G. McGehee (eds) *International Volunteer Tourism: Integrating Travellers and Communities* (pp. 70–83). Wallingford: CABI.

Graf, M. and Popesku, J. (2016) Cultural routes as innovative tourism products and possibilities of their development. *International Journal of Cultural and Digital Tourism* 3 (1), 24–44.

Graham, B. and Murray, M. (1997) The spiritual and the profane: The pilgrimage to Santiago de Compostela. *Ecumene* 4 (4), 389–409.

Graham, B., Ashworth, G.J. and Tunbridge, J.E. (2000) *A Geography of Heritage: Power, Culture and Economy*. London: Arnold.

Griffin, J. (2013) Local residents' responses to tourism as a framework to understand hosts' responses to short-term missions. *The Asbury Journal* 68 (2), 134–159.

Griffin, K. (2012) Pilgrimage through the eyes of the Irish 'traveller' community. *International Journal of Tourism Policy* 4 (2), 157–173.

Grondys, K., Ślusarczyk, B. and Kot, S. (2014) Logistics view on religious tourism. In R. Stefko, M. Frankovsky and J. Vravec (eds) *Management 2014: Business, Management and Social Sciences Research* (pp. 1–9). Presov: Bookman.

Gross, S. and Lück, M. (2012) Cruise line strategies for keeping afloat. In M. Vogel, A. Papathanassis and B. Wolber (eds) *The Business and Management of Ocean Cruises* (pp. 63–76). Wallingford: CABI.

Güçlü, Y. (1998) Turkey and faith tourism. *Perceptions: Journal of International Affairs* 3 (2), 1–3.

Gulatt-Whiteman, C. (2004) Volunteer tourism: A case study of a mobile medical mission. Unpublished MSc thesis, Arizona State University.

Gunner, G. (2017) Christian pilgrimage to sacred sites in the Holy Land: A Swedish perspective. In M. Leppäkari and K. Griffin (eds) *Pilgrimage and Tourism to Holy Cities: Ideological Perspectives and Practical Management* (pp. 43–58). Wallingford: CABI.

Gupta, R.K. (1986) *The Great Encounter: A Study of Indo-American Literary and Cultural Relations*. New Delhi: Abhinav Publications.

Gupta, V. (1999) Sustainable tourism: Learning from Indian religious traditions. *International Journal of Contemporary Hospitality Management* 11 (2/3), 91–95.

Gurgel, K. (1975) *Mormons in Canada and Religious Travel Patterns to the Mormon Culture Hearth*. Syracuse, NY: Department of Geography, Syracuse University.
Guter Y. (2000) Challenges and troubleshooting in tourism to Israel, Palestine and the West Bank: Special interest tours to the Holy Land. In R. French (ed.) *Challenged Tourism* (pp. 85–93). Girne, Cyprus: Girne American University Press.
Guter, Y. (1997) Mormon–Christian pilgrimage to Israel: Pilgrim's experience. Unpublished master's thesis, Bar-Ilan University (in Hebrew).
Guter, Y. (2004) Aspects of Christian pilgrimage to the Holy Land: The pilgrim's experience. Unpublished PhD dissertation, Bar Ilan University (in Hebrew).
Guter, Y. (2006) Pilgrims 'communitas' in the Holy Land: The case of Mormon pilgrimage. In M. Poorthuis and J. Schwartz (eds) *A Holy People: Jewish and Christian Perspectives on Religious Community* (pp. 337–348). Leiden: Brill.
Guter, Y. and Feldman, J. (2006) Holy Land pilgrimage as a site of inter-religious encounter. *Studia Hebraica* 6, 87–93.
Gutic, J., Caie, E. and Clegg, A. (2010) In search of hetertopia? Motivations of visitors to an English cathedral. *International Journal of Tourism Research* 12, 750–760.
Guttentag, D.A. (2009) The possible negative impacts of volunteer tourism. *International Journal of Tourism Research* 11 (6), 537–551.
Haddad, N., Waheeb, M. and Fakhoury, L. (2009) The baptism archaeological site of Bethany Beyond Jordan: Towards an assessment for a management plan. *Tourism and Hospitality Planning & Development* 6 (3), 173–190.
Hagstrom, A.A. and Vaisvilaite, I. (1999) *A Pilgrim Guide to Rome and the Holy Land for the Third Millennium*. Allen, TX: Thomas Moore.
Haładewicz-Grzelak, M. and Lubos-Kozieł, J. (2014) Story-ing memory in the Licheń Pilgrimage Centre (Poland). *European Journal of Cultural Studies* 17 (6), 647–664.
Hall, C.M. (2006a) Buddhism, tourism and the middle way. In D.J. Timothy and D.H. Olsen (eds) *Tourism, Religion and Spiritual Journeys* (pp. 172–185). London: Routledge.
Hall, C.M. (2006b) Travel and journeying on the sea of faith: Perspectives from religious humanism. In D.J. Timothy and D.H. Olsen (eds) *Tourism, Religion and Spiritual Journeys* (pp. 64–77). London: Routledge.
Hall, C.M. (ed.) (2007) *Pro-poor Tourism: Who benefits? Perspectives on Tourism and Poverty Reduction*. Clevedon: Channel View Publications.
Hall, C.M. and Tucker, H. (eds) (2004) *Tourism and Postcolonialism: Contested Discourses, Identities and Representations*. London: Routledge.
Hall, C.M., Ram, Y. and Shoval, N. (eds) (2018) *The Routledge International Handbook of Walking*. London: Routledge.
Halter, N. (2013) The Australian Catholic Church and the public sphere: World Youth Day 2008. *Journal of Religious History* 37 (2), 261–282.
Hamer, J. (2008) Mapping Mormon settlement in Caldwell County, Missouri. *Mormon Historical Studies* 9 (1), 15–38.
Hamilton, J. (2005) *Thomas Cook: The Holiday-Maker*. Stroud: Sutton.
Han, J.H.J. (2008) Missionary. *Aether: The Journal of Media Geography* 3, 58–83.
Hankinson, G. (2004) The brand images of tourism destinations: A study of the saliency of organic images. *Journal of Product & Brand Management* 13 (1), 6–14.
Hannigan, J. (1998) *Fantasy City: Pleasure and Profit in the Postmodern Metropolis*. London: Routledge.
Hanson, B.O. (2016) Branding faith: Do Christian ministries reach millennials with branding? Unpublished master's thesis, Liberty University.
Harpur, J. (2002) *Sacred Tracks: 2000 Years of Christian Pilgrimage*. Berkeley, CA: University of California Press.
Harris, A. (2013) Lourdes and holistic spirituality: Contemporary Catholicism, the therapeutic and religious thermalism. *Culture and Religion* 14 (1), 23–43.

Harris, P. (2002) Calling young people to missionary vocations in a 'Yahoo' world. *Missiology* 30 (1), 33–50.
Hartwig, M.J. (2006) Rome Belongs to You, Too! A Series of Historical Essays Exploring Christian Rome. See http://www.travelillume.com/documents/RomeBelongstoYou-Too.pdf (accessed 2 August 2010).
Hassan, A. and Rahman, M. (2015) World Heritage Site as a label in branding a place. *Journal of Cultural Heritage Management and Sustainable Development* 5 (3), 210–223.
Hassan, M.W. and Hall, C.M. (2003) The demand for halal food among Muslim travelers in New Zealand. In C.M. Hall, L. Sharples, R. Mitchell, B. Cambourne and N. Macionis (eds) *Food Tourism around the World: Development, Management and Markets* (pp. 81–101). Oxford: Butterworth Heinemann.
Hauck, F.R. and Hansen, V.E. (1988) *Deciphering the Geography of the Book of Mormon: Settlements and Routes in Ancient America*. Salt Lake City, UT: Deseret Book.
Hayes, D. and MacLeod, N. (2007) Packaging places: Designing heritage trails using an experience economy perspective to maximize visitor engagement. *Journal of Vacation Marketing* 13 (1), 45–58.
Head, R.J. (2006) Creating a Mormon Mecca in England: The Gadfield Elm Chapel. *Mormon Historical Studies* 7 (1–2), 89–102.
Heintzman, P. (2003) The wilderness experience and spirituality: What recent research tells us. *Journal of Physical Education, Recreation & Dance* 74 (6), 27–32.
Heintzman, P. (2009) Nature-based recreation and spirituality: A complex relationship. *Leisure Sciences* 32 (1), 72–89.
Henderson, J.C. (2016) Halal food, certification and halal tourism: Insights from Malaysia and Singapore. *Tourism Management Perspectives* 19, 160–164.
Hensel, C. (2012) Minimission-tourism in Ethiopia: A new subspecies of sustainable volunteer tourism? In P. Sloan, C. Simons-Kaufman and W. Legrand (eds) *Sustainable Hospitality and Tourism as Motors for Development: Case Studies from Developing Regions of the World* (pp. 242–262). London: Routledge.
Hepp, A. and Krönert, V. (2010) Religious media events: The Catholic 'World Youth Day' as an example for the mediatisation and individualisation of religion. In N. Couldry, A. Hepp and F. Krotz (eds) *Media Events in a Global Age* (pp. 265–282). London: Routledge.
Hercbergs, D. (2012) Narrating instability: Political detouring in Jerusalem. *Mobilities* 7 (3), 415–438.
Hermkens, A.K, Jansen, W. and Notermans, C. (eds) (2009) *Moved by Mary: The Power of Pilgrimage in the Modern World*. Aldershot: Ashgate.
Hernandez-Ramdwar, C. (2013) African traditional religions in the Caribbean and Brazil: Models of religious tourism and impacts of commodification. *Journal of Heritage Tourism* 8 (1), 81–88.
Herrero, N. (2008) Reaching 'Land's End': New social practices in the pilgrimage to Santiago de Compostela. *International Journal of Iberian Studies* 21 (2), 131–149.
Hess, A.C. (1978) *The Forgotten Frontier: A History of the Sixteenth-Century Ibero-African Frontier*. Chicago, IL: University of Chicago Press.
Higginbotham, G. (2012) Seeking roots and tracing lineages: Constructing a framework for reference for roots and genealogical tourism. *Journal of Heritage Tourism* 7 (3), 189–203.
Higgins, L. and Hamilton, K. (2011) Sacred places: An exploratory investigation of consuming pilgrimage. *Advances in Consumer Research* 38, 262–267.
Higgins, L. and Hamilton, K. (2016) Mini-miracles: Transformations of self from consumption of the Lourdes pilgrimage. *Journal of Business Research* 69 (1), 25–32.
Higgins-Desbiolles, F. (2009) International solidarity movement: A case study in volunteer tourism for justice. *Annals of Leisure Research* 12 (3–4), 333–349.

Higgins-Desbiolles, F. (2016) Walled off from the world: Palestine, tourism and resisting occupation. In R. Isaac, C.M. Hall and F. Higgins-Desbiolles (eds) *The Politics and Power of Tourism in Palestine* (pp. 178–194). London: Routledge.

Higgins-Desbiolles, F. and Russell-Mundine, G. (2008) Absences in the volunteer tourism phenomenon: The right to travel, solidarity tours and transformation beyond the one-way. In K.D. Lyons and S. Wearing (eds) *Journeys of Discovery in Volunteer Tourism* (pp. 182–194). Wallingford: CABI.

Hill, B.J. (1998) Reflections on an outdoor recreation experience. *Parks & Recreation* 33 (8), 58–63.

Hill, B.J. and Landon, M.N. (2000) Coming out of obscurity through the Pioneer Sesquicentennial Celebration. In S.E. Black (ed.) *Coming Out of Obscurity in the 20th Century* (pp. 76–89). Salt Lake City, UT: Deseret Book.

Hill, W. (1996) *The Mormon Trail: Yesterday and Today*. Boulder, CO: University Press of Colorado.

Hoade, E. (1984) *Guide to the Holy Land*. Jerusalem: Franciscan Printing Press.

Hobbs, J.J. (1992) Sacred space and touristic development at Jebel Musa (Mt Sinai), Egypt. *Journal of Cultural Geography* 12 (2), 99–113.

Hodgson, M.F. (2008) Personal interview conducted by Amos S. Ron, 26 October.

Holmes, K. and Smith, K. (2009) *Managing Volunteers in Tourism: Attractions, Destinations and Events*. Amsterdam: Butterworth Heinemann.

Holy Land Experience (2017) About the experience. See https://holylandexperience.com/about/ (accessed 18 December 2017).

Holy See (2018) The Holy See: Supreme Pontiffs. See http://w2.vatican.va/content/vatican/en.html (accessed 27 February 2018).

Horák, M., Kozumplíková, A., Somerlíková, K., Lorencová, H. and Lampartová, I. (2015) Religious tourism in the south-Moravian and Zlín regions: Proposal for three new pilgrimage routes. *European Countryside* 3, 167–178.

Horoszewicz, M. (2002) Great Judaic symbols of John Paul II. *Dialogue and Universalism* 6/7, 81–90.

Horsfall, S. (2000) The experience of Marian apparitions and the Mary Cult. *The Social Sciences Journal* 37 (3), 375–384.

Hostetler, D.M. (2005) Personal interview conducted by Amos S. Ron, 27 April.

Houlihan, M. (2000) Souvenirs with soul: 800 years of pilgrimage to Santiago de Compostela. In M. Hitchcock and K. Teague (eds) *Souvenirs: The Material Culture of Tourism* (pp. 18–24). Aldershot: Ashgate.

Howell, B. (2010) Roots of the Short-Term Missionary 1960–1985. See http://www.roundtripmissions.com/content/roots-short-term-missionary-1960-1985 (accessed 18 July 2012).

Howell, B. (2012) *Short-Term Mission: An Ethnography of Christian Travel Narrative and Experience*. Downers Grove, IL: IVP Academic.

Hsu, B., Reynolds, A., Hackett, C. and Gibbon, J. (2008) Estimating the religious composition of all nations: An empirical assessment of the World Christian Database. *Journal for the Scientific Study of Religion* 47 (4), 678–693.

Hudman, L.E. and Jackson, R.H. (1992) Mormon pilgrimage and tourism. *Annals of Tourism Research* 19 (1), 107–121.

Hughes, G. (1995) Authenticity in tourism. *Annals of Tourism Research* 22 (4), 781–803.

Hughes, K., Bond, N. and Ballantyne, R. (2013) Designing and managing interpretive experiences at religious sites: Visitors' perceptions of Canterbury Cathedral. *Tourism Management* 36, 210–220.

Hunt, E. (1984) Travel, tourism and piety in the Roman Empire: A context for the beginnings of Christian pilgrimage. *Echos du Monde Classique* 28, 391–417.

Hutton, A., Roderick, A. and Munt, R. (2010) Lessons learned at World Youth Day: Collecting data and using postcards at mass gatherings. *Prehospital and Disaster Medicine* 25 (3), 273–277.

Ioannides, D. (2003) The economics of tourism in host communities. In S. Singh, D.J. Timothy and R.K. Dowling (eds) *Tourism in Destination Communities* (pp. 37–54). Wallingford: CABI.

Ioannides, D. and Timothy, D.J. (2010) *Tourism in the USA: A Spatial and Social Synthesis*. London: Routledge.

Irimiás, A. and Michalkó, G. (2013) Religious tourism in Hungary: An integrative framework. *Hungarian Geographical Bulletin* 62 (2), 175–196.

Isaac, R.K. (2010) Palestinian tourism in transition: Hope, aspiration, or reality? *Journal of Tourism and Peace Research* 1 (1), 16–26.

Isaac, R.K. (2013) Palestine tourism under occupation. In R. Butler and W. Suntikul (eds) *Tourism and War* (pp. 143–157). London: Routledge.

Isaac, R.K. (2016) Pilgrimage tourism to Palestine. In R.K. Isaac, C.M. Hall and F. Higgins-Desbiolles (eds) *The Politics and Power of Tourism in Palestine* (pp. 124–136). London: Routledge.

Israel Revealed (2017) Your discovering the authentic Holy Land experience. See https://www.israelrevealed.com/ (accessed 1 December 2017).

Jabłoński, Z. (2009) Social and political context of pilgrimage of John Paul II to Jansą Góra. *Peregrinus Cracoviensis* 20, 65–88.

Jackowski, A. (1987) Geography of pilgrimages in Poland. *The National Geographical Journal of India* 33 (4), 422–429.

Jackowski, A. (1990) Pilgrimages in Poland versus pilgrimages in the world. *Problemy Turystyki* 1/2, 53–64.

Jackowski, A. and Marciniak (2000) The Holy Mount of Grabarka: The heart of the Polish Orthodox Church. *Peregrinus Cracoviensis* 10, 207–218.

Jackowski, A. and Smith, V.L. (1992) Polish pilgrim-tourists. *Annals of Tourism Research* 19 (1), 92–106.

Jackowski, A., Sołjan, I. and Mróz, F. (2009) The geography of the pilgrimages of John Paul II. *Peregrinus Cracoviensis* 20, 19–48.

Jackowski, A., Sołjan, I., Bilska-Wodecka, E., Liro, J., Trojnar, M. and Kostrzewa, E. (2017) *World Youth Day in Kraków in the Light of Experiences from around the World*. Kraków: Organizing Committee of World Youth Day in Kraków.

Jackson, R.H. and Hudman, L. (1995) Pilgrimage tourism and English cathedrals: The role of religion in travel. *The Tourist Review* 50 (4), 40–48.

Jacobs, A.S. (2002) 'The most beautiful Jewesses in the land': Imperial travel in the early Christian Holy Land. *Religion* 32 (3), 205–225.

James, J.D. (2010) *McDonaldisation, Masala McGospel and Om Economics: Televangelism in Contemporary India*. London: Sage.

Jansen, W. and Kühl, M. (2008) Shared symbols: Muslims, Marian pilgrimages and gender. *European Journal of Women's Studies* 15 (3), 295–311.

Jarrett, B. (1911) Pilgrimages. In *The Catholic Encyclopedia*. New York: Robert Appleton Company.

Jochnowitz, E. (2004) Flavors of memory: Jewish food as culinary tourism in Poland. In L.M. Long (ed.) *Culinary Tourism* (pp. 97–113). Lexington, KY: University Press of Kentucky.

John Paul II (2002) 'Ecotourism, the Key to Sustainable Development': Message of the Holy Father John Paul II for the 23rd World Day of Tourism. *Peregrinus Cracoviensis* 13, 7–10.

Johnson, D., Cooper, J. and Gasser, D. (2008) *An LDS Guide to Mesoamerica*. Springfield, UT: CFI.

Johnson, L.A. (2014) Can short-term mission trips reduce prejudice? *Journal for the Sociological Integration of Religion and Society* 4 (1), 10–22.

Johnston, A.M. (2003) Self-determination: Exercising indigenous rights in tourism. In S. Singh, D.J. Timothy and R.K. Dowling (eds) *Tourism in Destination Communities* (pp. 115–134). Wallingford: CABI.

Johnston, B. (2011) Constructing alternative Christian identity: An ethnography of Jesus people USA's Cornerstone Festival. Unpublished PhD dissertation, University of Southern Florida.

Jokela, S.E. (2014) Tourism and identity politics in the Helsinki churchscape. *Tourism Geographies* 16 (2), 252–269.

Jones, M.S. (2006) (Re)living the pioneer past: Mormon youth handcart trek re-enactments. *Theatre Topics* 16 (2), 113–130.

Josan, I. (2009) Pilgrimage: A rudimentary form of modern tourism. *GeoJournal of Tourism and Geosites* 2 (4), 160–168.

Josiam, B.M.B.M., Mattson, M. and Sullivan, P. (2004) The historaunt: Heritage tourism at Mickey's Dining Car. *Tourism Management* 25 (4), 453–461.

Jutla, R.S. (2006) Pilgrimage in Sikh tradition. In D.J. Timothy and D.H. Olsen (eds) *Tourism, Religion and Spiritual Journeys* (pp. 206–219). London: Routledge.

Kaelber, L. (2006) Paradigms of travel: From medieval pilgrimages to the postmodern virtual tour. In D.J. Timothy and D.H. Olsen (eds) *Tourism, Religion and Spiritual Journeys* (pp. 49–63). London: Routledge.

Kaell, H. (2010) Pilgrimage in the jet age: The development of the American evangelical Holy Land travel industry, 1948–1978. *Journal of Tourism History* 2 (1), 23–38.

Kaell, H. (2012) Of gifts and grandchildren: American Holy Land souvenirs. *Journal of Material Culture* 17 (2), 133–151.

Kaell, H. (2013) Evangelical ketubah, Messianic mezuzah: Judaica for Christians. *Religion & Politics* 12 March, np. See http://religionandpolitics.org/2013/03/12/evangelical-ketubah-messianic-mezuzah-judaica-for-christians/ (accessed 15 March 2018).

Kaell, H. (2014) *Walking Where Jesus Walked: American Christians and Holy Land Pilgrimage*. New York: New York University Press.

Kagan, R.L. (1990) *Lucrecia's Dreams: Politics and Prophecy in Sixteenth-Century Spain*. Berkeley, CA: University of California Press.

Kaiser, R.B. (2003) John Paul II frequent flyer, infrequent listener. *Catholic New Times* September 7, np.

Kamenidou, I. and Vourou, R. (2015) Motivation factors for visiting religious sites: The case of Lesvos Island. *European Journal of Tourism Research* 9, 78–91.

Kaplan, S. (2011) Pilgrimages, Christian. In S. Uhlig (ed.) *Encyclopaedia Aethiopica* (pp. 153–155). Wiesbaden: Harassowitz Verlag.

Kartal, B., Tepeci, M. and Atli, H. (2015) Examining the religious tourism potential of Manisa, Turkey with a marketing perspective. *Tourism Review* 70 (3), 214–231.

Kassis, R. (2004) The Palestinians and justice tourism. *Contours* 14 (2/3), 18–21.

Kassis, R. (2015) A kairos perspective of tourism and pilgrimage: Come and see. *This Week in Palestine* 204, 22–28.

Kassis, R., Solomon, R. and Higgins-Desbiolles, F. (2016) Solidarity tourism in Palestine: The alternative tourism group of Palestine as a catalyzing instrument of resistance. In R. Isaac, C.M. Hall and F. Higgins-Desbiolles (eds) *The Politics and Power of Tourism in Palestine* (pp. 37–53). London: Routledge.

Katz, K. (2003) Legitimizing Jordan as the Holy Land: Papal Pilgrimages – 1964, 2000. *Comparative Studies of South Asia, Africa and the Middle East* 23 (1–2), 181–189.

Kauffmann, J. and Hostetler, D.M. (2005) *The Nazareth Jesus Knew*. Harrison, NY: Bch Fulfillment & Distribution.

Kaufman, S.K. (2005) *Consuming Visions: Mass Culture and the Lourdes Shrine*. New York: Cornell University Press.

Keating, M. (2007) Plan to take a life-changing trip to Palestine in 2007. *The Washington Report on Middle East Affairs* 26 (2), 69–70.

Kelly, N. (2012) Pilgrimage and spiritual capital. In M. O'Sullivan and B. Flanagan (eds) *Spiritual Capital: A Moral Core for Social and Economic Justice* (pp. 147–158). Aldershot: Ashgate.

Kemp, A. and Raijman, R. (2003) Christian Zionists in the Holy Land: Evangelical churches, labor migrants, and the Jewish state. *Identities: Global Studies in Culture and Power* 10 (3), 295–318.

Kim, H. and Jamal, T. (2007) Touristic quest for existential authenticity. *Annals of Tourism Research* 34 (1), 181–202.

Kim, B. and Kim, S.S. (in press) Hierarchical value map of religious tourists visiting Vatican City/Rome. *Tourism Geographies*.

Kimball, S.B. (1988) *Historic Sites and Markers along the Mormon and Other Great Western Trails*. Champaign, IL: University of Illinois Press.

Kinder, T.N. (2002) *Cistercian Europe: Architecture of Contemplation*. Cambridge: Wm. B. Eerdmans.

King, G.G. (1920) *The Way of Saint James*. London: GP Putnam's Sons.

Kishkovsky, L. (2010) Following Christ with great joy: Christians called to reconciliation. *Transformation: An International Journal of Holistic Mission Studies* 27 (1), 55–62.

Kitiarsa, P. (2010) Toward a sociology of religious commodification. In B.S. Turner (ed.) *The New Blackwell Companion to the Sociology of Religion* (pp. 563–583). Oxford: Blackwell.

Klangwisan, Y. (2012) Educated guesses: Sacred journeys and transformational learning. *Stimulus: New Zealand Journal of Christian Thought and Practice* 19 (2), 40–42.

Klarin, T. (2014) Sacred heritage and cultural tourism: A case of Dalmatian region (Croatia). In M. Katić, T. Klarin and M. McDonald (eds) *Pilgrimage and Sacred Places in Southeast Europe: History, Religious Tourism and Contemporary Trends* (pp. 159–172). Zurich: Verlag.

Klimova, J. (2011) Pilgrimages of Russian Orthodox Christians to the Greek Orthodox monastery in Arizona. *Tourism* 59 (3), 305–318.

Klingelhofer, E. (2003) Cluniac architectural influences at Hyde Abbey Church, Winchester. *Medieval Archaeology* 47, 190–194.

Kliot, N. and Collins-Kreiner, N. (2003) Wait for us – we're not ready yet: Holy Land preparations for the new millennium – the year 2000. *Current Issues in Tourism* 6 (2), 119–149.

Kloek, M.E. (2009) Spirituele Ervaringen in Museumpark Orientalis. Unpublished master's thesis, University of Wageningen.

Kong, L. (2001) Mapping 'new' geographies of religion: Politics and poetics in modernity. *Progress in Human Geography* 25 (2), 211–233.

Konstantinovna, V.S. and Nikolayevich, P.M. (2014) Orthodox pilgrimage: History and modern age. *World Applied Sciences Journal* 30, 5–6.

Kormina, J. (2004) Pilgrims, priest and local religion in contemporary Russia: Contested religious discourses. *Folklore* 28, 25–40.

Korov, T. (2014) The contribution of the Catholic Church in the development of religious tourism and its implementation into the overall tourist offer. *Diacovensia* 22 (2), 233–253.

Kotsi, F. (1999) The enchantment of a floating pilgrimage: The case of Mount Athos, Greece. *Vrijetijdstudies* 17 (2), 5–20.

Kotsi, F. (2003) La communication enchantée: Une anthropologie réflexive du tourisme religieux autour du Mont Athos (Grèce). Unpublished PhD dissertation, École Normale Supérieure Lettres et Sciences Humaines, Lyon.

Kotsi, F. (2007) The religious souvenirs of Mount Athos. *Actes de la Recherche en Sciences Sociales* 170, 48–57.

Kotsi, F. (2012) Mount Athos: Development policies for short-term religious tourism. *International Journal of Tourism Anthropology* 2 (2), 149–163.

Krakover, S. (2017) A heritage site development model: Jewish heritage product formation in south-central Europe. *Journal of Heritage Tourism* 12 (1), 81–101.
Krebs, J.M. (2017) Contemporary Marian apparitions and devotional cultures. *Religion Compass* 11 (3–4), e12232.
Krešić, D., Mikulić, J. and Miličević, K. (2013) The factor structure of tourist satisfaction at pilgrimage destinations: The case of Medjugorje. *International Journal of Tourism Research* 15 (5), 484–494.
Kruger, M. and Saayman, M. (2016) Understanding the Zion Christian Church (ZCC) pilgrims. *International Journal of Tourism Research* 18 (1), 27–38.
Kselman, T. (2001) Lourdes: Body and spirit in the secular age. *The Catholic Historical Review* 87 (2), 337–339.
Kuiper, E. and Bryn, A. (2013) Forest regrowth and cultural heritage sites in Norway and along the Norwegian St Olav pilgrim routes. *International Journal of Biodiversity Science, Ecosystem Services and Management* 9 (1), 54–64.
Kušen, E. (2010) Modern pilgrimage routes in Croatia. *Tourism* 58 (3), 312–317.
Laga, B. (2010) In lieu of history: Mormon monuments and the shaping of memory. *Dialogue: A Journal of Mormon Thought* 43 (4), 131–153.
Laing, J. and Frost, W. (2016) Religious events and their impact: A new perspective for religious tourism. *International Journal of Religious Tourism and Pilgrimage* 4 (2), ii–iii.
Lamberty, K.M. (2012) Toward a spirituality of accompaniment in solidarity partnerships. *Missiology: An International Review* 40 (2), 181–193.
Lambouras, M. (1997) The Marian apparitions: Divine intervention or delusion? Orthodox Christian Information Center. See http://www.orthodoxinfo.com/inquirers/marian_apparitions.aspx (accessed 30 January 30, 2018).
Langelo, L. (2006) Place attachment and perceptions of ecological and social impacts on the Mormon Pioneer Historic Trail. Unpublished master's thesis, Arizona State University.
Lånke, B. (2012) The Route of St. Olav Ways: European cultural route and the pilgrimage path to the north. *Via Francigena* 34, 29–33.
Lanuza, G.M. (2017) Making and selling the 'Rock Star Pope': The celebritization of Pope Francis during his five-day visit to the Philippines. *Humanities Diliman* 14 (1), 1–45.
Larsen, T. (2000) Thomas Cook, Holy Land pilgrims, and the dawn of the modern tourist industry. In R.N. Swanson (ed.) *Holy Land, Holy Lands, and Christian Histories* (pp. 329–342). Woodbridge: Boydell Press.
Lehrhaupt, L.E. (1991) Pilgrimage in modern Ireland: A study in mise-en-scène and experience at Lough Derg, Croagh Patrick, and Knock Shrine. Unpublished PhD dissertation, New York University.
Levine, D.H. (2016) *Religion and Democratic Contestation in Latin America: What Pope Francis Brings to Latin America*. Washington, DC: Center for Latin American & Latino Studies, American University.
Lewon, D. (2012) The Jesus Trail: Hiking from Nazareth to the Sea of Galilee. *Backpacker* 40 (2), 70–80.
Liebelt, C. (2010) Becoming pilgrims in the Holy Land: On Filipina domestic workers' struggles and pilgrimages for a cause in Israel. *The Asia Pacific Journal of Anthropology* 11 (3/4), 245–267.
Liro, J., Soljan, I. and Bilska-Wodecka, E. (in press) Visitors' diversified motivations and behavior–the case of the pilgrimage center in Krakow (Poland). *Journal of Tourism and Cultural Change*.
Liutikas, D. (2014) Lithuanian valuistic journeys: Traditional and secular pilgrimage. *Journal of Heritage Tourism* 9 (4), 299–316.
Liutikas, D. (2015a) In search of miracles: Pilgrimage to the miraculous places. *Tourism Review* 70 (3), 197–213.

Liutikas, D. (2015b) Religious landscape and ecological ethics: Pilgrimage to the Lithuanian Calvaries. *International Journal of Religious Tourism and Pilgrimage* 3 (1), 12–24.

Liutikas, D. (2018) Catholic pilgrimage in Europe: Contemporary traditions and challenges. In H. El-Gohany, D.J. Edwards and R. Eid (eds) *Global Perspectives on Religious Tourism and Pilgrimage* (pp. 84–103). Hershey, PA: IGI Global.

Livermore, D. (2008) Cultural intelligence and short-term missions: The phenomenon of the fifteen-year-old missionary. In S. Ang and L. Van Dyne (eds) *Handbook of Cultural Intelligence: Theory, Measurement, and Applications* (pp. 271–287). Armonk, NY: M.E. Sharpe.

Livingstone, A. (2000) *The Concise Oxford Dictionary of the Christian Church*. Oxford: Oxford University Press.See http://www.encyclopedia.com/doc/1O95-OrientalOrthodoxChurches.html (accessed 9 September 2010).

Lo, A.S. and Lee, C.Y. (2011) Motivations and perceived value of volunteer tourists from Hong Kong. *Tourism Management* 32 (2), 326–334.

Lock, C. (2003) Bowing down to wood and stone: One way to be a pilgrim. In S. Coleman and J. Elsner (eds) *Pilgrim Voices: Narrative and Authorship in Christian Pilgrimage* (pp. 110–132). New York: Berghahn.

Logan, W.S. (2002) Vietnam's Highway No. 1: Corridor of power and patrimony. *Historic Environment* 16 (2), 23–26.

Lois González, R.C. (2013) The Camino de Santiago and its contemporary renewal: Pilgrims, tourists and territorial identities. *Culture and Religion* 14 (1), 8–22.

Lois González, R.C. and Santos, X.M. (2015) Tourists and pilgrims on their way to Santiago: Motives, caminos and final destinations. *Journal of Tourism and Cultural Change* 13 (2), 149–164.

Lois González, R.C., Castro Fernández, B.M. and Lopez, L. (2016) From sacred place to monumental space: Mobility along the Way to St. James. *Mobilities* 11 (5), 770–788.

LoMonaco, M.S. (2009) Mormon pageants as American historical performance. *Theatre Symposium* 17, 69–83.

Long, B.O. (2003) *Imagining the Holy Land: Maps, Models, and Fantasy Travels*. Bloomington, IN: Indiana University Press.

Lopez, L., Lois González, R.C. and Castro Fernández, B.M. (2017) Spiritual tourism on the way of Saint James: The current situation. *Tourism Management Perspectives* 24, 225–234.

Lough, B.J., Sherraden, M.S., McBride, A.M. and Xiang, X. (2014) The impact of international service on the development of volunteers' intercultural relations. *Social Science Research* 46, 48–58.

Lovan, D. (2016) Noah's ark of biblical proportions ready to open in Kentucky. *The Washington Times*, 5 July. See https://www.washingtontimes.com/news/2016/jul/5/christian-noahs-ark-attraction-ready-to-open-in-ke/ (accessed 10 November 2017).

Luhrmann, T.M. (2004) Metakinesis: How God becomes intimate in contemporary U.S. Christianity. *American Anthropologist* 106 (3), 518–528.

Lundgren, K.J. (2017) The paradox of the 'People's Pope': Pope Francis and the cult of authenticity. *International Journal of Media & Cultural Politics* 13 (3), 303–312.

Lux, R.C. (2010) *The Jewish People, the Holy Land, and the State of Israel: A Catholic View*. Mahwah, NJ: Paulist Press.

Ma, L. and Li, J. (2018) *Surviving the State, Remaking the Church: A Sociological Portrait of Christians in Mainland China*. Eugene, OR: Pickwick Publications.

MacCannell, D. (1973) Staged authenticity: Arrangements of social space in tourist settings. *American Journal of Sociology* 79, 589–603.

Mach, Z. (2009) Notes on the social significance of John Paul II's pilgrimages to Poland. *Peregrinus Cracoviensis* 20, 49–64 (in Polish).

MacLeod, N. (2017) The role of trails in the creation of tourist space. *Journal of Heritage Tourism* 12 (5), 423–430.

MacMullen, R. (1986) *Christianizing the Roman Empire, AD 100–400.* New Haven, CT: Yale University Press.

MacWilliams, M.W. (2002) Virtual pilgrimages on the Internet. *Religion* 32, 315–335.

Maddrell, A. and Della Dora, V. (2013) Crossing surfaces in search of the holy: Landscape and liminality in contemporary Christian pilgrimage. *Environment and Planning A: Economy and Space* 45 (5), 1105–1126.

Maddrell, A., Della Dora, V., Scafi, A. and Walton, H. (2015) *Christian Pilgrimage, Landscape, and Heritage: Journeying to the Sacred.* London: Routledge.

Madsen, M.H. (2003) Mormon meccas: The spiritual transformation of Mormon historical sites from points of interest to sacred space. Unpublished PhD dissertation, Syracuse University.

Madsen, M.H. (2006) The sanctification of Mormonism's historical geography. *Geographies of Religions and Belief Systems* 1 (1), 51–73.

Malezhki, L. (2011) The Phenomenon of Volunteering at Nazareth Village. Unpublished seminar paper in the Department of Tourism and Hotel Management, Kinneret College on the Sea of Galilee.

Mansfeld, Y. (2012) The Role of Religious Institutions in Sustainable Tourism Development and Operation. Paper presented at the Second International Conference on Sustainable Religious Tourism: Commandments, Obstacles and Challenges, 28 October, Lecce, Italy.

Mariñas Otero, E.J. (1990) El camino de Santiago en el arte y en la cultura europea. *Estudios Turísticos* 106, 29–42.

Marine-Roig, E. (2015) Religious tourism versus secular pilgrimage: The Basilica of La Sagrada Familia. *International Journal of Religious Tourism and Pilgrimage* 3 (1), 25–37.

Marine-Roig, E. (2016) The impact of the consecration of 'La Sagrada Familia' basilica in Barcelona by Pope Benedict XVI. *International Journal of Tourism Anthropology* 5 (1/2), 95–115.

Markwell, K. (ed.) (2015) *Animals and Tourism: Understanding Diverse Relationships.* Bristol: Channel View Publications.

Mashhadigholam Rojo, D. (2007) Religious tourism: The way to Santiago. Unpublished master's thesis, Bournemouth University.

Mathieson, A. and Wall, G. (1982) *Tourism: Economic, Physical and Social Impacts.* London: Longman.

McAlexander, J.H., Dufault, B.L., Martin, D.M. and Schouten, J.W. (2014) The marketization of religion: Field, capital, and consumer identity. *Journal of Consumer Research* 41 (3), 858–875.

McCabe, S. (2015) Are we all post-tourists now? Tourist categories, identities and postmodernity. In T.V. Singh (ed.) *Challenges in Tourism Research* (pp. 18–25). Bristol: Channel View Publications.

McCaul, K. (2005) World's first Hindu theme park. BBC News, 28 April. See http://news.bbc.co.uk/2/hi/south_asia/4494747.stm (accessed 6 August 2009).

McConkie, B.R. (1966) *Mormon Doctrine.* Salt Lake City: Bookcraft.

McDermott, J.C. (2008) The role of religious marketing in economic regeneration: A case study of Knock. *The Marketing Review* 8 (1), 75–82.

Mcelveen, B. (2010) Pastoral reflection. In 'One Spirit, Many Gifts' Christian Ecumenism: Pentecost. Raleigh, NC: North Carolina Council of Churches. See https://www.ncchurches.org/priorities/christian-unity/ (accessed 11 June 2018).

McGehee, N.G. (2014) Volunteer tourism: Evolution, issues and futures. *Journal of Sustainable Tourism* 22 (6), 847–854.

McGehee, N.G. and Andereck, K. (2008) 'Pettin' the critters': Exploring the complex relationship between volunteers and the volunteered in McDowell County, West Virginia, USA, and Tijuana, Mexico. In K.D. Lyons and S. Wearing (eds) *Journeys of Discovery in Volunteer Tourism: International Case Study Perspectives* (pp. 12–24). Wallingford: CABI.

McGehee, N.G. and Santos, C.A. (2005) Social change, discourse and volunteer tourism. *Annals of Tourism Research* 32 (3), 760–779.

McGuckin, J.A. (2010) *The Orthodox Church: An Introduction to Its History, Doctrine and Spiritual Culture*. London: Wiley.

McHale, E.E. (1985) 'Witnessing for Christ': The Hill Cumorah Pageant of Palmyra, New York. *Western Folklore* 44 (1), 34–40.

McIntosh, A. and Zahra, A. (2013) World Youth Day: Contemporary pilgrimage and tourism. Paper presented at the International Conference on Tourism (ICOT) 2013, Limassol, Cyprus.

McLennan, S. (2014) Medical voluntourism in Honduras: 'Helping' the poor? *Progress in Development Studies* 14 (2), 163–179.

Measham, T.G. and Barnett, G.B. (2008) Environmental volunteering: Motivations, modes and outcomes. *Australian Geographer* 39 (4), 537–552.

Meethan, K. (2004) 'To stand in the shoes of my ancestors': Tourism and genealogy. In T. Coles and D.J. Timothy (eds) *Tourism, Diasporas and Space* (pp. 139–150). London: Routledge.

Meinardus, O.F.A. (2002) *Two Thousand Years of Coptic Christianity*. Cairo: The American University in Cairo Press.

Meinardus, O.F.A. (2007) *Coptic Saints and Pilgrimages*. Cairo: The American University in Cairo Press.

Meskell, L. (2015) Transacting UNESCO World Heritage: Gifts and exchanges on a global stage. *Social Anthropology* 23 (1), 3–21.

Metreveli, M. and Timothy, D.J. (2010) Religious heritage and emerging tourism in the Republic of Georgia. *Journal of Heritage Tourism* 5 (3), 237–244.

Michalkó, G., Irimiás, A. and Timothy, D.J. (2015) Disappointment in tourism: Perspectives on tourism destination management. *Tourism Management Perspectives* 16, 85–91.

Mikula, M. (2013) The island monastery of Valaam in Finnish homeland tourism: Constructing a 'Thirdspace' in the Russian borderlands. *Fennia* 191 (1), 14–24.

Miller, K.E. (2006) *I Volunteered for This?! Life on an Archaeological Dig*. Washington, DC: Biblical Archaeology Society.

Miller, F.P., Vandome, A.F. and McBrewster, J. (2009) *Christian Denomination*. Saarbrücken: Verlag.

Milton, J. (1836) *The Poetical Works of John Milton*. Boston, MA: Hilliard, Gray, and Company.

Mitchell, H. (2001) 'Being there': British Mormons and the history trail. *Anthropology Today* 17 (2), 9–14.

Mitchell, H.J. (2003) Postcards from the edge of history: Narrative and the sacralisation of Mormon Historical Sites. In S. Coleman and J. Elsner (eds) *Pilgrim Voices: Narrative and Authorship in Christian Pilgrimage* (pp. 133–157). New York: Berghahn.

Mitchell, T. (1988) *Colonising Egypt*. Cambridge: Cambridge University Press.

Mitrašinović, M. (2006) *Total Landscape, Theme Parks, Public Space*. Aldershot: Ashgate.

Moal-Ulvoas, G. (2016) The tourism experience offered by religious theme parks: Taman Tamadun Islam (TTI) in Malaysia. *International Journal of Religious Tourism and Pilgrimage* 4 (5), 59–66.

Mohsin, A. and Ryan, C. (in press) Halal tourism. In D.J. Timothy (ed.) *The Routledge Handbook on Tourism in the Middle East and North Africa*. London: Routledge.

Mohsin, A., Ramli, N. and Alkhulayfi, B.A. (2016) Halal tourism: Emerging opportunities. *Tourism Management Perspectives* 19, 137–143.

Montgomery, E.J. (2011) Oberammergau Passion Play 2010. *Theatre Journal* 63 (2), 260–262.

Mooney, B. (2010) The pilgrim path to Rome, 75 days on foot. *Via Francigena* 32, 76–78.

Moore, H. (2003) The pilgrimage of passion in Sidney's Arcadia. In S. Coleman and J. Elsner (eds) *Pilgrim Voices: Narrative and Authorship in Christian Pilgrimage* (pp. 61–83). New York: Berghahn.

Morehead, J.W. (2008) Latter-day Saints, ritual, pilgrimage, and cultural symbolics: Neglected sources for understanding and engagement. *Sacred Tribes Journal* 3 (1), 59–71.

Morgan, N., Pritchard, A. and Pride, D. (2011) *Destination Brands: Managing Place Reputation* (3rd edn). Oxford: Butterworth Heinemann.

Morinis, E.A. (1992) Introduction: The territory of the anthropology of pilgrimage. In A. Morinis (ed.) *Sacred Journeys: The Anthropology of Pilgrimage* (pp. 1–28). Westport, CT: Greenwood.

Morpeth, N.D. (2007) Ancient and modern pilgrimage: El Camino Frances. In R. Raj and N.D. Morpeth (eds) *Religious Tourism and Pilgrimage Festivals Management: An International Perspective* (pp. 153–160). Wallingford: CABI.

Morpeth, N.D. (2011) Church tourism and faith tourism initiatives in Northern England: Implications for the management of religious tourism sites. *International Journal of Business and Globalisation* 7 (1), 93–101.

Morris, C. (2005) *The Sephulchre of Christ and the Medieval West: From the Beginning to 1600*. Oxford: Oxford University Press.

Morrison, I. (2014) The dig at the end of the world: Archaeology and apocalypse. Tourism in the Valley of Armageddon. In C. Moser and C. Feldman (eds) *Locating the Sacred: Theoretical Approaches to the Emplacement of Religion* (pp. 74–86). Oxford: Oxbow.

Mostafanezhad, M. (2013) The geography of compassion in volunteer tourism. *Tourism Geographies* 15 (2), 318–337.

Mostafanezhad, M. (2014) *Volunteer Tourism: Popular Humanitarianism in Neoliberal Times*. London: Routledge.

Motyer, S. (2004) Paul and pilgrimage. In C. Bartholomew and F. Hughes (eds) *Explorations in a Christian Theology of Pilgrimage* (pp. 50–70). Aldershot: Ashgate.

Moufakkir, O. (2010) Re-evaluating political tourism in the Holy Land: Towards a conceptualization of peace tourism. In O. Moufakkir and I. Kelly (eds) *Tourism, Progress and Peace* (pp. 162–178). Wallingford: CABI.

Moufakkir, O., Reisinger, Y. and AlSaleh, D. (in press) Much ado about halal tourism: Religion, religiosity, or none of the above? In D.J. Timothy (ed.) *Routledge Handbook on Tourism in the Middle East and North Africa*. London: Routledge.

Mowforth, M. and Munt, I. (2003) *Tourism and Sustainability: New Tourism in the Third World*. London: Routledge.

Mullins, E. (1974) *The Pilgrimage to Santiago*. London: Secker & Warburg.

Murray, M. and Graham, B. (1997) Exploring the dialectics of route-based tourism: The Camino de Santiago. *Tourism Management* 18, 513–524.

Murzyn, M.A. (2008) Heritage transformation in Central and Eastern Europe. In B. Graham and P. Howard (eds) *The Ashgate Research Companion to Heritage and Identity* (pp. 315–346). Aldershot: Ashgate.

Mustafa, M.H. (2014) Tourism development at the Baptism Site of Jesus Christ, Jordan: Residents' perspectives. *Journal of Heritage Tourism* 9 (1), 75–83.

Mustonen, P. (2006) Volunteer tourism: Postmodern pilgrimage? *Journal of Tourism and Cultural Change* 3 (3), 160–177.

Nakamura, Y. (1988) Some aspects of the Russian pilgrimage to the Mediterranean sacred places. *Studies in the Mediterranean World Past and Present: Collected Papers* 11, 25–35.

Narbona, J. and Arasa, D. (2016) The role and usage of apps and instant messaging in religious mass events. *International Journal of Religious Tourism and Pilgrimage* 4 (3), 29–42.

Neal, J.A. (2014) *Historic United Methodist Churches and Places in South Carolina*. Columbia, SC: Methodist Books.

Nichols, S.J. (2008) *Jesus: Made in America*. Downers Grove, IL: IVP Academic.

Nilsson, M. and Tesfahuney, M. (2016) Performing the 'post-secular' in Santiago de Compostela. *Annals of Tourism Research* 57 (1), 18–30.

Nolan, M.L. and Nolan, S. (1989) *Christian Pilgrimage in Modern Western Europe*. Chapel Hill, NC: University of North Carolina Press.

Nolan, M.L. and Nolan, S. (1992) Religious sites as tourism attractions in Europe. *Annals of Tourism Research* 19 (1), 68–78.

Norman, A. and Johnson, M. (2011) World Youth Day: The creation of a modern pilgrimage event for evangelical intent. *Journal of Contemporary Religion* 26 (3), 371–385.

Norris, J. (2013) Exporting the Holy Land: Aartisans and merchant migrants in Ottoman-era Bethlehem. *Mashriq & Mahjar* 2, 14–40.

Nyaupane, G. and Timothy, D.J. (2010) Power, regionalism and tourism policy in Bhutan. *Annals of Tourism Research* 37 (4), 969–988.

O'Flanagan, M. (1928) Memories of the pilgrimage. *The Irish Monthly* 56, 295–298.

O'Gorman, K.D. (2006) The legacy of monastic hospitality: The rule of Benedict and rise of western monastic hospitality. *The Hospitality Review* 8 (3), 35–44.

O'Gorman, K.D. and MacPhee, E. (2006) The legacy of monastic hospitality: The lasting influence. *The Hospitality Review* 8 (4), 16–25.

O'Mahony, A. (2005) The Vatican, Jerusalem, the State of Israel, and Christianity in the Holy Land. *International Journal for the Study of the Christian Church* 5 (2), 123–146.

O'Mahony, A. (2010) Between the local and the global: The modern papacy and Jerusalem: Catholic theological and ecclesiological perspectives on Christianity in the Holy Land. Presentation at a Conference on Transnationalism and the Contemporary Christian Communities in the Holy Land, 28–29 June, The Van Leer Jerusalem Institute and the CRFJ.

O'Mahony, A, and Bowe, P. (eds) (2006) *Catholics in Interreligious Dialogue: Monasticism, Theology and Spirituality*. Leominster: Gracewing Publishing.

Occhipinti, L. (2016) Not just tourists: Short-term missionaries and voluntourism. *Human Organization* 75 (3), 258–268.

Offutt, S. (2011) The role of short-term mission teams in the new centers of global Christianity. *Journal for the Scientific Study of Religion* 50 (4), 796–811.

Oficina del Peregrino (2018) *Informe estadístico Año Santo 2017*. Santiago de Compostela: Oficina del Peregrino.

Ołdakowski, K. (2002) The Pope-pilgrim on the ways of the world. *Peregrinus Cracoviensis* 13, 19–24.

Olsen, D.H. (2003) Heritage, tourism and the commodification of religion. *Tourism Recreation Research* 28 (3), 99–104.

Olsen, D.H. (2006a) Management issues for religious heritage attractions. In D.J. Timothy and D.H. Olsen (eds) *Tourism, Religion and Spiritual Journeys* (pp. 104–118). London: Routledge.

Olsen, D.H. (2006b) Tourism and informal pilgrimage among the Latter-day Saints. In D.J. Timothy and D.H. Olsen (eds) *Tourism, Religion and Spiritual Journeys* (pp. 254–270). London: Routledge.

Olsen, D.H. (2008) Contesting identity, space and sacred site management at Temple Square in Salt Lake City, Utah. Unpublished PhD dissertation, University of Waterloo.

Olsen, D.H. (2009) 'The strangers within our gates': Managing visitors at Temple Square. *Journal of Management, Spirituality & Religion* 6 (2), 121–139.

Olsen, D.H. (2010) Pilgrims, tourists and Max Weber's 'ideal types'. *Annals of Tourism Research* 37 (3), 848–851.

Olsen, D.H. (2011) Towards a religious view of tourism: Negotiating faith perspectives on tourism. *Tourism, Culture & Communication* 11 (1), 17–30.

Olsen, D.H. (2012a) Negotiating identity at religious sites: A management perspective. *Journal of Heritage Tourism* 7 (4), 359–366.

Olsen, D.H. (2012b) Teaching truth in 'third space': The use of religious history as a pedagogical instrument at Temple Square in Salt Lake City, Utah. *Tourism Recreation Research* 37 (3), 227–237.

Olsen, D.H. (2013) Touring sacred history: The Latter-day Saints and their historical sites. In J.M. Hunter (ed.) *Mormons and American Popular Culture: The Global Influence of an American Phenomenon* (Vol. 2; pp. 225–242). Santa Barbara, CA: Praeger.

Olsen, D.H. (2014) A scalar comparison of motivations and expectations of experience within the religious tourism market. *International Journal of Religious Tourism and Pilgrimage* 1 (1), 41–61.

Olsen, D.H. (2017) Social politics on the move: The case of the Marian Ocean to Ocean pilgrimage. In M.S.C. Mariani and A. Trono (eds) *The Ways of Mercy: Arts, Culture and Marian Routes between East and West* (pp. 405–430). Galatina: Mario Congedo.

Olsen, D.H. (in press) Religion, pilgrimage and tourism in the Middle East and North Africa. In D.J. Timothy (ed.) *The Routledge Handbook on Tourism in the Middle East and North Africa*. London: Routledge.

Olsen, D.H. and Guelke, J.K. (2004a) 'Nourishing the soul': Geography and matters of meaning. In D.G. Janelle, B. Warf and K. Hansen (eds) *Worldminds: Geographical Perspectives on 100 Problems* (pp. 595–599). Dordrecht: Kluwer.

Olsen, D.H. and Guelke, J.K. (2004b) Spatial transgression and the BYU Jerusalem Center controversy. *The Professional Geographer* 56 (4), 503–515.

Olsen, D.H. and Ron, A.S. (2013) Managing religious heritage attractions: The case of Jerusalem. In B. Garrod and A. Fyall (eds) *Contemporary Cases in Heritage: Volume 1* (pp. 51–78). Oxford: Goodfellow.

Olsen, D.H. and Timothy, D.J. (1999) Tourism 2000: Selling the Millennium. *Tourism Management* 20, 389–392.

Olsen, D.H. and Timothy, D.J. (2002) Contested religious heritage: Differing views of Mormon heritage. *Tourism Recreation Research* 27 (2), 7–15.

Olsen, D.H. and Timothy, D.J. (2006) Tourism and religious journeys. In D.J. Timothy and D.H. Olsen (eds) *Tourism, Religion and Spiritual Journeys* (pp. 1–21). London: Routledge.

Olsen, D.H. and Timothy, D.J. (2018) Tourism, Salt Lake City and the cultural heritage of Mormonism. In R. Butler and W. Suntikul (eds) *Tourism and Religion: Issues and Implications* (pp. 250–269). Bristol: Channel View Publications.

Olsen, D.H. and Trono, A. (eds) (2018) *Religious Pilgrimage Routes and Trails: Sustainable Development and Management*. Wallingford: CABI.

Opera Romana Pellegrinaggi (ORP) (2015) *Programmi 2015*. Rome: Opera Romana Pelegrinaggi.

Orcutt, A. (2012) World's most-visited sacred sites. *Travel & Leisure*. See http://www.travelandleisure.com/slideshows/worlds-most-visited-sacred-sites/12 (accessed 13 January 2018).

Ortiz, E. (2017) Museum of the Bible opens in Washington, D.C., with celebration amid cynicism. *NBC News*, 18 November. See https://www.nbcnews.com/news/religion/

museum-bible-opens-washington-d-c-celebration-amid-cynicism-n821996 (accessed 22 February 2018).
Ostrometskaia, E. and Griffin, K. (2018) Religious tourism and pilgrimage in Russia. In R. Butler and W. Suntikul (eds) *Tourism and Religion: Issues and Implications* (pp. 182–196). Bristol: Channel View Publications.
Ostrowski, M. (1997) Turystyka w myśli Jana Pawła II (Tourism in the views of John Paul II). *Peregrinus Cracoviensis* 5, 139–153.
Öter, Z. and Çetinkaya, M.Y. (2016) Interfaith tourist behaviour at religious heritage sites: House of the Virgin Mary case in Turkey. *International Journal of Religious Tourism and Pilgrimage* 4 (4), 1–18.
Otterstrom, S.M. (2008) Genealogy as religious ritual: The doctrine and practice of family history in the Church of Jesus Christ of Latter-day Saints. In D.J. Timothy and J.K. Guelke (eds) *Geography and Genealogy: Locating Personal Pasts* (pp. 137–152). Aldershot: Ashgate.
Ouellette, P., Kaplan, R. and Kaplan, S. (2005) The monastery as a restorative environment. *Journal of Environmental Psychology* 25 (2), 175–188.
Pack, C. (2008) Personal interview conducted by Amos S. Ron, 23 October.
Pack, C. (2013) Personal interview conducted by Amos S. Ron, 25 April.
Pack, S.D. (2010) Revival of the pilgrimage to Santiago de Compostela: The politics of religious, national, and European patrimony, 1879–1988. *The Journal of Modern History* 82 (2), 335–367.
Pagliaroli, J.C. (2004) Kodak Catholicism: Miraculous photography and its significance at a post-conciliar Marian apparition site in Canada. *CCHA Historical Studies* 70, 71–93.
Paradis, T.W. (2004) Theming, tourism and fantasy city. In A.A. Lew, C.M. Hall and A.M. Williams (eds) *A Companion to Tourism* (pp. 195–208). Oxford: Blackwell.
Paraskevaidis, P. and Antriotis, K. (2015) Values of souvenirs as commodities. *Tourism Management* 48, 1–10.
Park, C.C. (1994) *Sacred Worlds: An Introduction to Geography and Religion*. London: Routledge.
Parker, G. (2001) *Europe in Crisis: 1598–1648*. Chichester: Wiley.
Pastoor, C., Caton, K., Belhassen, Y., Collins, B. and Wallin, M.R. (2014) Let there be rock! A tale of two Christian music festivals. In O. Moufakkir and T. Pernecky (eds) *Ideological, Social and Cultural Aspects of Events* (pp. 47–59). Wallingford: CABI.
Pastoor, C., Caton, K., Belhassen, Y., Collins, B. and Wallin, M.R. (2018) Rock of our salvation: Ideological production at the Christian youth music festival. *Annals of Leisure Research* 21 (4), 440–461.
Pavicic, J., Alfirevic, N. and Batarelo, V.J. (2007) The management and marketing of religious sites, pilgrimage and religious events: Challenges for Roman Catholic pilgrimages in Croatia. In R. Raj and N.D. Morpeth (eds) *Religious Tourism and Pilgrimage Festivals Management: An International Perspective* (pp. 48–63). Wallingford: CABI.
Pentecostal World Fellowship (2011) Pentecostal World Conference. See http://www.pentecostalworldfellowship.org/about/aboutus.htm#history (accessed 15 August 2011).
Peters, K. (2011) Negotiating the 'place' and 'placement' of banal tourist souvenirs in the home. *Tourism Geographies* 13 (2), 234–256.
Peterson, J.L. (1998) *A Walk in Jerusalem: Stations of the Cross*. Harrisburg, PA: Morehouse.Pew Research Center (2011) Global Christianity – A Report on the Size and Distribution of the World's Christian Population. See http://www.pewforum.org/2011/12/19/global-christianity-exec/ (accessed 11 June 2018).
Pfaffenberger, B. (1983) Serious pilgrims and frivolous tourists: The chimera of tourism in the pilgrimage of Sri Lanka. *Annals of Tourism Research* 10 (1), 57–74.
Pfanner, J.H. (2011) Archaeological sieving as creative tourism? Unpublished master's thesis, University of Warwick.

Pilegrimsleden (2014) St. Olav Ways: The pilgrim paths to Trondheim. See http://pilegrimsleden.no/en/map (accessed 3 April 2017).

Pilgrim Tours (2016) Footsteps of Paul & John. See http://www.pilgrimtours.com/greece/sched_tours/footsteps_of_paul16day.htm. (accessed 11 June 2018).

Pine, B.J. and Gilmore, J.H. (1998) Welcome to the experience economy. *Harvard Business Review* July–August, 97–105.

Pine, B.J. and Gilmore, J.H. (1999) *The Experience Economy: Work is Theatre & Every Business a Stage*. Boston, MA: Harvard Business School Press.

Pinsky, M.I. (2007) *The Gospel According to The Simpsons: BIGGER and Possibly Even BETTER!* (2nd edn). Louisville, KY: Westminster John Knox Press.

Pinto, H. (2004) Personal interview with Amos S. Ron, 10 December.

Poon, A. (1993) *Tourism, Technology and Competitive Strategies*. Wallingford: CABI.

Poon, A. (1994) The 'new tourism' revolution. *Tourism Management* 15 (2), 91–92.

Poon, A. (2003) Competitive strategies for a 'new tourism'. In C. Cooper (ed.) *Classic Reviews in Tourism* (pp. 130–142). Clevedon: Channel View Publications.

Poria, Y., Butler, R.W. and Airey, D. (2003) Tourism, religion and religiosity: A holy mess. *Current Issues in Tourism* 6 (4), 340–363.

Poria, Y., Reichel, A. and Cohen, R. (2011) World Heritage Site: An effective brand for an archaeological site? *Journal of Heritage Tourism* 6 (3), 197–208.

Post, P., Pieper, J., and van Uden, M. (1998) *The Modern Pilgrim: Multidisciplinary Explorations of Christian Pilgrimage*. Leuven: Peeters.

Potter, J.H. (1982) *Pilgrim's Trail*. London: Hale.

Poulston, J. and Pernecky, T. (2017) Accommodating New Age: Understanding the needs of a growing segment. *Hospitality & Society* 7 (3), 245–262.

Probasco, L. (2013) Giving time, not money: Long-term impacts of short-term mission trips. *Missiology* 41 (2), 202–224.

Pruess, J.B. (1976) Merit-seeking in public: Buddhist pilgrimage in northeastern Thailand. *Journal of the Siam Society* 64 (1), 167–206.

Przybył, E. (2002) Major Orthodox pilgrimage destinations in the past and present Poland. *Peregrinus Cracoviensis* 13, 167–177.

Przybylska, L. and Sołjan, I. (2010) Polish pilgrimages to Santiago de Compostela: Ways of St. James in Poland. *GeoJournal of Tourism and Geosites* 6 (2), 211–218.

Ptaszycka-Jackowska, D. (2000) Religious tourism and the protection of the natural environment and nature conservation. *Peregrinus Cracoviensis* 10, 83–99.

Pusztai, B. (2004) Religious tourists: Constructing authentic experiences in late modern Hungarian Catholicism. Unpublished PhD dissertation, University of Jyväskylä.

Qurashi, J. (2017) Commodification of Islamic religious tourism: From spiritual to touristic experience. *International Journal of Religious Tourism and Pilgrimage* 5 (1), 89–104.

Raheb, M. (2002) Sailing through troubled waters: Palestinian Christians in the Holy Land. *Dialog* 41 (2), 97–102.

Rahkala, M.J. (2010a) In the sphere of the holy: Pilgrimage to a contemporary Greek convent. In R. Gothóni (ed.) *Pilgrims and Travellers in Search of the Holy* (pp. 69–95). Oxford: Peter Lang.

Rahkala, M.J. (2010b) Pilgrimage as a lifestyle: A contemporary Greek nunnery as a pilgrimage site. Unpublished PhD dissertation, University of Helsinki.

Raivo, P.J. (2002) The peculiar touch of the East: Reading the post-war landscapes of the Finnish Orthodox Church. *Social & Cultural Geography* 3 (1), 11–24.

Ramos, C.M., Henriques, C. and Lanquar, R. (2016) Augmented reality for smart tourism in religious heritage itineraries: Tourism experiences in the technological age. In J. Rodrigues, P. Cardoso, J. Monteiro and M. Figueiredo (eds) *Handbook of Research on Human–Computer Interfaces, Developments, and Applications* (pp. 245–272). Hershey, PA: IGI Global.

Ramsay, J. and Truscott, M.C. (2003) Tracking through Australian forests. *Historic Environment* 16 (2), 32–38.

Reader, I. (2007) Pilgrimage growth in the modern world: Meanings and implications. *Religion* 37, 210–229.

Reader, I. (2014) *Pilgrimage in the Marketplace*. London: Routledge.

Redfield, R. (1956) *Peasant Society and Culture: An Anthropological Approach to Civilization*. Chicago, IL: University of Chicago Press.

Reeve, W.P. (2010) Word of wisdom. In W.P. Reeve and A.E. Parshall (eds) *Mormonism: A Historical Encyclopedia* (pp. 122–123). Santa Barbara, CA: ABC-CLIO.

Richards, G. and Fernandes, C. (2011) Religious tourism in northern Portugal. In G. Richards (ed.) *Cultural Tourism: Global and Local Perspectives* (pp. 215–237). London: Routledge.

Rinschede, G. (1986) The pilgrimage town of Lourdes. *Journal of Cultural Geography* 7 (1), 21-34.

Rinschede, G. (1992) Forms of religious tourism. *Annals of Tourism Research* 19 (1), 51–67.

Rivera, M.A., Shani, A. and Severt, D. (2009) Perceptions of service attributes in a religious theme site: An importance-satisfaction analysis. *Journal of Heritage Tourism* 4 (3), 227–243.

Rizzello, K. and Trono, A. (2013) The pilgrimage to the San Nicola Shrine in Bari and its impacts. *International Journal of Religious Tourism and Pilgrimage* 1 (1), 24–40.

Robertson, R. (1992) *Globalization: Social Theory and Global Culture*. London: Sage.

Rodosthenous, N. and Varvounis, M. (2014) Contemporary parish and pilgrimage travel: Preconditions and targeting. *Tourism Today* 14, 164–172.

Rodrigues, S. and McIntosh, A. (2014) Motivations, experiences and perceived impacts of visitation at a Catholic monastery in New Zealand. *Journal of Heritage Tourism* 9 (4), 271–284.

Rogers, S.S. (2003) American Protestant pilgrimage: Nineteenth-century impressions of Palestine. *Koinonia Journal: The Princeton Seminary Graduate Forum* 15 (1), 60–80.

Roitershtein, A. (2009) Christian Orthodox Tourism: Its Impact on Tourism and Hospitality Landscapes in Israel. Seminar paper at Kinneret College on the Sea of Galilee, Israel.

Ron, A.S. (2002) Representational and symbolic landscapes of the early Zionist rural settlement in the Kinneret (Sea of Galilee) Valley. Unpublished PhD dissertation, Hebrew University of Jerusalem (in Hebrew).

Ron, A.S. (2009) Towards a typological model of contemporary Christian travel. *Journal of Heritage Tourism* 4 (4), 287–297.

Ron, A.S. (2010a) Banneux: Catholic Spirituality and Diasporic Christian Identities. Unpublished manuscript in possession of A.S. Ron.

Ron, A.S. (2010b) Holy Land Protestant themed environments and the spiritual experience. In J. Schlehe, M. Uike-Bormann, C. Oesterle and W. Hochbruck (eds) *Staging the Past: Themed Environments in Transcultural Perspectives* (pp. 111–133). Bielefeld: Verlag.

Ron, A.S. (2011) Notes from the Field: A Diary of Guiding Christians in the Holy Land. Unpublished manuscript in possession of A.S. Ron.

Ron, A.S. (2018) Religious needs in the tourism industry: The perspective of Abrahamic traditions. In R. Butler and W. Suntikul (eds) *Tourism and Religion: Issues and Implications* (pp. 270–287). Bristol: Channel View Publications.

Ron, A.S. and Feldman, J. (2009) From spots to themed sites: The evolution of the Protestant Holy Land. *Journal of Heritage Tourism* 4 (3), 201–216.

Ron, A.S. and Timothy, D.J. (2013) The Land of Milk and Honey: Biblical foods, heritage and Holy Land tourism. *Journal of Heritage Tourism* 8 (2/3), 234–247.

Ron, A.S. and Timothy, D.J. (2016) Archaeology and contemporary Christian travel: The challenge and the potential. Paper presented at the international symposium, Galilean Archaeology – Research Education and Religion, Nazareth, Israel, 24 July.

Roseman, S.R. (2004) Santiago de Compostela in the Year 2000: From religious center to European City of Culture. In E. Badone and S.R. Roseman (eds) *Intersecting Journeys: The Anthropology of Pilgrimage and Tourism* (pp. 68–88). Urbana, IL: University of Illinois Press.

Roseman, S.R. and Fife, W. (2008) Souvenirs and cultural politics in Santiago de Compostela. *International Journal of Iberian Studies* 21 (2), 109–130.

Rosenblum, I. (2008) Tourists may tread 'Pilgrim's Route', visit W. Bank Christian sites by next year. *Haaretz*, June 21, np.

Ross, B. (2009) Church in America marked by decline. *The Christian Chronicle* 66 (2), 1, 18.

Ross, G. (2014) Meaning making, life transitional experiences and personal well-being within the contexts of religious and spiritual travel. In S. Filep and P.L. Pearce (eds) *Tourist Experience and Fulfilment: Insights from Positive Psychology* (pp. 91–109). London: Routledge.

Roth, S. (2008) Personal interview with Amos Ron, 12 May.

Rotherham, I.D. (2007) Sustaining tourism infrastructures for religious tourists and pilgrims within the UK. In R. Raj and N.D. Morpeth (eds) *Religious Tourism and Pilgrimage Festivals Management: An International Perspective* (pp. 64–77). Wallingford: CABI.

Rotkovitz, M. (2004) Kashering the melting pot: Oreos, sushi restaurants, 'Kosher Treif', and the observant American Jew. In L.M. Long (ed.) *Culinary Tourism* (pp. 157–185). Lexington, KY: University Press of Kentucky.

Rowan, Y. (2004) Repacking the pilgrimage: Visiting the Holy Land in Orlando. In Y. Rowan and U. Baram (eds) *Marketing Heritage: Archaeology and the Consumption of the Past* (pp. 249–266). Walnut Creek, CA: AltaMira.

Rubin, R. (2000) When Jerusalem was built in St. Louis: A large-scale model of Jerusalem in the Louisiana Purchase Exposition 1904. *Palestine Exploration Quarterly* 132, 59–70.

Rubio Gill, A. and de Esteban Curiel, J. (2008) Religious events as special interest tourism: A Spanish experience. *PASOS: Revista de Turismo y Patrimonio Cultural* 6 (3), 419–433.

Rudolf, C. (2004) *Pilgrimage to the End of the World: The Road to Santiago de Compostela*. Chicago, IL: University of Chicago Press.

Ruini, C. (2007) Cultural-religious significance of the ancient pilgrims ways. *Via Francigena* 26, 30–33.

Russell, P. (1999) Religious travel in the new Millennium. *Travel & Tourism Analyst* 5, 39–68.

Ruthven, M. (2012) *The Divine Supermarket: Travels in Search of the Soul in America*. London: Tauris.

Ryan, M. and McKenzie, F. (2003) A monastic tourist experience: The packaging of a place. *Tourism Geographies* 5 (1), 54–70.

Saayman, A., Saayman, M. and Gyekye, A. (2014) Perspectives on the regional economic value of pilgrimage. *International Journal of Tourism Research* 16 (4), 407–414.

Sacred Destinations (2014) Via Dolorosa, Jerusalem. See http://www.sacred-destinations.com/israel/jerusalem-via-dolorosa (accessed 3 December 2014).

Sallnow, M.J. (2000) Pilgrimage and cultural fracture in the Andes. In J. Eade and M.J. Sallnow (eds) *Contesting the Sacred: The Anthropology of Christian Pilgrimage* (pp. 137–153). Urbana, IL: University of Illinois Press.

Salman, H.K. (2006) The olive wood industry: Year 2000. See http://admusallam.bethlehem.edu (accessed 1 November 2016).

San Filippo, M. (2001) The religious niche. *Travel Weekly* 60 (18), 12.
Sánchez y Sánchez, S. and Hesp, A. (eds) (2015) *The Camino de Santiago in the 21st Century: Interdisciplinary Perspectives and Global Views*. London: Routledge.
Sandberg, K. (2009) 60 Ft. Jesus resurrected: A glimpse of Tierra Santa theme park in Buenos Aires. See http://gogreentravelgreen.com/green-travel-stories/tierra_santa_religious_theme_park_buenos_aires/ (accessed 2 July 2015).
Santos, C.A. and Yan, G. (2010) Genealogical tourism: A phenomenological examination. *Journal of Travel Research* 49 (1), 56–67.
Santos, M.G.M.P. (2003) Religious tourism: Contributions towards a clarification of concepts. In C. Fernandes, F. McGettigan and J. Edwards (eds) *Religious Tourism and Pilgrimage, ATLAS Special Interest Group, 1st Expert Meeting* (pp. 27–42). Fátima: Tourism Board of Leiria/Fátima.
Santos, M.G.M.P. (2009) Visitor profiles and market segmentation: A contribution to the renewal of an almost centennial religious destination (Fátima). In A. Trono (ed.) *Proceedings of the International Conference Tourism, Religion & Culture: Regional Development through Meaningful Tourism Experiences* (pp. 307–328). Lecce: University of Salento.
Santos, X.M. (2002) Pilgrimage and tourism at Santiago de Compostela. *Tourism Recreation Research* 27 (2), 41–50.
Scandolara, P. (2008) Towards Santiago de Compostela. *Via Francigena* 27, 30–33.
Scheer, M. (2007) The symbolic representation of religion, culture and heritage and their implications on the tourism experience: The example of the 'Ciudad de Cultura' in Santiago de Compostela. In R. Raj and N.D. Morpeth (eds) *Religious Tourism and Pilgrimage Festivals Management: An International Perspective* (pp. 161–169). Wallingford: CABI.
Scheyvens, R. (1999) Ecotourism and the empowerment of local communities. *Tourism Management* 20, 245–249.
Schmidt, K. (2000) Göbekli Tepe, southeastern Turkey: A preliminary report on the 1995–1999 excavations. *Paléorient* 26 (1), 45–54.
Schmidt, W.S. (2012) *Walking with Stones: A Spiritual Odyssey on the Pilgrimage to Santiago*. Bloomington, IN: Trafford.
Schmisek, B. (2017) *The Rome of Peter and Paul: A Pilgrim's Handbook to New Testament Sites in the Eternal City*. Eugene, OR: Wipf and Stock.
Schott, S.B. (2008) *Religious Tourism in America: Identity Formation of Sites and Visitors*. Chicago, IL: University of Chicago Press.
Sekerdej, K. (2005) The Amazing Lichen. See http://www.ccrit.ro/Pdf/ResearchReports/ResearchReportKingaSekerdej.pdf (accessed 19 July 2010).
Sekerdej, K., Pasieka, A. and Warat, M. (2007) Popular religion and postsocialist nostalgia: Licheń as a polysemic pilgrimage centre in Poland. *Polish Sociological Review* 4, 431–444.
Shachar, A. and Shoval, N. (1999) Tourism in Jerusalem: A place to play. In D.R. Judd and S.S. Fainstein (eds) *The Tourist City* (pp. 198–211). New Haven, CT: Yale University Press.
Shackley, M. (1998) A golden calf in sacred space: The future of St Katherine's Monastery, Mount Sinai (Egypt). *International Journal of Heritage Studies* 4 (3/4), 123–134.
Shackley, M. (2001) *Managing Sacred Sites: Service Provision and Visitor Experience*. London: Continuum.
Shackley, M. (2002) Space, sanctity and service; The English cathedral as heteropia. *International Journal of Tourism Research* 4 (5), 345-352.
Shackley, M. (2003) Management challenges for religion-based attractions. In A. Fyall, B. Garrod and A. Leask (eds) *Managing Visitor Attractions: New Directions* (pp. 159–170). Oxford: Butterworth Heinemann.
Shackley, M. (2004) Accommodating the spiritual tourist: The case of religious retreat houses. In R. Thomas (ed.) *Small Firms in Tourism: International Perspectives* (pp. 225–238). London: Elsevier.

Shackley, M. (2006a) Costs and benefits: The impact of cathedral tourism in England. *Journal of Heritage Tourism* 1 (2), 133–141.
Shackley, M. (2006b) Empty bottles at sacred sites: Religious retailing at Ireland's national shrine. In D.J. Timothy and D.H. Olsen (eds) *Tourism, Religion and Spiritual Journeys* (pp. 94–103). London: Routledge.
Shackley, M. (2008) Management challenges for religion-based attractions. In A. Fyall, B. Garrod, A. Leask and S. Wanhill (eds) *Managing Visitor Attractions: New Directions* (2nd edn; pp. 253–263). Oxford: Butterworth Heinemann.
Shai, I. and Uziel, J. (2016) All for archaeology and archaeology for all: The Tel Burna archaeology project's approach to community archaeology. *Journal of Community Archaeology & Heritage* 3 (1), 57–69.
Shani, A. and Logan, R. (2010) Walt Disney's world of entertainment attractions. In R.W. Butler and R. Russell (eds) *Giants of Tourism* (pp. 155–169). Wallingford: CABI.
Shani, A., Rivera, M.A. and Severt, D. (2007) To bring God's word to all people: The case of a religious theme-site. *Tourism* 55 (1), 39–50.
Shapiro, F.L. (2008) To the apple of God's eye: Christian Zionist travel to Israel. *Journal of Contemporary Religion* 23 (3), 307–320.
Shapiro, F.L. (2010) Taming Tehran: Evangelical Christians and the Iranian threat to Israel. *Studies in Religion/Sciences Religieuses* 39 (3), 363–377.
Shapiro, J.S. (2000) *Oberammergau: The Troubling Story of the World's Most Famous Passion Play*. New York: Pantheon.
Sharif, R. (1976) Christians for Zion, 1600–1919. *Journal of Palestine Studies* 5 (3/4), 123–141.
Sharpley, R. (2009) Tourism, religion and spirituality. In T. Jamal and M. Robinson (eds) *The Sage Handbook of Tourism Studies* (pp. 237–253). London: Sage.
Sharpley, R. and Jepson, D. (2011) Rural tourism: A spiritual experience? *Annals of Tourism Research* 38 (1), 52–71.
Shaw, G. and Williams, A.M. (2002) *Critical Issues in Tourism: A Geographical Perspective* (2nd edn). Oxford: Blackwell.
Shaw, G. and Williams, A.M. (2004) *Tourism and Tourism Spaces*. London: Sage.
Shenhav-Keller, S. (1993) The Israeli souvenir: Its text and context. *Annals of Tourism Research* 20 (1), 182–196.
Sherrard, P. (1977) The paths of Athos. *Eastern Churches Review* 9 (1), 100–107.
Shi, F. (2007) Commoditised religious souvenirs and visitor experience at Chinese Buddhist sites. Unpublished PhD dissertation, Nottingham Trent University.
Shi, F. (2011) Business at religious sites: Blessing or sin? Paper presented at the conference, Tourism in an Era of Uncertainty, Rhodes, Greece, 27–30 April.
Shinde, K.A. (2007) Visiting sacred sites in India: Religious tourism or pilgrimage? In R. Roj and N.D. Morpeth (eds) *Religious Tourism and Pilgrimage Management: An International Perspective* (pp. 184–197). Wallingford: CABI.
Shoval, N. (2000) Commodification and theming of the sacred: Changing patterns of tourist consumption in the 'Holy Land'. In M. Gottdiener (ed.) *New Forms of Consumption: Consumers, Culture and Commodification* (pp. 251–263). Boulder, CO: Rowman and Littlefield.
Shunnaq, M., Schwab, W.A. and Reid, M.F. (2008) Community development using a sustainable tourism strategy: A case study of the Jordan River Valley touristway. *International Journal of Tourism Research* 10 (1), 1–14.
Simone-Charteris, M.T. and Boyd, S.W. (2010) The development of religious heritage tourism in Northern Ireland: Opportunities, benefits and obstacles. *Tourism* 58 (3), 229–257.
Sin, H.L. (2009) Volunteer tourism: 'Involve Me and I Will Learn'? *Annals of Tourism Research* 36 (3), 480–501.
Singh, R.P.B. (2006) Pilgrimage in Hinduism: Historical context and modern perspectives. In D.J. Timothy and D.H. Olsen (eds) *Tourism, Religion and Spiritual Journeys* (pp. 220–236). London: Routledge.

Singh, T.V. (ed.) (2004) *New Horizons in Tourism: Strange Experiences and Stranger Practices*. Wallingford: CABI.

Sizer, S. (2003) Christian Zionism and the road map to Armageddon. Unpublished PhD dissertation, University of Oxford.

Sizer, S.R. (1999) The ethical challenges of managing pilgrimages to the Holy Land. *International Journal of Contemporary Hospitality Management* 11 (2/3), 85–90.

Skrbiš, Z. (2007) From migrants to pilgrim tourists: Diasporic imagining and visits to Medjugorje. *Journal of Ethnic and Migration Studies* 33 (2), 313–329.

Slavin, S. (2003) Walking as spiritual practice: The pilgrimage to Santiago de Compostela. *Body and Society* 9 (3), 1–18.

Smelser, N.J. (2009) *The Odyssey Experience: Physical, Social, Psychological, and Spiritual Journeys*. Berkeley, CA: University of California Press.

Smith, R.K. and Olson, L.S. (2001) Tourist shopping activities and development of travel sophistication. *Visions in Leisure and Business* 20 (1), 23-33.

Smith, V.L. (1992) Introduction: The quest in guest. *Annals of Tourism Research* 19 (1), 1–17.

Smolčić Jurdana, D. and Soldić Frleta, D. (2017) Satisfaction as a determinant of tourist expenditure. *Current Issues in Tourism* 20 (7), 691–704.

Snell, T.L. and Simmonds, J.G. (2012) 'Being in that environment can be very therapeutic': Spiritual experiences in nature. *Ecopsychology* 4 (4), 326–335.

Sørensen, A. and Sundbo, J. (eds) (2008) *Cases from the Experience Economy*. Nykøbing Falster: CELF Center for Leisure Management Research.

Sorenson, J.L. (1985) *An Ancient American Setting for the Book of Mormon*. Salt Lake City, UT: Deseret Book.

Southern Baptist Convention (2018) 2018 SBC Annual Meeting. See http://www.sbcannualmeeting.net/sbc18/ (accessed 22 February 2018).

Spano, S. (2008) Lourdes celebrates 150th anniversary of Bernadette's visions. *Los Angeles Times*, 7 September. See http://www.latimes.com/travel/la-tr-lourdes7-2008sep07-story.html (accessed 22 October 2017).

Speake, G. (2005) The Importance of Mount Athos and Monastic Revival. See http://www.benedictines.org.uk/theology/2005/speake.rtf (accessed 22 August 2010).

Spencer, R. (2008) Lessons from Cuba: A volunteer army of ambassadors. In K.D. Lyons and S. Wearing (eds) *Journeys of Discovery in Volunteer Tourism: International Case Study Perspectives* (pp. 36–47). Wallingford: CABI.

Spencer, R. (2010) *Development Tourism: Lessons from Cuba*. Aldershot: Ashgate.

St Justin Martyr (2003) *Dialogue with Trypho* (trans. T.B. Falls). Washington DC: The Catholic University of America Press.

Stănciulescu, G.C. and Țîrca, A.M. (2010) Implications of commercial activity within monastic settlements as a way to maintain the sustainable development of religious tourism in Romania. *Amfiteatru Economic Journal* 11, 129–144.

Stausberg, M. (2011) *Religion and Tourism: Crossroads, Destinations and Encounters*. London: Routledge.

Stefko, R., Jencova, S. and Litavcová, E. (2013) Selected aspects of marketing pilgrimage sites. *Polish Journal of Management Studies* 8, 280–287.

Steil, C.A. (2017) Studies of Catholicism and pilgrimage in Brazil: Continuities and ruptures over the long-term. In D. Albera and J. Eade (eds) *New Pathways in Pilgrimage Studies: Global Perspectives* (pp. 162–180). London: Routledge.

Steinmetz, T. (2009) Religious travel market shows resilience. *eTurboNews*, 23 November. See http://www.eturbonews.com/print/12933 (accessed 30 July 2010).

Stemberger, G. (2000) *Jews and Christians in the Holy Land: Palestine in the Fourth Century*. Edinburgh: T&T Clark.

Stephanopoulos, R.G. (1973) Guidelines for Orthodox in Ecumenical Relations. See http://www.assemblyofbishops.org/assets/files/news/scoba/guide_for_orthodox.pdf (accessed 23 February 2018).

Stevenson, J. (2011) Oberammergau's Passion Play 2010 performance and context, July 22, 2010, Oberammergau, Germany. *Material Religion* 7 (2), 304–307.

Stevenson, J. (2015) Affect, medievalism and temporal drag: Oberammergau's passion play event. In S.D. Brunn (ed.) *The Changing World Religion Map: Sacred Places, Identities, Practices and Politics* (pp. 2491–2515). Dordrecht: Springer.

Stirrat, R.L. (2000) Place and person in Sinhala Catholic pilgrimage. In J. Eade and M.J. Sallnow (eds) *Contesting the Sacred: The Anthropology of Christian Pilgrimage* (pp. 122–136). Urbana, IL: University of Illinois Press.

Stoddart, H. and Rogerson, C.M. (2004) Volunteer tourism: The case of Habitat for Humanity South Africa. *GeoJournal* 60 (3), 311–318.

Stone, M.E. (1986) Holy Land pilgrimage of Armenians before the Arab conquest. *Revue Biblique Jérusalem* 93 (1), 93–110.

Stopford, J. (1994) Some approaches to the archaeology of Christian pilgrimage. *World Archaeology* 26 (1), 57–72.

Stoykova, B. (2009) Contemporary tendencies in development of sacred tourism in Bulgaria. *International Review on Public and Nonprofit Marketing* 6 (1), 1–9.

Stringer, A.L. and McAvoy, L.H. (1992) The need for something different: Spirituality and wilderness adventure. *Journal of Environmental Education* 15 (1), 13–20.

Suleiman, J.S.H. and Mohamed, B. (2011) Factors impact on religious tourism market: The case of the Palestinian territories. *International Journal of Business and Management* 6 (7), 254–260.

Suntikul, W. and Butler, R. (2018) Tourism and religion: Origins, interactions and issues. In R. Butler and W. Suntikul (eds) *Tourism and Religion: Issues and Implications* (pp. 1–9). Bristol: Channel View Publications.

Swanson, K.K. and Timothy, D.J. (2012) Souvenirs: Icons of meaning, commercialization, and commoditization. *Tourism Management* 33, 489–499.

Swatos, W.H. and Tomasi, L. (2002) *From Medieval Pilgrimage to Religious Tourism: The Social and Cultural Economics of Piety*. London: Praeger.

Sznajder, M., Przezbórska, L. and Scrimgeour, F. (2009) *Agritourism*. Wallingford: CABI.

Taylor, M.C. (1999) *About Religion: Economies of Faith in Virtual Culture*. Chicago, IL: University of Chicago Press.

Tencer, N.J. (2011) Via Francigena: Walking Europe's oldest pilgrimage trail. *Tourism-Review.com*. April, 33–35.

Terzidou, M. (2010) Religion as a Motivation to Travel: The Case of Tinos island in Greece. Paper presented at Management of International Business and Economic Systems conference, June 4-6 2010, Greece.

Terzidou, M., Scarles, C. and Saunders, M.N. (2017) Religiousness as tourist performances: A case study of Greek Orthodox pilgrimage. *Annals of Tourism Research* 66, 116–129.

Terzidou, M., Stylidis, D. and Szivas, E. (2008) Residents' perceptions of religious tourism and its socio-economic impacts on the island of Tinos. *Tourism and Hospitality Planning & Development* 5 (2), 113–129.

Thomas, S. (2016) Promoting the sacred: The potential for pilgrimage-touristic growth in Wales: A theoretical and applied analysis. In G. Hooper (ed.) *Heritage and Tourism in Britain and Ireland* (pp. 37–51). London: Palgrave Macmillan.

Thomas-Penette, M. (2010) Cultural route: A solidarity march towards St James of Compostela. *Via Francigena* 32, 66–69.

Thomas-Penette, M. (2011) The pilgrim pathways for Europe. *Via Francigena* 33, 8–9.

Thue, S. (2008) *On the Pilgrim Way to Trondheim*. Trondheim: Tapir Academic Press.

Tilson, D.J. (2005) Religious-spiritual tourism and promotional campaigning: A church–state partnership for St. James and Spain. *Journal of Hospitality & Leisure Marketing* 12 (1/2), 9–40.

Timothy, D.J. (1997) Tourism and the personal heritage experience. *Annals of Tourism Research* 34 (3), 751–754.

Timothy, D.J. (1999) Participatory planning: A view of tourism in Indonesia. *Annals of Tourism Research* 26 (2), 371–391.
Timothy, D.J. (2001) Postage stamps, microstates and tourism. *Tourism Recreation Research* 26 (3), 85–88.
Timothy, D.J. (2002) Sacred journeys: Religious heritage and tourism. *Tourism Recreation Research* 27 (2), 3–6.
Timothy, D.J. (2005) *Shopping Tourism, Retailing and Leisure*. Clevedon: Channel View Publications.
Timothy, D.J. (2007) Empowerment and stakeholder participation in tourism destination communities. In A. Church and T. Coles (eds) *Tourism, Power and Space* (pp. 199–216). London: Routledge.
Timothy, D.J. (2008) Genealogical mobility: Tourism and the search for a personal past. In D.J. Timothy and J.K. Guelke (eds) *Geography and Genealogy: Locating Personal Pasts* (pp. 115–135). Aldershot: Ashgate.
Timothy, D.J. (2010) Foreword. In R.P.B. Singh (ed.) *Sacredscapes and Pilgrimage Landscapes* (pp. 1–4). New Delhi: Shubhi Publications.
Timothy, D.J. (2011) *Cultural Heritage and Tourism: An Introduction*. Bristol: Channel View Publications.
Timothy, D.J. (2012) Historical geographies of tourism. In J. Wilson (ed.) *The Routledge Handbook of Tourism Geographies* (pp. 157–162). London: Routledge.
Timothy, D.J. (2013) Religious views of the environment: Sanctification of nature and implications for tourism. In A. Holden and D. Fennell (eds) *The Routledge Handbook of Tourism and the Environment* (pp. 31–42). London: Routledge.
Timothy, D.J. (2014) Contemporary cultural heritage and tourism: Development issues and emerging trends. *Public Archeaology* 13 (1–3), 1–18.
Timothy, D.J. (2018a) Geography: The substance of tourism. *Tourism Geographies* 20 (1), 166–169.
Timothy, D.J. (2018b) Making sense of heritage tourism: Research trends in a maturing field of study. *Tourism Management Perspectives* 25, 177–180.
Timothy, D.J. (2018c) Producing and consuming heritage tourism: Recent trends. In S. Gmelch and A. Kaul (eds) *Tourists and Tourism: A Reader* (3rd edn; pp. 167–178). Long Grove, IL: Waveland Press.
Timothy, D.J. and Boyd, S.W. (2003) *Heritage Tourism*. London: Prentice Hall.
Timothy, D.J. and Boyd, S.W. (2006) Heritage tourism in the 21st century: Valued traditions and new perspectives. *Journal of Heritage Tourism* 1 (1), 1–17.
Timothy, D.J. and Boyd, S.W. (2015) *Tourism and Trails: Cultural, Ecological and Management Issues*. Bristol: Channel View Publications.
Timothy, D.J. and Conover, P.J. (2006) Nature religion, self-spirituality and New Age tourism. In D.J. Timothy and D.H. Olsen (eds) *Tourism, Religion and Spiritual Journeys* (pp. 139–155). London: Routledge.
Timothy, D.J. and Daher, R.F. (2009) Heritage tourism in Southwest Asia and North Africa: Contested pasts and veiled realities. In D.J. Timothy and G.P. Nyaupane (eds) *Cultural Heritage and Tourism in the Developing World: A Regional Perspective* (pp. 146–164). London: Routledge.
Timothy, D.J. and Emmett, C.F. (2014) Jerusalem, tourism, and the politics of heritage. In M. Adelman and M.F. Elman (eds) *Jerusalem: Conflict & Cooperation in a Contested City* (pp. 276–290). Syracuse, NY: Syracuse University Press.
Timothy, D.J. and Iverson, T. (2006) Tourism and Islam: Considerations of culture and duty. In D.J. Timothy and D.H. Olsen (eds) *Tourism, Religion and Spiritual Journeys* (pp. 186–205). London: Routledge.
Timothy, D.J. and Olsen, D.H. (2006) Conclusion: Whither religious tourism? In D.J. Timothy and D.H. Olsen (eds) *Tourism, Religion and Spiritual Journeys* (pp. 271–278). London: Routledge.

Timothy, D.J. and Olsen, D.H. (2018) Religious routes, pilgrim trails: Spiritual pathways as tourism resources. In R. Butler and W. Suntikul (eds) *Tourism and Religion: Issues and Implications* (pp. 220–235). Bristol: Channel View Publications.
Timothy, D.J. and Ron, A.S. (2013) Understanding heritage cuisines and tourism: Identity, image, authenticity, and change. *Journal of Heritage Tourism* 8 (2–3), 99–104.
Timothy, D.J. and Ron, A.S. (2016) Religious heritage, spiritual aliment and food for the soul. In D.J. Timothy (ed.) *Heritage Cuisines: Traditions, Identities and Tourism* (pp. 104–118). London: Routledge.
Timothy, D.J. and Ron, A.S. (in press) Christian tourism in the Middle East. In D.J. Timothy (ed.) *Routledge Handbook on Tourism in the Middle East and North Africa*. London: Routledge.
Timothy, D.J. and Saarinen, J. (2013) Cross-border cooperation and tourism in Europe. In C. Costa, D. Buhalis and E. Panyik (eds) *European Tourism Planning and Organisation Systems, Volume I: New Perspectives and Emerging Issues* (pp. 64–74). Bristol: Channel View Publications.
Timothy, D.J. and Schmidt, K. (2011) Personal heritage and return visits to American colonies in Mexico. *Tourism Review International* 14 (4), 179–188.
Timothy, D.J. and Teye, V.B. (2009) *Tourism and the Lodging Sector*. Oxford: Butterworth Heinemann.
Tirca, A. and Stanciulescu, G.C. (2011) Managing the religious tourism experience in Romanian Christian Orthodoxy. *International Journal of Business and Globalisation* 7 (1), 40–63.
Țîrca, A.M. and Stănciulescu, G.C. (2009) Aspects Regarding the Religious Tourism Experience in Romanian Christian Orthodoxy: Monasteries Abbots' Perceptions. Unpublished manuscript in possession of Amos Ron.
Țîrca, A.M., Stănciulescu, G.C., Chiş, A. and Băcilă, M.F. (2010) Managing the visitor experience on Romanian religious sites: Monasteries abbots' perceptions. *Management and Marketing Journal* 8, 1–16.
Todd, J.R. (1984) *Whither Pilgrimage: A Consideration of Holy Land Pilgrimage Today*. Jerusalem: Notre Dame Center.
Todras-Whitehall, E. (2007) Mormon faith and spectacle at Hill Cumorah in Palmyra, NY. *New York Times*, 27 July. See http://www.nytimes.com/2007/07/27/travel/escapes/27palmyra.html (accessed 3 December 2017).
Tomasi, L. (2002) Homo viator: From pilgrimage to religious tourism via the journey. In W.H. Swatos and L. Tomasi (eds) *From Medieval Pilgrimage to Religious Tourism: The Social and Cultural Economics of Piety* (pp. 1–24). London: Praeger.
Tomazos, K. and Butler, R. (2010) The volunteer tourist as 'hero'. *Current Issues in Tourism* 13 (4), 363–380.
Tomazos, K. and Cooper, W. (2012) Volunteer tourism: At the crossroads of commercialisation and service? *Current Issues in Tourism* 15 (5), 405–423.
Tomlin, G. (2004) Protestants and pilgrimage. In C. Bartholomew and F. Hughes (eds) *Explorations in a Christian Theology of Pilgrimage* (pp. 110–125). Aldershot: Ashgate.
TotusTuus (2017) TotusTuus – Totus2us. See http://www.totus2us.com/home/ (accessed 30 January 2018).
Tourism Review (2011) New trail in Israel: In the footsteps of Jesus. *Tourism Review*, 19 December. See www.tourism-review.com/israel-opened-a-new-trail-in-the-footsteps-of-jesus-news3052 (accessed 3 November 2014).
Triantafillidou, A., Koritos, C., Chatzipanagiotou, K. and Vassilikopoulou, A. (2010) Pilgrimages: The 'promised land' for travel agents? *International Journal of Contemporary Hospitality Management* 22 (3), 382–398.
Trinitapoli, J. and Vaisey, S. (2009) The transformative role of religious experience: The case of short-term missions. *Social Forces* 88 (1), 121–146.

Troen, I. and Rabineau, S. (2014) Competing concepts of land in Eretz Israel. *Israel Studies* 19 (2), 162–186.
Trono, A. (2017) Logistics at holy sites. In M. Leppäkari and K.A. Griffin (eds) *Pilgrimage and Tourism to Holy Cities: Ideological and Management Perspectives* (pp. 113–128). Wallingford: CABI.
Trono, A. and Oliva, L. (2017) Cultural tourism and historical routes: The Way of St Peter from Jerusalem to Rome. *Methaodos: Revista de Ciencias Sociales* 5 (1), 10–29.
Turkson, P. (2017) Vatican releases message for World Tourism Day 2017. *Vatican Radio*, 29 June. See http://en.radiovaticana.va/news/2017/08/01/vatican_releases_message_for_world_tourism_day_2017/1328261 (accessed 23 January 2018).
Turner, V. (1973) The center out there: Pilgrim's goal. *History of Religions* 12 (3), 191–230.
Turner, V. and Turner, E. (1978) *Image and Pilgrimage in Christian Culture: Anthropological Perspectives*. New York: Columbia University Press.
Tweed, T.A. (1997) *Our Lady of the Exile: Diasporic Religion at a Cuban Catholic Shrine in Miami*. Oxford: Oxford University Press.
Tyndall. J. (2011) Personal interview with Amos S. Ron, 26 March.
United States Conference of Catholic Bishops (2018) World Youth Day. See http://www.usccb.org/about/world-youth-day/index.cfm (accessed 30 January 2018).
UNWTO (1995) *Collection of Tourism Expenditure Statistics*. Madrid: World Tourism Organization.
UNWTO (2011) *Religious Tourism in Asia and the Pacific*. Madrid: World Tourism Organization.
Urry, J. (1995) *Consuming Places*. London: Routledge.
Urry, J. (2002) *The Tourist Gaze* (2nd edn). London: Sage.
Uysal, M., Sirgy, M.J., Woo, E. and Kim, H.L. (2016) Quality of life (QOL) and well-being research in tourism. *Tourism Management* 53, 244–261.
van der Plancke, C. (1992) La rencontre mondiale des jeunes Czestochowa et la construction de l'Europe. *Lumen Vitae* 47, 61–66.
Ventresca, R.A. (2003) The Virgin and the bear: Religion, society and the Cold War in Italy. *Journal of Social History* 37 (2), 439–456.
Vernitski, A. (2003) The way of the pilgrim: Literary reading of a religious text. *Slavonica* 9 (2), 113–122.
Vidal, D., Aulet, S. and Creus, N. (2013) Structuration and branding of a religious tourism product: Catalonia Sacra. *PASOS: Revista de Turismo y Patrimonio Cultural* 11 (3), 135–145.
Vijayanand, S. (2013) Pilgrimage tourism and its economic dimensions in tourism management. *Journal of Radix International Educational and Research Consortium* 2 (1), 1–31.
Vilaça, H. (2010) Pilgrims and pilgrimages: Fatima, Santiago de Compostela and Taize. *Nordic Journal of Religion and Society* 23 (2), 137–155.
Voase, R. (2007) Visiting a cathedral: The consumer psychology of a rich experience. *International Journal of Heritage Studies* 13 (1), 41–55.
Vodopivec, B. and Jaffe, R. (2011) Save the world in a week: Volunteer tourism, development and difference. *European Journal of Development Research* 23 (1), 111–128.
Vogel, L.I. (1993) *To See a Promised Land: Americans and the Holy Land in the Nineteenth Century*. University Park, PA: Pennsylvania State University.
VolunTourism (2014) What is voluntourism? See http://voluntourism.org (accessed 15 January 2018).
Vukonić, B. (1992) Medjugorje's religion and tourism connection. *Annals of Tourism Research* 19 (1), 79–91.
Vukonić, B. (1996) *Tourism and Religion*. Oxford: Elsevier.
Vukonić, B. (2002) Religion, tourism and economics: A convenient symbiosis. *Tourism Recreation Research* 27 (2), 59–64.
Vukonić, B. (2006) Sacred places and tourism in the Roman Catholic tradition. In D.J. Timothy and D.H. Olsen (eds) *Tourism, Religion and Spiritual Journeys* (pp. 237–253). London: Routledge.

Wagner, D. (2002) For Zion's sake. *Middle East Report* 223, 52–57.
Waheeb, M. (2008) The discovery of Bethany Beyond the Jordan River (Wadi Al-Kharrar). *Disarat, Human and Social Sciences* 35 (1), 115–126.
Wahlquist, W. (2014) Pioneer trails. In B.S. Plewe, S.K. Brown, D.Q. Cannon and R.H. Jackson (eds) *Mapping Mormonism: An Atlas of Latter-day Saint History* (pp. 80–83). Provo, UT: BYU Press.
Walker, P. (1999) *The Weekend that Changed the World: The Mystery of Jerusalem's Empty Tomb*. Louisville, KY: Westminster John Knox Press.
Wall, G. (1997) Tourism attractions: Points, lines, and areas. *Annals of Tourism Research* 24 (1), 249–243.
Walton, S. (2000) *Leadership and Lifestyle: The Portrait of Paul in the Miletus Speech and 1 Thessalonians*. Cambridge: Cambridge University Press.
Wan, E. and Hartt, G. (2008) Complementary aspects of short-term missions and long-term missions: Case studies for a win-win situation. In R.J. Priest (ed.) *Effective Engagement in Short-Term Missions: Doing it Right!* (pp. 63–98). Pasadena, CA: William Carey Library.
Wang, N. (1999) Rethinking authenticity in tourism experience. *Annals of Tourism Research* 26 (2), 349–370.
Ward, A. (2008) Faith-based theme parks and museums: Multidimensional media. In Q.J. Schultze and R.H. Woods Jr. (eds) *Understanding Evangelical Media: The Changing Face of Christian Communication* (pp. 161–172). Downers Grove, IL: InterVarsity Press.
Watson, J. (2006) Walking pilgrimage as caritas action in the world. *Journal of Holistic Nursing* 24 (4), 289–296.
Wearing, S. (2001) *Volunteer Tourism: Experiences that Make a Difference*. Wallingford: CABI.
Wearing, S. and McGehee, N.G. (2013) Volunteer tourism: A review. *Tourism Management* 38, 120–130.
Weber, T.P. (2010) American evangelicals and Israel: A complicated alliance. In J. Frankel and E. Mendelsohn (eds) *The Protestant Jewish Conundrum* (pp. 141–157). New York: Oxford University Press.
Weidenfeld, A. (2006) The religious needs of the hospitality industry. *Tourism and Hospitality Research* 6 (2), 143-159.
Weidenfeld, A. and Ron, A.S. (2008) Religious needs in the tourism industry. *Anatolia* 19 (2), 357–361.
Weiler, B. and Black, R. (2015) *Tour Guiding Research: Insights, Issues and Implications*. Bristol: Channel View Publications.
West, B. (2006) Consuming national themed environments abroad: Australian working holidaymakers and symbolic national identity in 'Aussie' theme pubs. *Tourist Studies* 6 (2), 139–155.
Wetmore, K.J. (ed.) (2017) *The Oberammergau Passion Play: Essays on the 2010 Performance and the Centuries-Long Tradition*. Jefferson, NC: McFarland & Company.
Whalen, B.E. (ed.) (2011) *Pilgrimage in the Middle Ages: A Reader*. Toronto: University of Toronto Press.
Wharton, A.J. (2006) *Selling Jerusalem: Relics, Replicas, Theme Parks*. Chicago, IL: The University of Chicago Press.
Wilkinson, J. (1977) *Jerusalem Pilgrims before the Crusades*. Warminster: Aris & Phillips.
Williams, A. (2010) Spiritual therapeutic landscapes and healing: A case study of St. Anne de Beaupre, Quebec, Canada. *Social Science & Medicine* 70 (10), 1633–1640.
Williams, E., Francis, L.J., Robbins, M. and Annis, J. (2007) Visitor experiences of St Davids Cathedral: The two worlds of pilgrims and secular tourists. *Rural Theology* 5 (2), 111–123.
Willis, K.G. (1994) Paying for heritage: What price for Durham Cathedral? *Journal of Environmental Planning and Management* 37 (3), 267–278.
Wiltshier, P. (2011) Religious tourism. In P. Robinson, S. Heitmann, and P.U.C. Dieke (eds) *Research Themes for Tourism* (pp. 249–265). Wallingford: CABI.

Wiltshier, P. (2014) Volunteers: Their role in the management of the visitor and pilgrimage experience. *International Journal of Religious Tourism and Pilgrimage* 2 (2), 50–60.

Wiltshier, P. (2015) Derby Cathedral as a beacon: The role of the Church of England in tourism management. *International Journal of Religious Tourism and Pilgrimage* 3 (2), 65–76.

Wiltshier, P. and Clarke, A. (2012) Tourism to religious sites, case studies from Hungary and England: Exploring paradoxical views on tourism, commodification and cost benefits. *International Journal of Tourism Policy* 4 (2), 132–145.

Wiltshier, P. and Griffiths, M. (2016) Management practices for the development of religious tourism sacred sites: Managing expectations through sacred and secular aims in site development; report, store and access. *International Journal of Religious Tourism and Pilgrimage* 4 (7), 1–8.

Winter, M. and Gasson, R. (1996) Pilgrimage and tourism: Cathedral visiting in contemporary England. *International Journal of Heritage Studies* 2 (3), 172–182.

Woodward, S.C. (2004) Faith and tourism: Planning tourism in relation to places of worship. *Tourism and Hospitality Planning & Development* 1 (2), 173–186.

Wright, J.B. (2014) The pilgrimage to Santiago de Compostela, Spain. *Focus on Geography* 57 (1), 25–40.

Wright, K.J. (2008) *The Christian Travel Planner*. Nashville, TN: Thomas Nelson, Inc.

Wright, N.T. (1999) *The Way of the Lord: Christian Pilgrimage Today*. Grand Rapids, MI: William B. Eerdmans.

Wuthnow, R. (2009) *Boundless Faith: The Global Outreach of American Churches*. Berkeley, CA: University of California Press.

Wuthnow, R. and Offutt, S. (2008) Transnational religious connections. *Sociology of Religion* 69 (2), 209–232.

Xie, P.F. (2015) *Industrial Heritage Tourism*. Bristol: Channel View Publications.

Yadin, Y. (1966) *Masada: Herod's Fortress and the Zealots' Last Stand*. London: Widenfeld and Nicolson.

Ynetnews (2008) Now tourists can follow 'Jesus Trail'. *eTurbo News*, 9 September.

Yoo, K-H. and Lee, W. (2015) Use of Facebook in the US heritage accommodations sector: An exploratory study. *Journal of Heritage Tourism* 10 (2), 191–201.

Zahra, A. (2006) The unexpected road to spirituality via volunteer tourism. *Tourism* 54 (2), 173–185.

Zahra, A. (2011) Volunteer tourism as a life-changing experience. In A.M. Benson (ed.) *Volunteer Tourism: Theoretical Frameworks and Practical Applications* (pp. 90–101). London: Routledge.

Zahra, A. and McIntosh, A. (2007) Volunteer tourism: Evidence of cathartic tourist experiences. *Tourism Recreation Research* 32 (1), 115–119.

Zaidman, N. (2003) Commercialization of religious objects: A comparison between traditional and New Age religions. *Social Compass* 50 (3), 345–360.

Zamani-Farahani, H. and Henderson, J.C. (2010) Islamic tourism and managing tourism development in Islamic societies: The cases of Iran and Saudi Arabia. *International Journal of Tourism Research* 12 (1), 79–89.

Zehner, E. (2013) Short-term missions: Some perspectives from Thailand. *Missiology* 41 (2), 130–145.

Zhou, X., Wang, M. and Li, D. (2017) From state to play: A travel planning tool based on crowdsourcing user-generated contents. *Applied Geography* 78, 1–11.

Zimdars-Swartz, S.L. (1991) *Encountering Mary: From La Salette to Medjugorje*. Princeton, NJ: Princeton University Press.

Zwi Werblowsky, R.J. (1983) *The Meaning of Jerusalem to Jews, Christians and Muslims*. Jerusalem: Israel Universities Study Group for Middle Eastern Affairs.

Index

accommodations 4, 5, 30, 41, 48, 52, 59, 62, 65, 68, 70, 72, 73–74, 75, 94–95, 101, 104, 114, 119, 123, 129, 136
  See also hospitality
  See also food
acculturation 58
Africa 2, 9, 37, 84, 148
Albania 138, 148
alcohol, prohibitions against 75
altruism 83–85, 102, 158, 160
amusement parks *see* theme parks
Anabaptists 7
Andorra 138
Anglican Church 79, 155
anthropology 10
Antioch 22
apostles 9, 13, 27, 32, 50, 77, 83, 138
Arab Christians 69–70, 82, 116
Arab Spring 41
archaeological sites *see* archaeology
archaeology 1, 16, 51, 52, 54, 65, 72, 76, 82, 83, 85, 92, 93–96, 112, 114, 115, 127, 133, 158
  See also volunteer tourism
architecture 5, 12, 14, 17, 33, 75, 78, 124, 142–143, 147
Argentina 103, 110, 114, 118–119
Ark Encounter (Kentucky, USA) 14, 112
Armenia 67
Armenian Catholic Church 7
Armenian Orthodox Church 22
  See also Orthodox Christians
art 12, 14, 17, 23, 30, 33, 55, 75, 108, 147
Asia 2, 4, 31, 37, 50, 103, 114, 158
  East Asia 2
  South Asia 1, 84
  Southeast Asia 2, 51, 148

atheism 24, 90
attractions, tourist 4, 12–16, 24, 26–27, 33, 45, 47, 50, 64, 67, 72, 79–80, 82, 101, 104–105, 108, 112, 113, 116–119, 124, 125–126, 145, 147, 150, 156
augmented reality 162
Australia 3, 83
Austria 138, 143
authenticity 32, 62, 75–77, 81, 103, 105–106, 109, 111–112, 115–116, 140, 154
Azerbaijan 148

Bangladesh 148
Basilica of Saint Paul Outside the Walls 27
basilicas *see* cathedrals, *see also* churches
baptismal site (of Jesus) 52–54, 76
Baptists 7, 14, 71, 99, 101, 112, 150, 155
  See also Southern Baptist Convention
Belgium 127, 128, 138, 142
Belize 51
Bethlehem 8, 22, 55, 69, 77, 140
Bible 6, 13, 15, 32, 35, 49, 50, 55, 69, 70, 71, 74, 75, 95, 98, 102, 108–109, 111–112, 118, 158, 160
biblical gardens 108–109, 158
Biblical History Center 113
biblical meals 14, 49–50, 67, 68, 70, 77, 114
Biblical Resources Museum 113, 115, 119
biblical sites 10, 13, 16, 35, 38, 42, 92, 107
  See also historic sites
  See also sacred sites
  See also themed environments
biblicism 7
blessings 2, 3, 10, 34, 61, 88, 127, 147
blogs 22, 72
Book of Mormon 12, 13, 35, 50–51, 155

203

Book of Mormon tours 36
Bosnia and Herzegovina 79–80, 138
branding 65, 78–82, 151, 159–160
Brazil 14, 84, 110, 153
Buddhism 4, 146, 160
Bulgaria 23, 138
Bulgarian Orthodox Church 7
business travel *see* MICE tourism,
    see conferences
Byzantine Empire 22

Cairo 25
    See also Egypt
Calvin, John 68
Camino de Santiago *see* Way of St James
camps 10, 145
Canada 83
Canterbury Cathedral 14, 79, 80
career missionaries *see* long-term
    missionaries
Caribbean 11, 51, 148
Catalonia 67, 81
cathedrals (as attractions) 13, 14, 22, 67,
    72, 136, 143
    See also churches (as attractions)
Catholicism *see* Roman Catholicism
Catholics *see* Roman Catholicism
cemeteries 67, 96
Central America *see* Latin America
charitable giving 88
China 11, 42, 51, 70, 90, 102, 110
Church of St Lazarus 23
Christ of the Ozarks statue (Arkansas, USA) 14
Christ the Redeemer statue (Rio de Janeiro, Brazil) 14
Christianization process 2, 8
Christian rock 153–154, 161
    See also music
Christian Zionists 13, 69, 74, 91–92
Christmas 56, 134, 156
church attendance 2
churches (as attractions) 13, 14, 22,
    24–25, 32, 46–47, 51, 60, 64, 67,
    69, 72, 77, 79, 92, 96, 101, 117,
    118, 122, 125, 127, 138, 142
    See also shrines
Churches of Christ 88
church headquarters 9, 12, 13, 27

church history sites *see* historic sites
church history tours 36–37
Church of Christ 155
Church of Christ, Scientist 7
Church of Jesus Christ of Latter-day Saints
    7, 13, 14, 15, 18, 19, 33, 34–37,
    50–51, 71, 75, 97, 101, 136–137,
    150–151, 155
Church of the Holy Sepulcher 19, 25, 57,
    59, 97, 133
Church of the Nativity 55, 80
church leaders 145–150, 156, 159
    See also Pope
civic engagement 89
commercialization of Christianity 16,
    43–63, 84, 115, 117, 157, 160
commoditization of Christianity *see*
    commercialization of Christianity
communion, with God 3, 50, 157, 158,
    160
communism 24, 90
communitas see solidarity
community Christian theater *see* liturgical
    theater
conferences 10, 12, 14, 33, 73, 145–146,
    150–151
    See also MICE tourism
conflict, Israel-Palestine *see* Israel, *see*
    Palestine
Congregationalists 7
conservation *see* preservation
Constantine, conversion of 8
Constantinople *see* Istanbul
contested spaces 25, 61, 67, 74
conventions *see* conferences
conversionism 7
Coptic Orthodox Church 22, 25–26
    See also Orthodox Christians
Cornerstone Full Gospel 155
Costa Rica 84
creationism 108, 119
credentials, pilgrim 129–131, 133
Croatia 31, 138, 143
cruises 11, 48–51, 63, 68, 70, 71, 160
Crusaders 9
cultural geography 10
cultural landscapes 104, 139
cultural tourism *see* heritage tourism
customer service 73–74

Cyprus 13, 19, 22–23, 33, 38, 42, 50, 138
Czech Republic 138, 142

Dead Sea 13, 52
Dead Sea Scrolls 13
Denmark 83, 135, 138, 142
denominational differences in travel 18–37, 71, 86, 162
dependency relationships 85, 89
Derby Cathedral 14
desecularizing 151–152, 155, 160
destination management organizations (DMOs) 48, 63, 64–67, 72, 73, 75, 81
developing countries 2, 84–85
diaspora, Orthodox 26
disabilities, physical 100–101
Disney/Disneyland 104, 108, 110–111
Disneyization/Disneyfication 104–106, 115–116, 118, 158
doctrines 2, 6–7, 36, 42, 93
drama *see* liturgical theater

Easter 15, 26, 134, 145, 154–156
Eastern Catholicism 7
Eastern Orthodox Church *see* Orthodox Christians
economic value of religious tourism 62, 64, 65–66, 135, 139, 146, 157, 159
ecotourists 5, 30
Ecuador 84
ecumenical movement 21, 24, 64, 70
Ecumenical Patriarch of Istanbul 22
England 9, 14, 67, 132
  See also United Kingdom
  See also Walsingham
Egypt 9, 13, 23, 25, 42, 48, 68
entertainment 51, 70, 105, 112, 118, 150
environmental stewardship 29–30, 84
Eritrea 26
Estonia 138
eternal life 1, 6, 102, 162
Ethiopia 26
Ethiopian Orthodox Church 22, 26
  See also Orthodox Christians
Europe 2, 3, 4, 8–9, 10, 14, 15, 18, 27, 31, 37, 38, 50, 55, 65, 68, 77, 78, 82, 97, 103–104, 117, 126, 138, 142, 152, 154–155, 157, 158

Eastern Europe 2, 68, 84
  See also individual countries
European Cultural Routes *see* trails
evangelical Christians 6, 32–33, 50, 61, 82, 91, 103, 112, 119
  See also Protestanism
evangelical movement *see* evangelical Christians
evangelizing *see* missions
events 10, 16, 27, 37, 51–54, 61, 96, 129, 145–156, 161

Facebook 72
faith-building 2
family markets 68, 83, 99
Fatima (Portugal) 9, 13, 31, 60, 80, 110
feeling the spirit *see* spiritual growth
fellowshipping *see* solidarity
festivals 105, 146, 161
Fields of the Wood Bible Park (North Carolina, USA) 14
Finland 24, 138
Finnish Orthodox Church 7
folk shrines 9–10
  See also shrines
folk religiosity 9
food 3, 5, 58, 74, 75, 78, 119, 123, 129
  See also restaurants
  See also biblical meals
footsteps of Jesus, in the 27, 28–29, 32, 33, 35, 68, 69, 76, 95, 136, 158, 160
footsteps of Paul, in the 33, 50, 68, 144
forgiveness 1, 3, 34, 159, 160
France 14, 31, 68, 78–79, 80, 83, 99–101, 114, 127–130, 135, 138, 142–143
funerals 5, 47, 57

Garden Tomb 15, 32, 82, 97–98, 99, 113
Gaza Strip *see* Palestine
genealogy 37, 68
geopolitics 19, 40–42
Georgia, Republic of 23, 67, 143
Germany 13, 15, 68, 83, 110, 128, 135, 138, 142–143, 153
  See also Oberammergau
gentrification, urban 52
Ghana 84
global awareness 89

globalization 39–42, 62
global positioning systems (GPS) 133
Gospel Trail 140–142
grace 6–7
Grand Tour 9
graves *see* tombs
'great traditions' 19
Greece 13, 18, 19, 22–25, 32–33, 38, 42, 50, 68, 138, 148
Greek Orthodox Church 7, 18, 22, 24, 55, 75
Greenland 135
grottos 59–60, 125
Guatemala 51
guides *see* tour guides
guidebooks 29, 36, 57, 72, 129, 136

Habitat for Humanity 83
　See also humanitarian aide
Hagia Sophia 22
hajj 4, 146
　see also Islam
halal tourism 74, 157
handicrafts *see* souvenirs
healing 1, 3, 10, 20, 34, 68, 73, 100–101, 129, 133
health and wellness 45, 46, 75, 126, 129, 133, 157, 161
health spas 46, 133
heaven 3
Helsinki 79
heritage tourism 5, 37, 133
Hinduism 1, 4, 108, 146, 160
　See also Kumbh Mela
historians 10
historic sites 5, 9, 10, 11, 13, 16, 18, 19, 34–36, 51, 69, 82, 96, 101, 155, 158
　See also archaeology
　See also churches
　See also heritage tourism
　See also shrines
Holy Land 8–10, 12–13, 14, 18–19, 22, 24, 25–26, 28, 29, 32–33, 35, 37–38, 40–41, 48, 49, 52–54, 55–59, 61, 62, 66, 68–70, 74, 77–78, 90–94, 102, 103, 106, 108, 113–117, 128, 134–135, 136, 139–142, 157, 158–159, 160

definition of 28–29, 42
　See also Israel
　See also Palestine
　See also Jordan
Holy Land Experience (Florida, USA) 14, 106, 110–112
holy places *see* sacred spaces
　See also shrines
　See also churches
Holy See 27, 29–30
　See also Vatican City
Hong Kong 48, 114, 119
hospitality 3, 8, 30, 104, 129
hotels *see* accommodations
humanitarian aid 15, 33, 39, 82, 88, 90, 97, 102
　See also volunteer tourism
human rights *see* social justice
humility, as characteristic of pilgrims 4, 159
Hungary 138
hyper-reality 158
hyper-spirituality 117

Iceland 138
icons *see* relics
impacts, negative 84–85
indigenous churches 9
India 4, 42, 84, 107, 146
Indonesia 3
intangible heritage 125
internet 10, 48, 72
　See also social media
intifada, second 41, 52
inward journey/inner pilgrimage 3, 4, 9, 11, 162
Iraq 13, 112
Ireland 13, 18, 57, 68, 138, 139
Islam 4, 58, 59, 71, 74–75, 79, 108, 146, 157, 160
Israel 13, 15–16, 28, 32–33, 38, 52–54, 61, 66, 68–69, 73, 75, 77, 90–93, 95, 103, 110, 113–117, 139–142, 158
　See also Holy Land
　See also Jerusalem
Istanbul 22
Italy 13, 19, 30, 33, 38, 50, 68, 108, 127–128, 132–133, 138, 142–143

Japan 83
Jehovah's Witnesses 7, 51, 73
Jerusalem 15, 18, 19, 22, 26, 30, 32, 55–57, 59, 65, 69, 77, 79, 92, 97, 109, 113, 127, 132, 133–134, 135
    See also Holy Land
    See also Israel
    See also Palestine
Jesus Christ,
    as Savior 6, 52
    baptism of 52–54, 76–77
    birth of 8, 38, 51, 52, 73
    crucifixion of 8, 15, 38, 97, 133, 134, 157, 159
    divinity of 6–7, 162
    gospel of 15, 17, 27, 40, 45, 50, 71, 88, 119, 138, 153, 158
    ministry of 9, 17, 52, 55, 76, 91, 97, 108, 118, 140, 153, 158
    resurrection of 15, 97, 134
Jesus Trail 140–142
Jewish Christians 7
Jewish guides *see* Jews; *see* guides
Jews 8, 32, 59, 71, 74–75,91
John the Baptist 52–54, 113
Jordan 13, 28–29, 38, 42, 52, 68
Jordan River 52–54, 76–77, 140
jubilee year 52, 129
Judaism 79, 160
    See also Jews
justice tourism 93

Kenya 84
Knock (Ireland) 9, 31, 57, 59, 60, 80, 97
Knox, John 68
Korea 148
Kumbh Mela 4, 146
    See also Hinduism

Land of Milk and Honey 50
    See also Holy Land
Last Supper 49
Last Supper re-enactments 50, 113
Latin America 2, 4, 9, 13, 14, 31, 36, 38, 51, 148
    see also individual countries
Latvia 138
Lebanon 13, 33, 38, 42
leisure activities *see* recreation

Liechtenstein 138
Lithuania 138, 143
'little traditions' 19, 24
liturgical theater 11–12, 14, 15, 16, 33, 39, 145–147, 153–156, 160
Living Stones 15, 69, 92–93, 116, 140
    See also solidarity tourism
    See also volunteer tourism
lodging *see* accommodations
long-term missions 16, 82, 89–90, 158
Lourdes (France) 9, 13, 18, 31, 58, 59–60, 62, 71, 82, 97, 99–101
Lutheranism 7, 13, 18, 24, 135, 144, 155
Lutherans *see* Lutheranism
    See also Reformation, the
Luxembourg 128, 138

Macedonia 33, 38, 138
Macedonian Orthodox Church 7
Malaysia 108
Malta 18, 33, 38, 41, 50, 138
Mamertine Prison 27–28, 77
    See also Rome
Marian apparitions 9, 20, 31, 61, 79, 99, 159
Marian pilgrimages *see* Marian shrines
Marian shrines 9, 12, 13, 30–31, 79–80, 99–101, 143
    See also shrines
Marija Bistrica (Croatia) 31
marketing 16, 64–81, 78, 103, 129, 133, 151
market segments 49, 66–67, 79
marketing tools 71–73
Martin Luther 8, 31, 68
    See also Lutheranism
    See also Reformation, the
mass tourism 39, 42, 84, 102
match-making/singles travel 51, 68
materialism 47, 105, 152
medieval times 3, 7, 9, 14, 63, 65, 96, 108, 121, 132
Medjugorje (Bosnia and Herzegovina) 9, 13, 18, 31, 58, 60, 71, 79–80
Mediterranean region 4, 8–9, 10, 12–13, 33, 38, 40–41, 83, 143, 157
meetings *see* conferences
mega-events *see* events
Mennonites 98–99, 114

Meteora 22–23
Methodism 7, 13, 18, 73, 101, 155
Methodists *see* Methodism
Mexico 20–21, 51, 68
MICE tourism (meetings, incentives, conferences and exhibitions) 146, 150–151, 159
  See also conferences
Millennialism 2, 7
millennium, new (1999–2000) 52, 73, 114
mini-missions *see* short-term missions
miracles 1, 9, 26, 30, 34, 138
missionaries *see* missions
missions 10, 13, 15, 16, 32–33, 35, 36, 39, 62, 73, 82, 85–88, 97, 101, 112, 114, 145, 151, 153, 158
  outcomes of serving 88–90, 101
  See also short-term missions
  See also long-term missions
mobile phone apps 125, 133, 162
mobility 40, 63, 69, 122, 162
model of contemporary Christian travel 11–16
Moldova 23, 138
Monaco 138
monasteries 8, 23, 24, 26, 67, 81, 138, 142, 160
Montenegro 138
Mormon Trail 36, 136–137
Mormonism *see* Church of Jesus Christ of Latter-day Saints
motivations for travel 5, 83, 160
Mount Athos 22–23, 75–76
Mount Sinai 22–23
multisectoral destinations 19–22
Museum of the Bible 112
museums 5, 68, 101, 105, 108, 110–111, 125, 158
music 47, 68, 118, 150, 153, 156
  See also Christian rock
Muslims *see* Islam

Nativity Trail 139–140
Nazareth 14, 77, 97–98, 113–114, 140–141
Nazareth Village (themed environment) 14, 82, 97–99, 114–115, 119
neocolonialism 84–85

Nepal 4, 84
Netherlands, the 83, 138
New Age movement 2
New Testament 11–13, 33, 38, 42, 50, 82, 97, 115, 118, 154–155
  See also Bible
  See also Old Testament
New Valamo Monastery 24–25
New Zealand 3, 83
Noah's Ark Park (Hong Kong) 119
non-government organizations (NGO) 48, 69, 103, 115, 140
Nontrinitarian 7
North America 2, 3, 4, 9, 10, 14, 15, 37, 50, 82, 148, 155
  See also individual countries
North Carolina Council of Churches 21
Northern Ireland 13, 139
  See also United Kingdom
Norway 13, 18, 83, 134–136, 138
Notre Dame Cathedral 14

Oberammergau 15, 153–155
  See also liturgical theater
Old Testament 11, 12–13, 42, 82
  See also Bible
  See also New Testament
Opera Romana Pellegrinaggi 30, 49
Oriental Orthodox Churches *see* Orthodox Christians
Orthodox Christians 7, 9, 14, 21, 22–26, 32, 71, 77, 92, 101, 113, 134, 138, 148, 162
  See also individual Orthodox churches
Our Lady of Guadalupe shrine 21

Pacific Islands 2, 10, 37, 84
pageants *see* liturgical theater
Palestine 9, 13, 15–16, 28–29, 38, 48, 52–54, 61, 69, 73, 78, 90–93, 139–142, 158–159
  See also Jerusalem
papal visits *see* Pope
Paris 14, 78
passion plays *see* liturgical theater
Passover meals *see* biblical meals
peace 16, 84, 93
Peace Corps 83
penitence *see* forgiveness

Pentecostals *see* Pentecostalism
Pentecostalism 7, 14, 20, 71, 73
Pentecostal World Fellowship 14
Peru 84, 88
Philippines 3, 147, 153
piety 5, 11, 63, 109
pilgrimage, ancient 8
pilgrimage and tourism, relationship between 4–5
pilgrimage routes *see* trails
Pinterest 72
place branding *see* branding
Poland 10, 103, 110, 114, 117–118, 119, 138, 142, 147, 155
political instability 19, 25, 40–42, 78
  See also war
  See also terrorism
Pope as tourist attraction 147–150, 159
Pope, the 21, 29, 52, 59, 77, 132, 146–150, 159
Pope Benedict XVI 29, 30, 149, 150
Pope Francis 30, 147–150
Pope John Paul II 21, 29, 39, 51–52, 128, 139, 147–151, 156
Portugal 68, 127–128, 131, 138, 142–143
Presbyterianism 7
Presbyterians *see* Presbyterianism
preservation, heritage 67, 97, 102
promotion of tourism *see* marketing
Protestantism 2, 7–9, 14, 18, 20, 21, 22, 31–34, 39, 61, 68, 71, 74, 77, 97, 101, 103, 108, 109, 113–116, 119, 121, 135, 154, 157, 162
  See also individual denominations
  See also Reformation, the
Protestants *see* Protestantism

Quakers 7
Qumran 13

recreation 11, 69, 74, 86, 90, 121–122, 127, 151, 157, 161
re-enactments *see* liturgical theater
Reformation, the 7, 8–9, 32, 68, 101, 127–128, 135, 157, 159
relics 8, 9, 23, 26, 55, 56, 131
religious needs of travelers 74–75
religious obligation 3
repentance *see* forgiveness

resorts 11, 44
restaurants 5, 48, 59, 70, 73, 104, 105
  see also food
rest houses, pilgrim *see* accommodations
Restorationism 2, 7, 13, 101, 157
retail zone *see* shopping
retreats 10, 14
revival meetings 14, 145, 150, 155, 159
rituals 1, 2, 4, 6, 37, 44, 125
Roman Catholicism 4, 7, 9, 13, 14, 15, 18, 20, 22, 26–31, 32, 52, 57–58, 61, 67, 68, 71, 75, 77, 79, 92, 99–101, 103, 108, 113, 118, 128–131, 134–135, 138–139, 143, 145, 147–151, 154–155, 157, 159, 162
Roman Empire 8
Romania 23, 138, 143
Romanian Orthodox Church 7
Rome 8, 18, 20, 27, 31, 49, 66, 77, 78, 79, 127, 128, 132–133, 135, 160
routes *see* trails
Routes of Santiago *see* Way of St James
Russia 22, 23, 42, 135
Russian Catholic Church 7
Russian Orthodox Church 7, 18, 24

Sabbath-Keeping churches 7
sacred spaces/places 3, 5, 9–10, 19, 27, 32, 34, 38–39, 54, 56, 59, 65, 67–68, 76, 79, 82, 99, 105, 138, 150, 158
safaris 11
safety *see* security
Saint Martin of Tours Route 138
saints 8, 25, 135, 138
Salt Lake City 14, 35–37, 38, 137, 150–151
salvation *see* eternal life
Santiago de Compostela 27, 60, 67, 77, 79, 80, 122, 127–131, 132, 135, 160
  See also Spain
satisfaction, tourist 67, 73–78, 116
Saudi Arabia 4, 146
Scotland 9
Sea of Galilee 114
sectoral destinations 18, 19–37
secular pilgrims 5
security 48, 70, 78, 92, 142, 150
Serbia 23, 138, 143

Seventh-day Adventists 7, 75
short-term missions 15–16, 39, 40, 82, 86–89, 158
shopping 4, 5, 6, 56–59, 90, 101, 104, 125
  See also souvenirs
shops *see* shopping
shrines 8, 9, 13, 20–21, 34, 59, 62, 64, 68, 72, 75, 77, 79, 96, 97, 99–101, 122, 125–126, 127, 150, 158–159
  See also folk shrines
sightseeing 5, 6, 8, 90, 159
Slovakia 138
Slovenia 138
smart tourism 162
Smith's continuum of sacred and profane tourism 5–6
social justice 14, 83, 90–91, 148
social media 22, 72, 77, 162
solidarity 10, 11, 16, 30, 36, 48, 51, 61, 66, 69, 76, 78, 127, 144, 145, 151, 153, 159, 160, 161
solidarity tourism 14, 15–16, 33, 69, 90–94, 158
  See also justice tourism
South Africa 42, 84, 145
South America 37, 51, 158
  See also Latin America
Southern Baptist Convention 14, 150
  See also Baptists
souvenirs 5, 31, 48, 54–61, 65, 77, 92, 116, 123, 131, 141, 144, 154
  See also shopping
Soviet Union 24
Spain 27, 67, 68, 79, 127–131, 138, 142–143, 150
special events *see* events
spiritual experiences *see* spiritual growth
spiritual growth 50, 54, 64, 68–69, 76, 88, 97, 119, 125, 136–137, 158, 161
sport tourists 5
Sri Lanka 4
St Andrews (Scotland) 9
St Catherine's Monastery 23
St Francis 29–30
St James 27
St John 50

St Olaf 13, 18
St Olav's Way 13–14, 134–136
St Patrick 13, 18
St Patrick's Trail 139
St Paul 28, 32–33, 50, 132
St Peter 27–28, 132
St Peter's Basilica 27, 79
  See also Vatican City
Sweden 135, 138, 144
Switzerland 127–128, 132, 138, 142
Syria 13, 33, 38
Syrian Orthodox Church 22
  See also Orthodox Christians

tangible heritage 35, 67, 78, 125
technology 10, 161
  See also augmented reality
  See also geographic positioning systems
  See also internet
  See also mobile phone apps
  See also social media
  See also smart tourism
televangelists 47, 70
temples 12, 13, 34, 37, 108
terrorism 40, 150
testimony development *see* spiritual growth
Thailand 4, 76, 84
theme parks 48, 71, 102, 103–104, 109–110, 116, 118, 158
themed environments 14–15, 16, 33, 39, 63, 72, 82, 98, 103–120, 104–120, 158, 161
themed landscapes *see* themed environments
Thomas Cook 9, 48, 65
Tibet 4
Tierra Santa theme park (Buenos Aires, Argentina) 14
Timor Leste 3
Tinos island 24
tombs 8, 13, 25, 26, 27, 35, 127, 135
tour companies/tour operators 10, 11, 22, 30, 32, 41, 48–51, 63, 64–65, 68–70, 81, 94, 116, 154
  See also travel agents
tour guides 41, 48–49, 70–71, 72, 74–76, 81, 82, 91, 94, 97–98, 117
tour packages *see* tours

tourist, definition of 5
tours 4, 11, 15, 35–36, 48–51, 65, 68–69, 71, 74, 78, 92, 133, 154, 160
trails 3, 4, 16, 27, 48, 77, 80–81, 105, 121–144, 159, 161
transnationalism *see* globalization
transportation 4, 9, 30, 48, 49, 66, 68, 70, 72–73, 77, 95, 121, 123–124, 126, 132
travel agents 11, 48–51, 64, 65, 68–69, 81
 See also tour companies
travel writers 77, 79
TripAdvisor 72
Turkey 1, 13, 19, 22, 26, 32–33, 38, 50, 68, 148
Twitter 72

Ukraine 138
Ukrainian Orthodox Church 7
UNESCO List of Intangible Cultural Heritage 80
UNESCO World Heritage Sites 10, 23–24, 53, 80–81, 126, 147
United churches 7
United Kingdom 67, 68, 83, 97, 127, 135, 138, 142, 155
 See also England
 See also Northern Ireland
 See also Scotland
 See also Wales
United Methodist Church *see* Methodism
United States of America 37, 83, 103–104, 110–112, 114, 117, 136–137, 155, 158
 Alabama 150
 Alaska 42
 Arizona 15, 68, 155
 Arkansas 14, 15
 California 150
 Florida 150
 Georgia 113
 Hawaii 42
 Illinois 35–36, 136
 Indiana 150
 Iowa 36, 136
 Kentucky 112
 Missouri 18, 19
 Nebraska 36, 136
 New York 18, 35–36, 108, 155
 North Carolina 150
 Ohio 18, 36
 Tennessee 13, 150
 Texas 150
 Utah 34–36, 38, 136–137
 Vermont 36
 Washington, DC 112
 Wyoming 36, 136

Vatican City 27, 30, 39, 49, 68, 79, 109, 147–148
Via Dolorosa 133–134
Via Francigena 132–133, 143, 159
Virgin Mary 9, 13, 24, 25, 61, 113
 See also Marian apparitions
 See also Marian shrines
virtual pilgrimage 4, 47
visitor centers 82, 96
volunteer tourism 10, 12, 14, 15–16, 33, 39, 72, 82–102, 113, 115, 158, 161

Wales 67
Walsingham (England) 9
war 40, 71
water to wine miracle 49, 52, 140
Way of St James 54, 80–81, 122, 126, 127–131, 133, 143, 159
webcams *see* technology
websites 22, 77
Wesley, John 68
West Bank *see* Palestine
World Heritage Sites *see* UNESCO World Heritage Sites
World Religious Travel Association 10–11, 19
World Tourism Day 30
World Tourism Organization 5, 19, 89–90
World War Two 29, 86, 102, 154
World Youth Day 14, 128, 151–153

youth ministries 151–152
YouTube 72

Zimbabwe 73
Zionism *see* Christian Zionists
Zwingli, Ulrich 68

For Product Safety Concerns and Information please contact our EU Authorised Representative:

Easy Access System Europe

Mustamäe tee 50

10621 Tallinn

Estonia

gpsr.requests@easproject.com

www.ingramcontent.com/pod-product-compliance
Ingram Content Group UK Ltd.
Pitfield, Milton Keynes, MK11 3LW, UK
UKHW021823220426

5349IPUK00003B/54